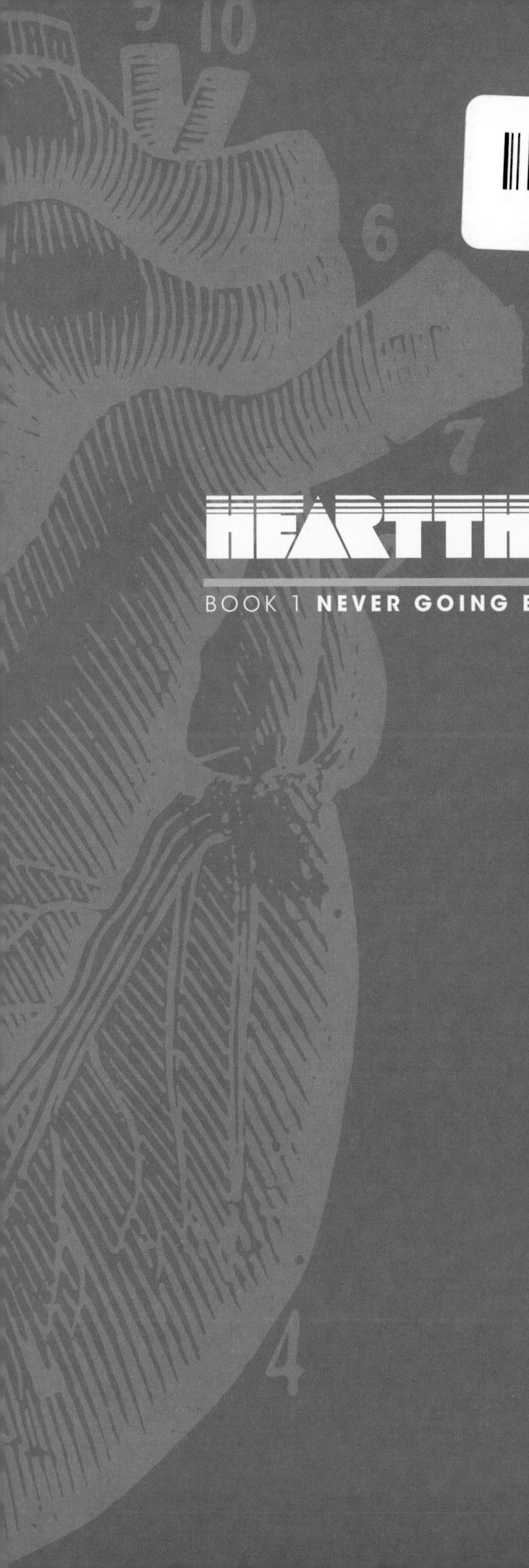
9 10
6
7
4



# HEARTTHROB

BOOK 1 **NEVER GOING BACK AGAIN**

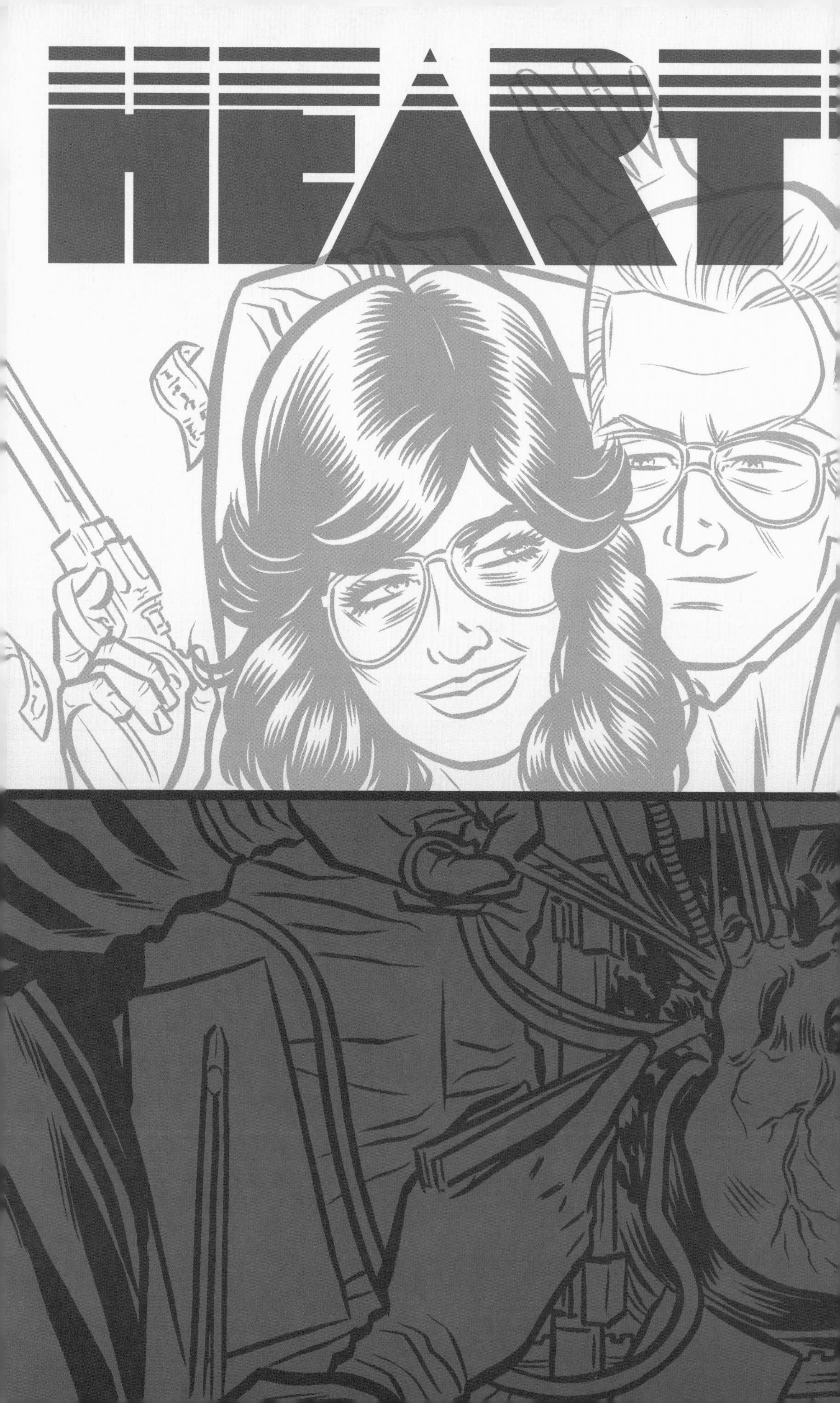
HEART

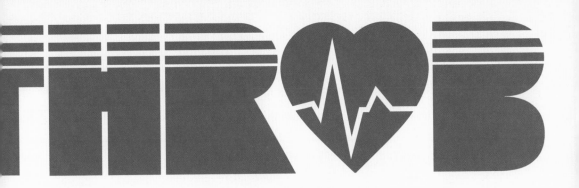

# THROB

## BOOK 1 **NEVER GOING BACK AGAIN**

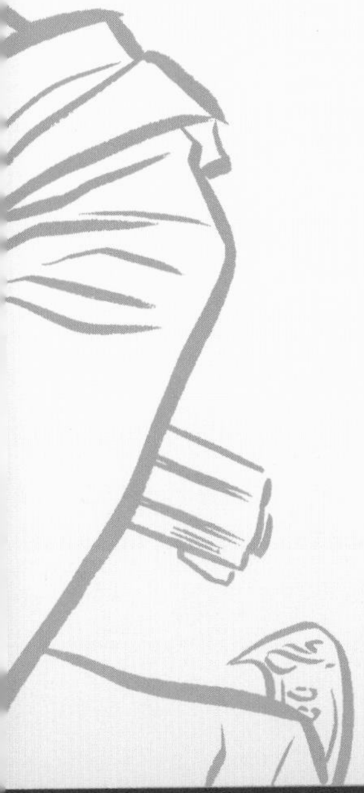


WRITTEN BY
**CHRISTOPHER SEBELA**

ILLUSTRATED BY
**ROBERT WILSON IV**

COLORED BY
**NICK FILARDI**

LETTERED BY **CRANK!**

DESIGNED BY **DYLAN TODD**

EDITED BY **CHARLIE CHU**



ONI PRESS

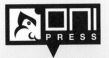

AN ONI PRESS PUBLICATION


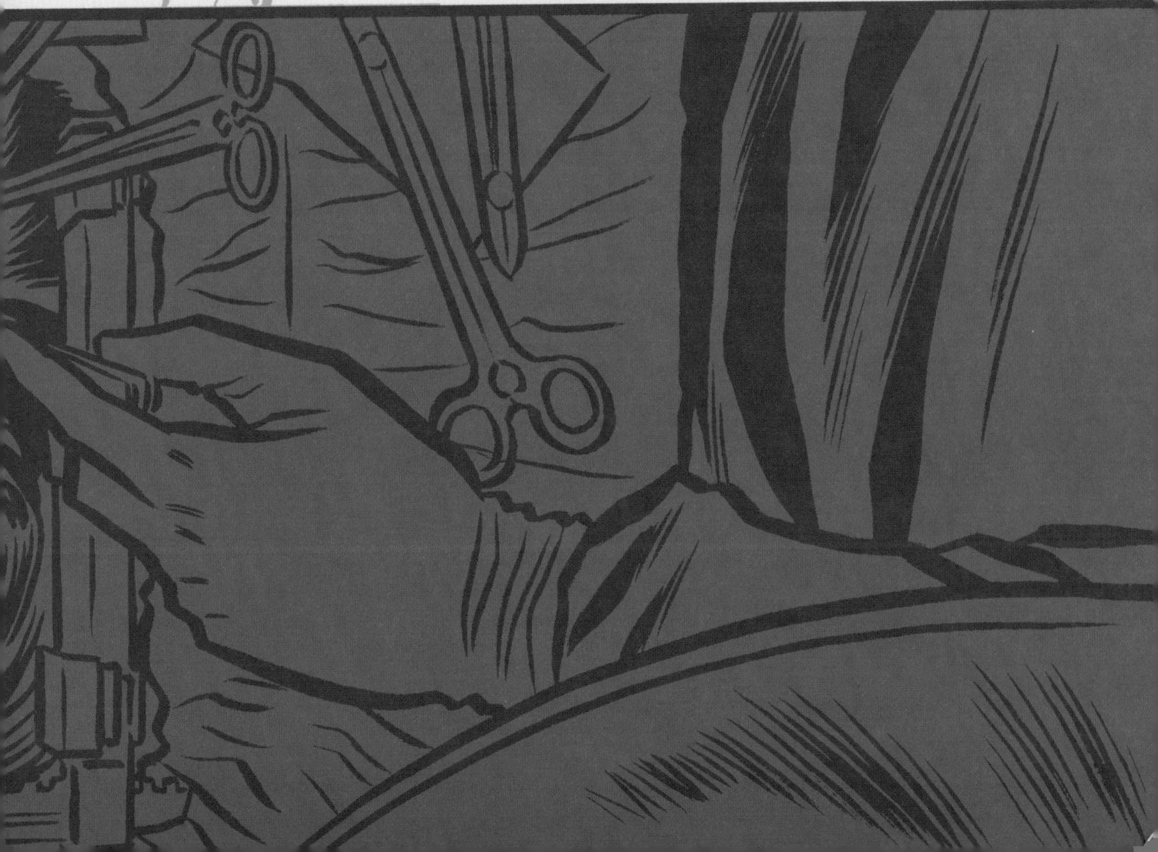

**HEARTTHROB**
BY CHRISTOPHER SEBELA, ROBERT WILSON IV,
NICK FILARDI

PUBLISHED BY ONI PRESS, INC.
Joe Nozemack PUBLISHER
James Lucas Jones EDITOR IN CHIEF
Andrew McIntire V.P. OF MARKETING & SALES
Rachel Reed PUBLICITY COORDINATOR
Troy Look DIRECTOR OF DESIGN & PRODUCTION
Hilary Thompson GRAPHIC DESIGNER
Jared Jones DIGITAL ART TECHNICIAN
Ari Yarwood MANAGING EDITOR
Charlie Chu SENIOR EDITOR
Robin Herrera EDITOR
Bess Pallares EDITORIAL ASSISTANT
Brad Rooks DIRECTOR OF LOGISTICS
Jung Lee LOGISTICS ASSOCIATE

Oni Press, Inc
1305 SE Martin Luther King, Jr. Blvd
Suite A
Portland, OR 97214
onipress.com
facebook.com/onipress
twitter.com/onipress
onipress.tumblr.com
instagram.com/onipress

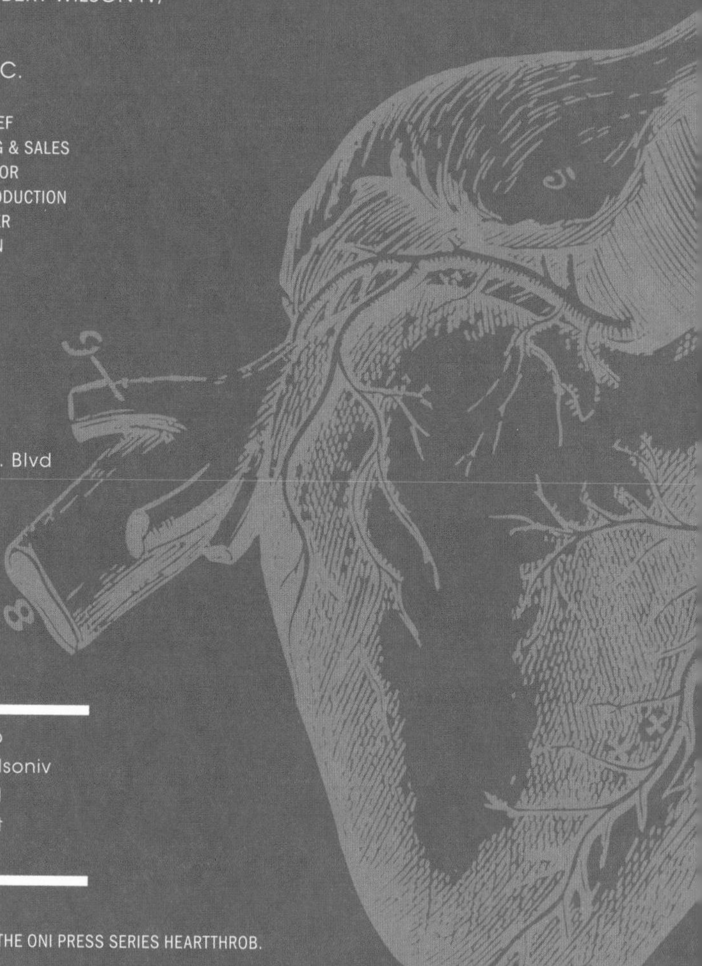
8

christophersebela.com / @xtop
robertwilsoniv.com / @robertwilsoniv
nickfilardi.tumblr.com / @nickfil
bigredrobot.net / @bigredrobot
@ccrank

THIS VOLUME COLLECTS ISSUES #1-5 OF THE ONI PRESS SERIES HEARTTHROB.

FIRST EDITION: DECEMBER 2016

ISBN 978-1-62010-338-8
EISBN 978-1-62010-339-5



LIBRARY OF CONGRESS CONTROL NUMBER: 2016903942

1 2 3 4 5 6 7 8 9 10

PRINTED IN CHINA.

# CHAPTER 1

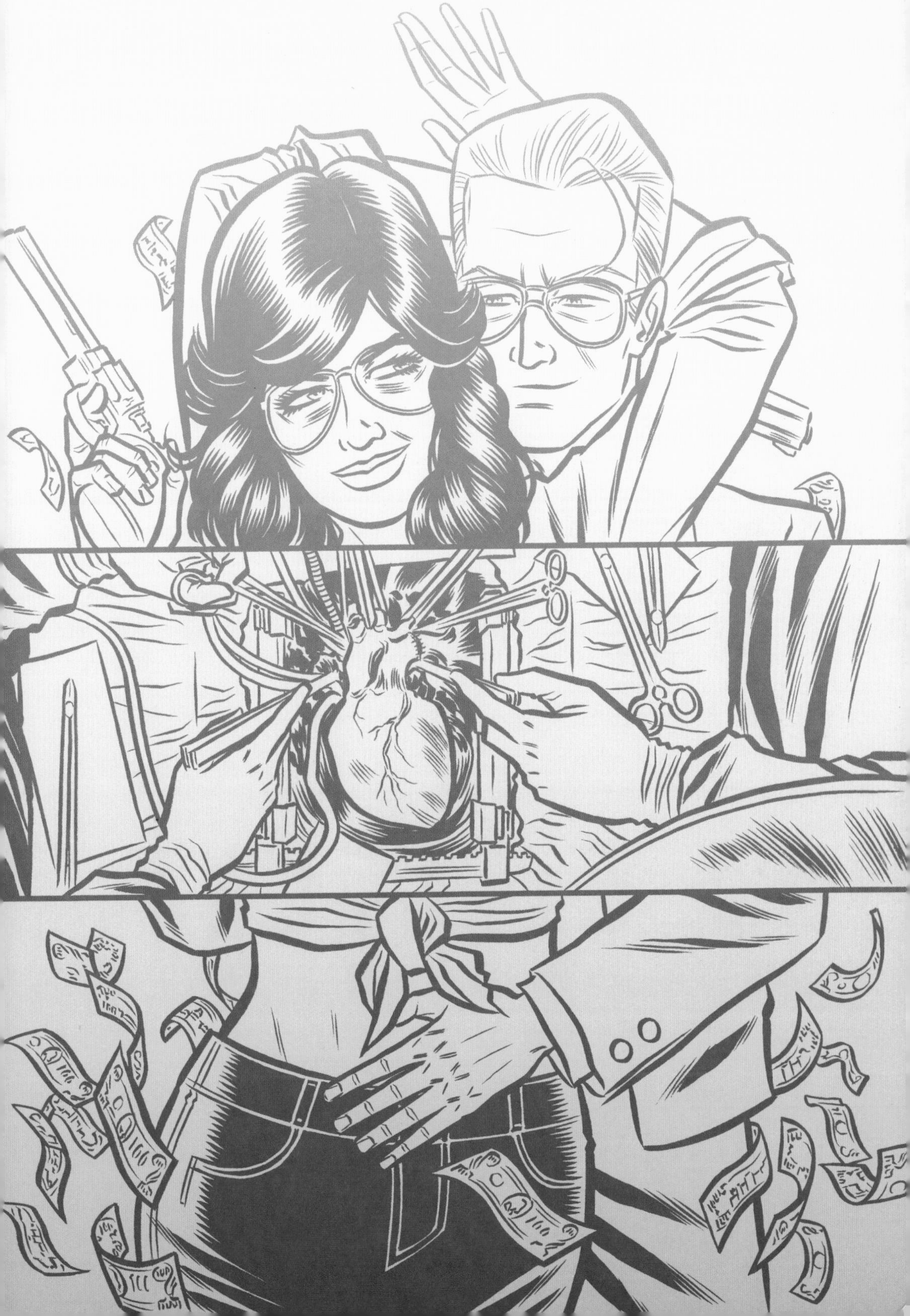

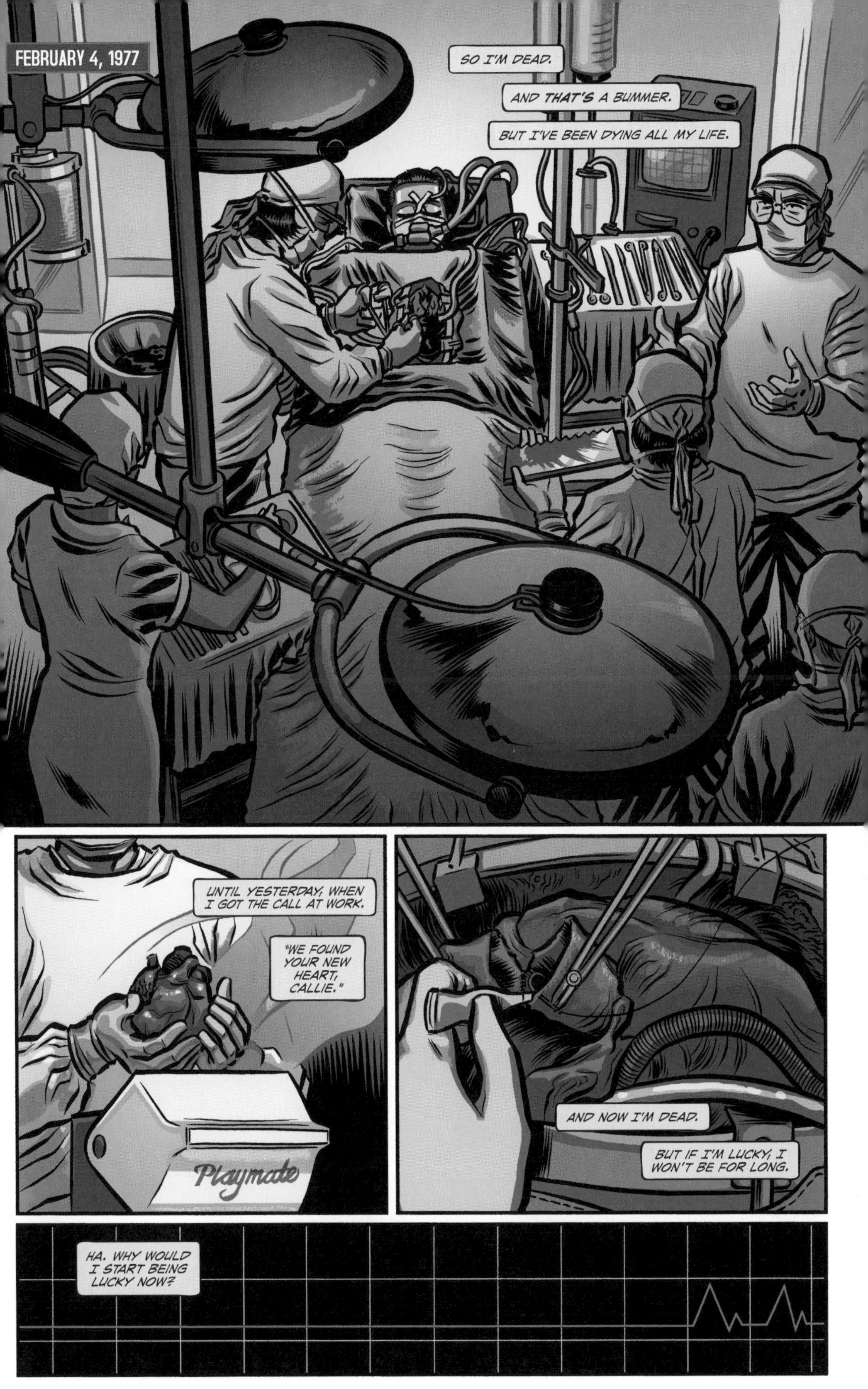
FEBRUARY 4, 1977
SO I'M DEAD.
AND THAT'S A BUMMER.
BUT I'VE BEEN DYING ALL MY LIFE.
UNTIL YESTERDAY, WHEN I GOT THE CALL AT WORK.
"WE FOUND YOUR NEW HEART, CALLIE."
Playmate
AND NOW I'M DEAD.
BUT IF I'M LUCKY, I WON'T BE FOR LONG.
HA. WHY WOULD I START BEING LUCKY NOW?

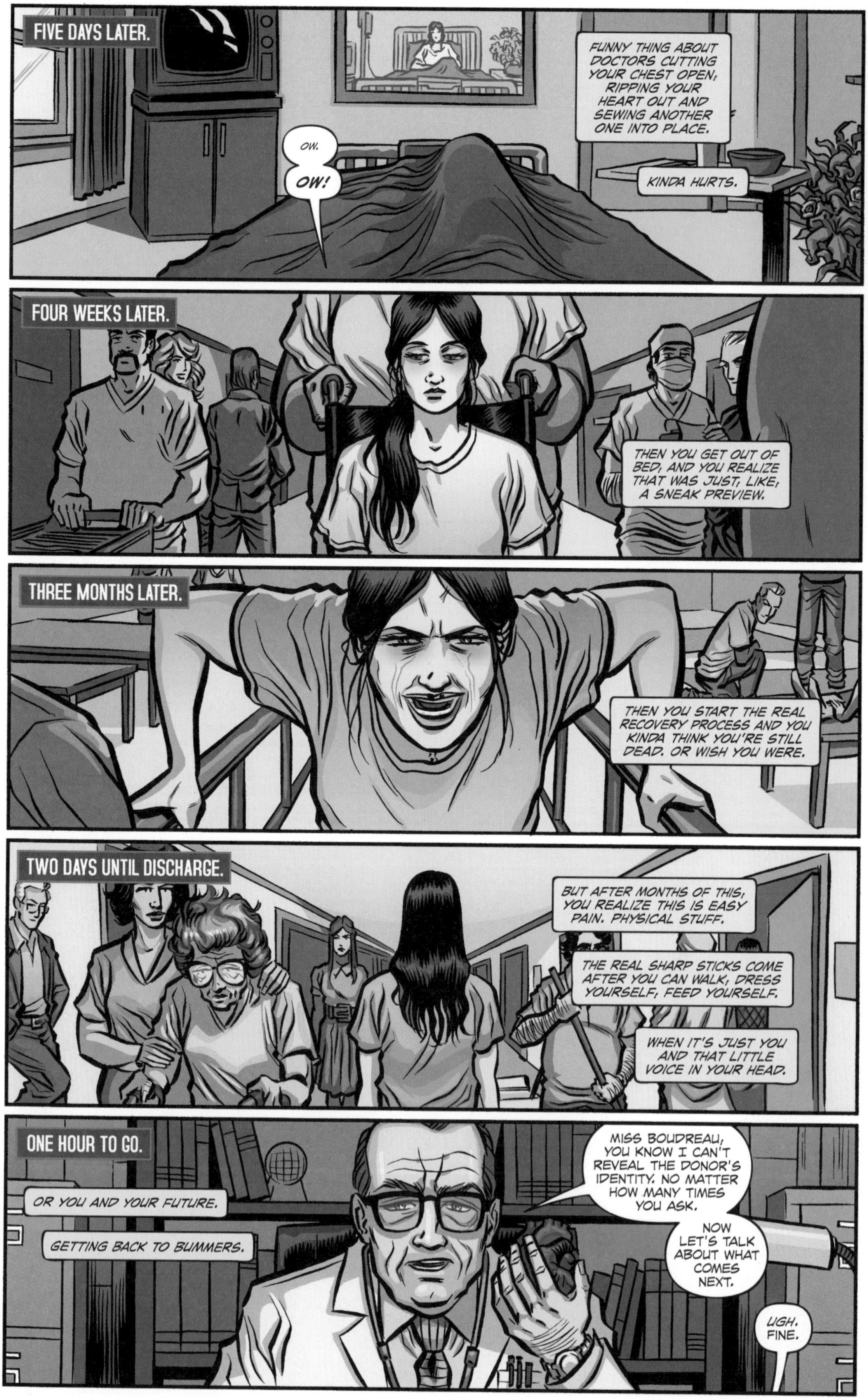
FIVE DAYS LATER.
OW.
OW!
FUNNY THING ABOUT DOCTORS CUTTING YOUR CHEST OPEN, RIPPING YOUR HEART OUT AND SEWING ANOTHER ONE INTO PLACE.
KINDA HURTS.
FOUR WEEKS LATER.
THEN YOU GET OUT OF BED, AND YOU REALIZE THAT WAS JUST, LIKE, A SNEAK PREVIEW.
THREE MONTHS LATER.
THEN YOU START THE REAL RECOVERY PROCESS AND YOU KINDA THINK YOU'RE STILL DEAD. OR WISH YOU WERE.
TWO DAYS UNTIL DISCHARGE.
BUT AFTER MONTHS OF THIS, YOU REALIZE THIS IS EASY PAIN. PHYSICAL STUFF.
THE REAL SHARP STICKS COME AFTER YOU CAN WALK, DRESS YOURSELF, FEED YOURSELF.
WHEN IT'S JUST YOU AND THAT LITTLE VOICE IN YOUR HEAD.
ONE HOUR TO GO.
OR YOU AND YOUR FUTURE.
GETTING BACK TO BUMMERS.
MISS BOUDREAU, YOU KNOW I CAN'T REVEAL THE DONOR'S IDENTITY. NO MATTER HOW MANY TIMES YOU ASK.
NOW LET'S TALK ABOUT WHAT COMES NEXT.
UGH. FINE.

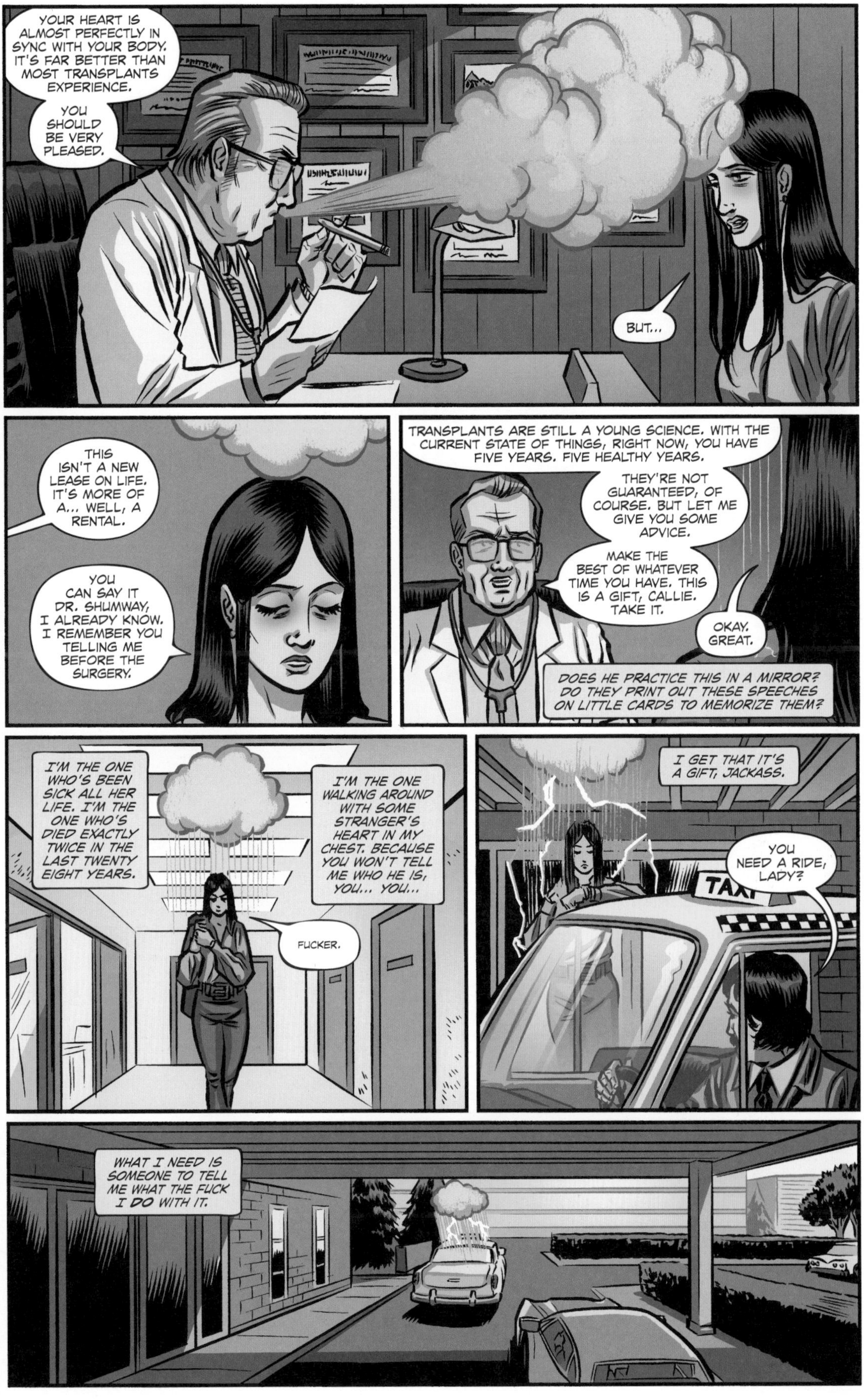

YOUR HEART IS ALMOST PERFECTLY IN SYNC WITH YOUR BODY. IT'S FAR BETTER THAN MOST TRANSPLANTS EXPERIENCE.
YOU SHOULD BE VERY PLEASED.
BUT...
THIS ISN'T A NEW LEASE ON LIFE. IT'S MORE OF A... WELL, A RENTAL.
YOU CAN SAY IT DR. SHUMWAY, I ALREADY KNOW. I REMEMBER YOU TELLING ME BEFORE THE SURGERY.
TRANSPLANTS ARE STILL A YOUNG SCIENCE. WITH THE CURRENT STATE OF THINGS, RIGHT NOW, YOU HAVE FIVE YEARS. FIVE HEALTHY YEARS.
THEY'RE NOT GUARANTEED, OF COURSE. BUT LET ME GIVE YOU SOME ADVICE.
MAKE THE BEST OF WHATEVER TIME YOU HAVE. THIS IS A GIFT, CALLIE. TAKE IT.
OKAY. GREAT.
DOES HE PRACTICE THIS IN A MIRROR? DO THEY PRINT OUT THESE SPEECHES ON LITTLE CARDS TO MEMORIZE THEM?
I'M THE ONE WHO'S BEEN SICK ALL HER LIFE. I'M THE ONE WHO'S DIED EXACTLY TWICE IN THE LAST TWENTY EIGHT YEARS.
I'M THE ONE WALKING AROUND WITH SOME STRANGER'S HEART IN MY CHEST. BECAUSE YOU WON'T TELL ME WHO HE IS, YOU... YOU...
FUCKER.
I GET THAT IT'S A GIFT, JACKASS.
YOU NEED A RIDE, LADY?
TAXI
WHAT I NEED IS SOMEONE TO TELL ME WHAT THE FUCK I DO WITH IT.

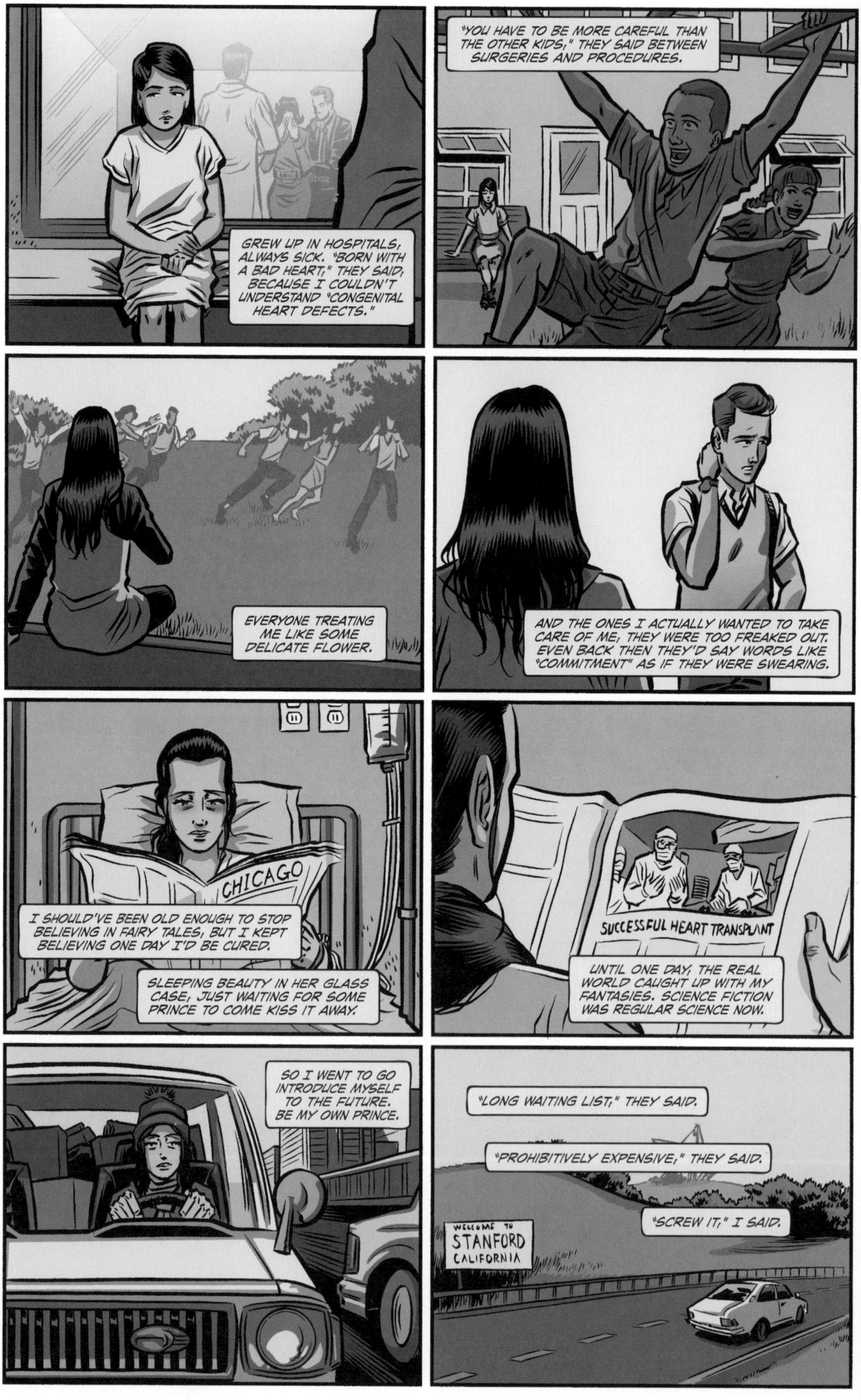
GROW UP IN HOSPITALS, ALWAYS SICK. "BORN WITH A BAD HEART," THEY SAID, BECAUSE I COULDN'T UNDERSTAND "CONGENITAL HEART DEFECTS."
"YOU HAVE TO BE MORE CAREFUL THAN THE OTHER KIDS," THEY SAID BETWEEN SURGERIES AND PROCEDURES.
EVERYONE TREATING ME LIKE SOME DELICATE FLOWER.
AND THE ONES I ACTUALLY WANTED TO TAKE CARE OF ME; THEY WERE TOO FREAKED OUT. EVEN BACK THEN THEY'D SAY WORDS LIKE "COMMITMENT" AS IF THEY WERE SWEARING.
CHICAGO
I SHOULD'VE BEEN OLD ENOUGH TO STOP BELIEVING IN FAIRY TALES, BUT I KEPT BELIEVING ONE DAY I'D BE CURED.
SLEEPING BEAUTY IN HER GLASS CASE, JUST WAITING FOR SOME PRINCE TO COME KISS IT AWAY.
SUCCESSFUL HEART TRANSPLANT
UNTIL ONE DAY, THE REAL WORLD CAUGHT UP WITH MY FANTASIES. SCIENCE FICTION WAS REGULAR SCIENCE NOW.
SO I WENT TO GO INTRODUCE MYSELF TO THE FUTURE. BE MY OWN PRINCE.
"LONG WAITING LIST," THEY SAID.
"PROHIBITIVELY EXPENSIVE," THEY SAID.
"SCREW IT," I SAID.
WELCOME TO
STANFORD
CALIFORNIA

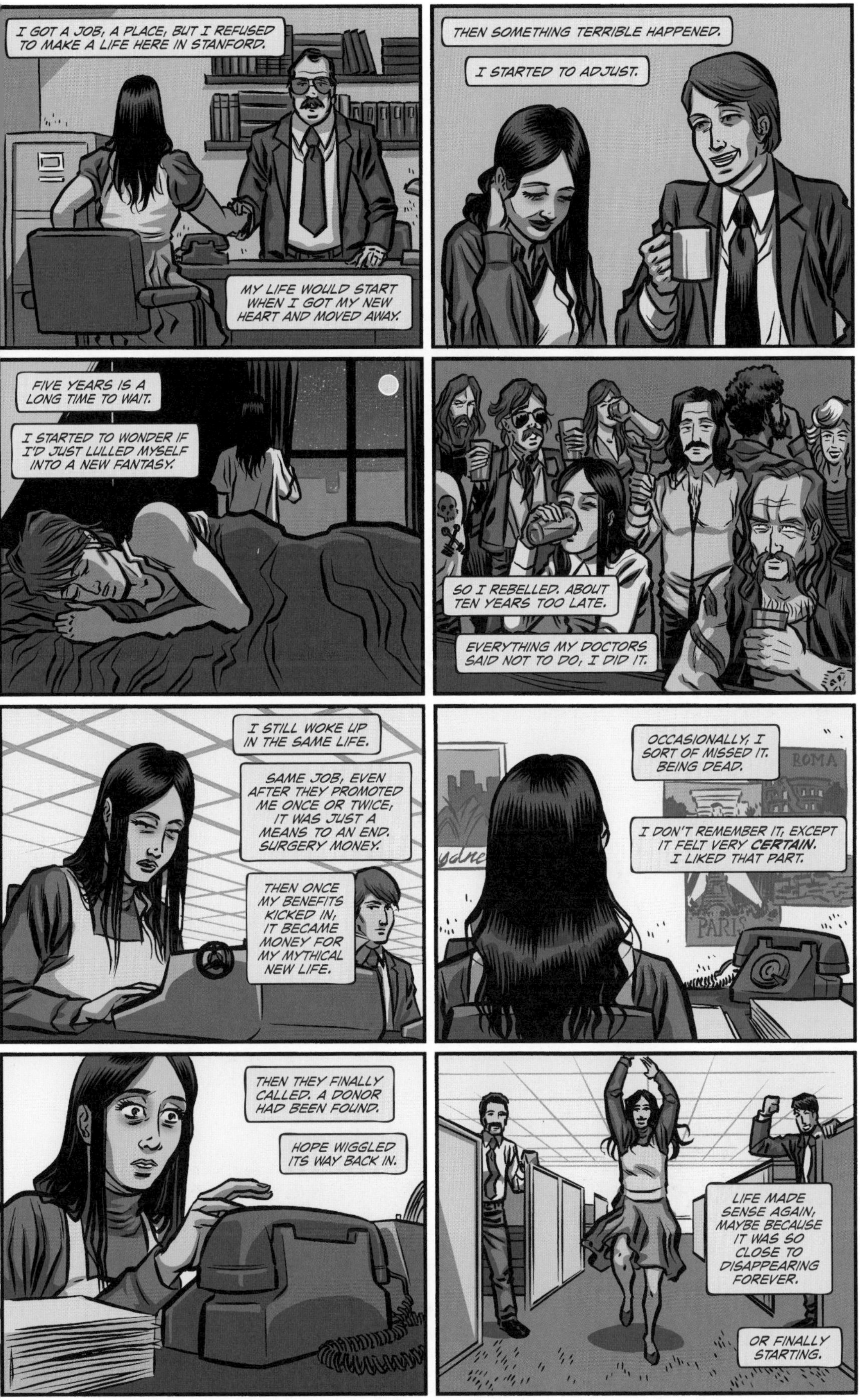

I GOT A JOB, A PLACE, BUT I REFUSED TO MAKE A LIFE HERE IN STANFORD.
MY LIFE WOULD START WHEN I GOT MY NEW HEART AND MOVED AWAY.
THEN SOMETHING TERRIBLE HAPPENED.
I STARTED TO ADJUST.
FIVE YEARS IS A LONG TIME TO WAIT.
I STARTED TO WONDER IF I'D JUST LULLED MYSELF INTO A NEW FANTASY.
SO I REBELLED. ABOUT TEN YEARS TOO LATE.
EVERYTHING MY DOCTORS SAID NOT TO DO, I DID IT.
I STILL WOKE UP IN THE SAME LIFE.
SAME JOB, EVEN AFTER THEY PROMOTED ME ONCE OR TWICE; IT WAS JUST A MEANS TO AN END. SURGERY MONEY.
THEN ONCE MY BENEFITS KICKED IN, IT BECAME MONEY FOR MY MYTHICAL NEW LIFE.
OCCASIONALLY, I SORT OF MISSED IT. BEING DEAD.
ROMA
I DON'T REMEMBER IT, EXCEPT IT FELT VERY CERTAIN. I LIKED THAT PART.
PARIS
THEN THEY FINALLY CALLED. A DONOR HAD BEEN FOUND.
HOPE WIGGLED ITS WAY BACK IN.
LIFE MADE SENSE AGAIN, MAYBE BECAUSE IT WAS SO CLOSE TO DISAPPEARING FOREVER.
OR FINALLY STARTING.

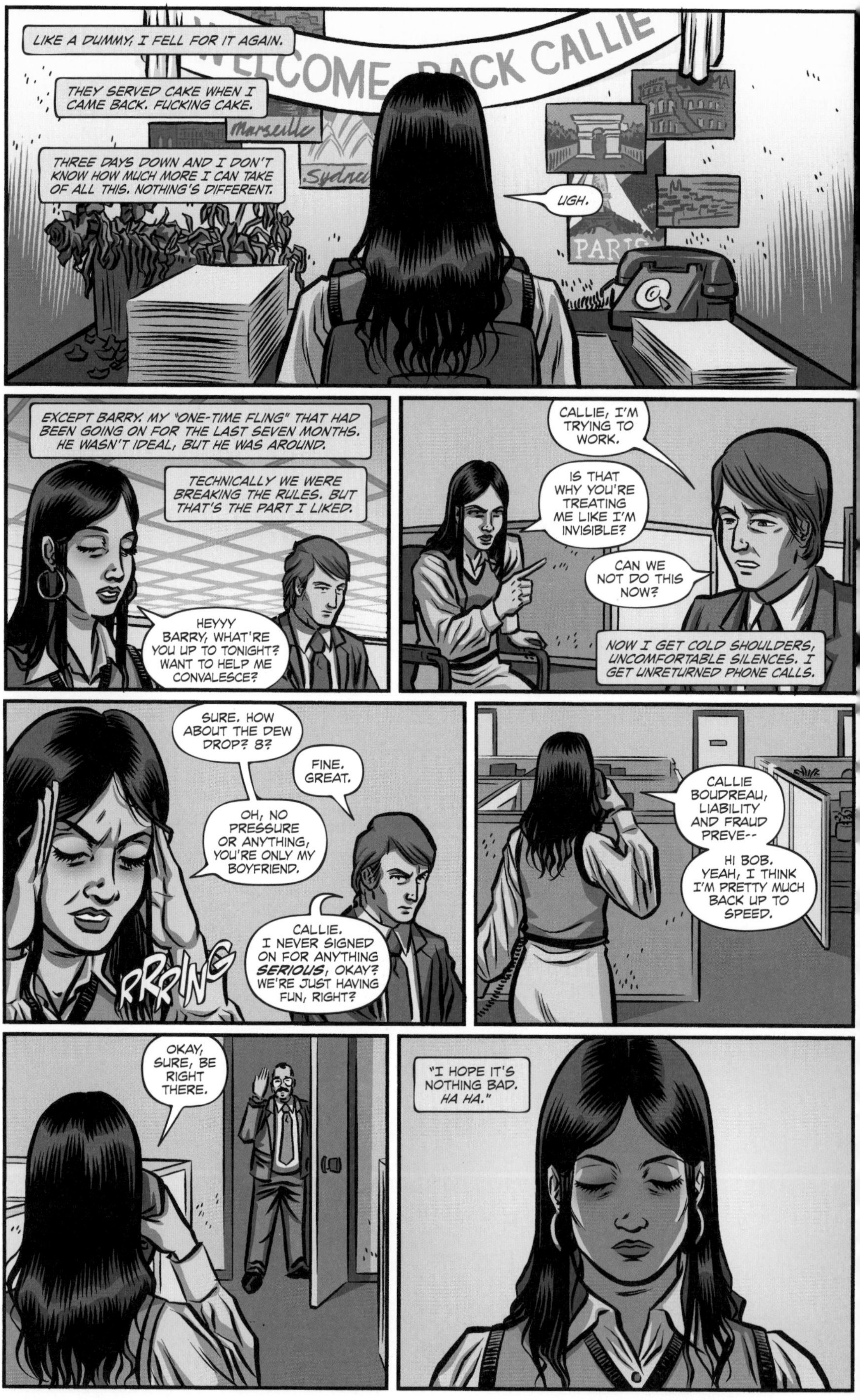

LIKE A DUMMY, I FELL FOR IT AGAIN.
WELCOME BACK CALLIE
THEY SERVED CAKE WHEN I CAME BACK. FUCKING CAKE.
Marseille
THREE DAYS DOWN AND I DON'T KNOW HOW MUCH MORE I CAN TAKE OF ALL THIS. NOTHING'S DIFFERENT.
UGH.
PARIS
EXCEPT BARRY. MY "ONE-TIME FLING" THAT HAD BEEN GOING ON FOR THE LAST SEVEN MONTHS. HE WASN'T IDEAL, BUT HE WAS AROUND.
TECHNICALLY WE WERE BREAKING THE RULES. BUT THAT'S THE PART I LIKED.
HEYYY BARRY, WHAT'RE YOU UP TO TONIGHT? WANT TO HELP ME CONVALESCE?
CALLIE, I'M TRYING TO WORK.
IS THAT WHY YOU'RE TREATING ME LIKE I'M INVISIBLE?
CAN WE NOT DO THIS NOW?
NOW I GET COLD SHOULDERS, UNCOMFORTABLE SILENCES. I GET UNRETURNED PHONE CALLS.
SURE. HOW ABOUT THE DEW DROP? 8?
FINE. GREAT.
OH, NO PRESSURE OR ANYTHING, YOU'RE ONLY MY BOYFRIEND.
CALLIE. I NEVER SIGNED ON FOR ANYTHING SERIOUS, OKAY? WE'RE JUST HAVING FUN, RIGHT?
RRRING
CALLIE BOUDREAU, LIABILITY AND FRAUD PREVE--
HI BOB. YEAH, I THINK I'M PRETTY MUCH BACK UP TO SPEED.
OKAY, SURE, BE RIGHT THERE.
"I HOPE IT'S NOTHING BAD. HA HA."

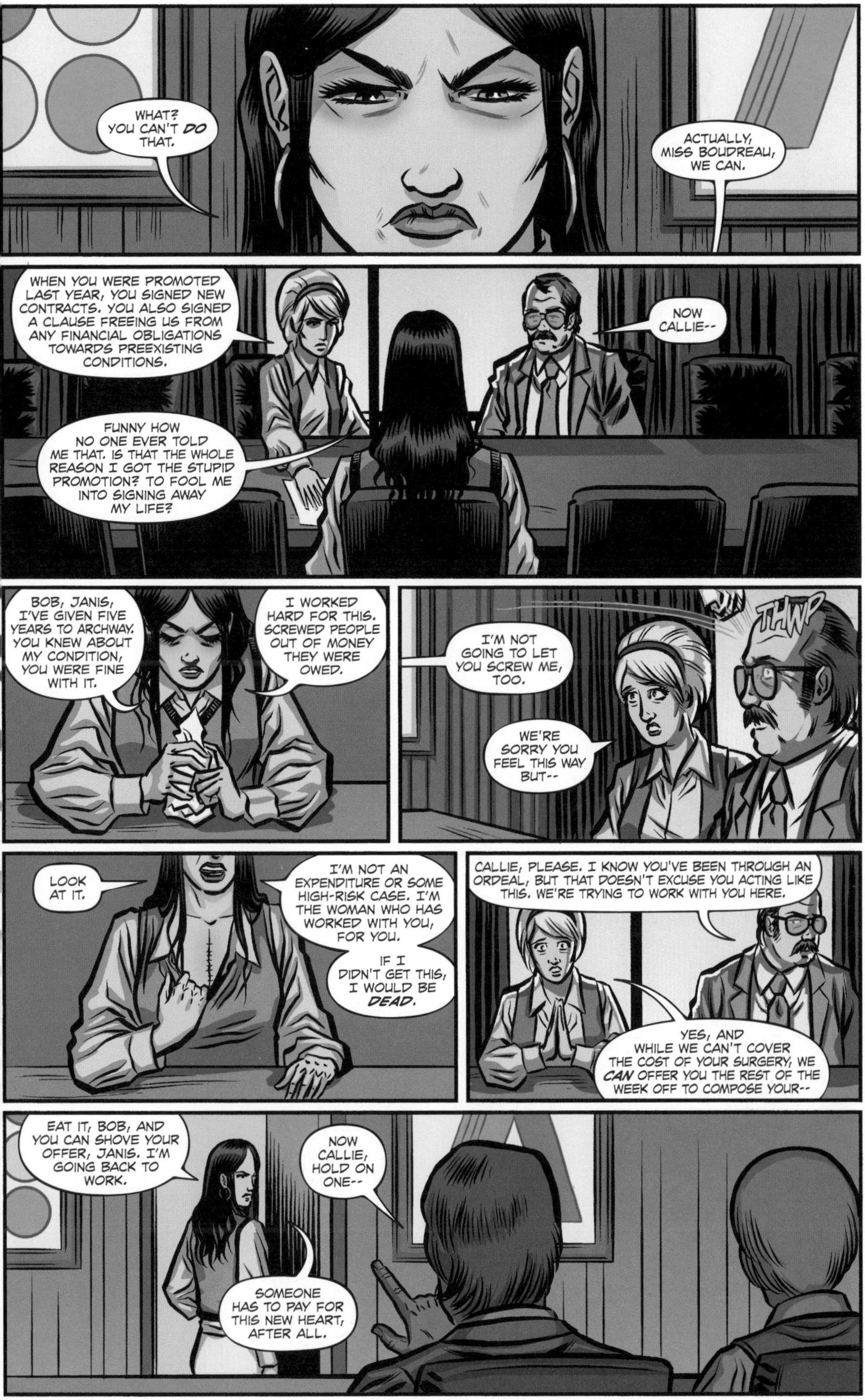

WHAT? YOU CAN'T *DO* THAT.
ACTUALLY, MISS BOUDREAU, WE CAN.
WHEN YOU WERE PROMOTED LAST YEAR, YOU SIGNED NEW CONTRACTS. YOU ALSO SIGNED A CLAUSE FREEING US FROM ANY FINANCIAL OBLIGATIONS TOWARDS PREEXISTING CONDITIONS.
NOW CALLIE--
FUNNY HOW NO ONE EVER TOLD ME THAT. IS THAT THE WHOLE REASON I GOT THE STUPID PROMOTION? TO FOOL ME INTO SIGNING AWAY MY LIFE?
BOB, JANIS, I'VE GIVEN FIVE YEARS TO ARCHWAY. YOU KNEW ABOUT MY CONDITION, YOU WERE FINE WITH IT.
I WORKED HARD FOR THIS. SCREWED PEOPLE OUT OF MONEY THEY WERE OWED.
I'M NOT GOING TO LET YOU SCREW ME, TOO.
THWP
WE'RE SORRY YOU FEEL THIS WAY BUT--
LOOK AT IT.
I'M NOT AN EXPENDITURE OR SOME HIGH-RISK CASE. I'M THE WOMAN WHO HAS WORKED WITH YOU, FOR YOU.
IF I DIDN'T GET THIS, I WOULD BE *DEAD*.
CALLIE, PLEASE. I KNOW YOU'VE BEEN THROUGH AN ORDEAL, BUT THAT DOESN'T EXCUSE YOU ACTING LIKE THIS. WE'RE TRYING TO WORK WITH YOU HERE.
YES, AND WHILE WE CAN'T COVER THE COST OF YOUR SURGERY, WE *CAN* OFFER YOU THE REST OF THE WEEK OFF TO COMPOSE YOUR--
EAT IT, BOB, AND YOU CAN SHOVE YOUR OFFER, JANIS. I'M GOING BACK TO WORK.
NOW CALLIE, HOLD ON ONE--
SOMEONE HAS TO PAY FOR THIS NEW HEART, AFTER ALL.

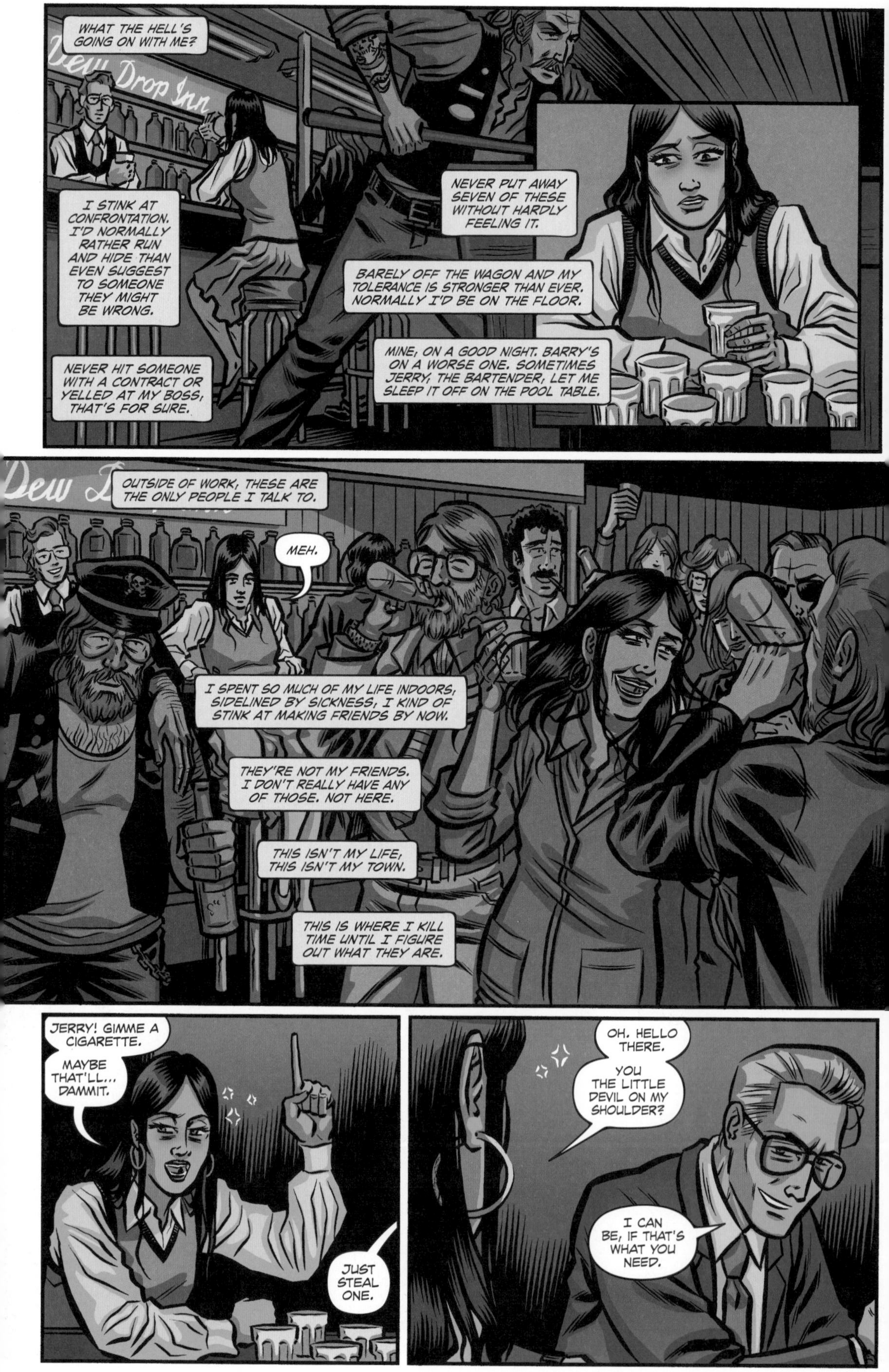

WHAT THE HELL'S GOING ON WITH ME?
Dew Drop Inn
I STINK AT CONFRONTATION. I'D NORMALLY RATHER RUN AND HIDE THAN EVEN SUGGEST TO SOMEONE THEY MIGHT BE WRONG.
NEVER HIT SOMEONE WITH A CONTRACT OR YELLED AT MY BOSS, THAT'S FOR SURE.
NEVER PUT AWAY SEVEN OF THESE WITHOUT HARDLY FEELING IT.
BARELY OFF THE WAGON AND MY TOLERANCE IS STRONGER THAN EVER. NORMALLY I'D BE ON THE FLOOR.
MINE, ON A GOOD NIGHT. BARRY'S ON A WORSE ONE. SOMETIMES JERRY, THE BARTENDER, LET ME SLEEP IT OFF ON THE POOL TABLE.
OUTSIDE OF WORK, THESE ARE THE ONLY PEOPLE I TALK TO.
MEH.
I SPENT SO MUCH OF MY LIFE INDOORS, SIDELINED BY SICKNESS, I KIND OF STINK AT MAKING FRIENDS BY NOW.
THEY'RE NOT MY FRIENDS. I DON'T REALLY HAVE ANY OF THOSE. NOT HERE.
THIS ISN'T MY LIFE, THIS ISN'T MY TOWN.
THIS IS WHERE I KILL TIME UNTIL I FIGURE OUT WHAT THEY ARE.
JERRY! GIMME A CIGARETTE.
MAYBE THAT'LL... DAMMIT.
JUST STEAL ONE.
OH. HELLO THERE.
YOU THE LITTLE DEVIL ON MY SHOULDER?
I CAN BE, IF THAT'S WHAT YOU NEED.

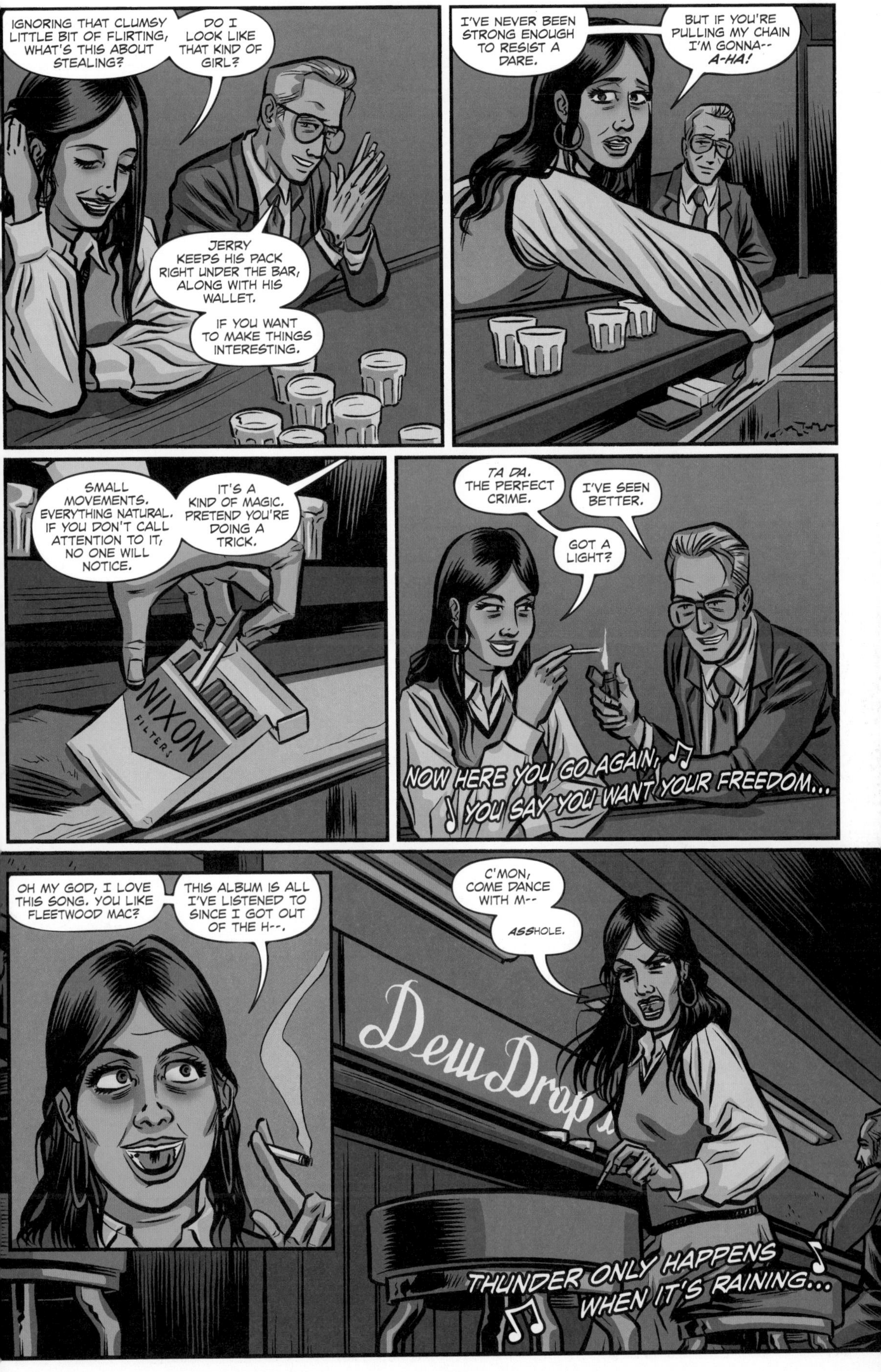
IGNORING THAT CLUMSY LITTLE BIT OF FLIRTING, WHAT'S THIS ABOUT STEALING?
DO I LOOK LIKE THAT KIND OF GIRL?
JERRY KEEPS HIS PACK RIGHT UNDER THE BAR, ALONG WITH HIS WALLET.
IF YOU WANT TO MAKE THINGS INTERESTING.
I'VE NEVER BEEN STRONG ENOUGH TO RESIST A DARE.
BUT IF YOU'RE PULLING MY CHAIN I'M GONNA-- *A-HA!*
SMALL MOVEMENTS. EVERYTHING NATURAL. IF YOU DON'T CALL ATTENTION TO IT, NO ONE WILL NOTICE.
IT'S A KIND OF MAGIC. PRETEND YOU'RE DOING A TRICK.
NIXON
FILTERS
*TA DA.* THE PERFECT CRIME.
I'VE SEEN BETTER.
GOT A LIGHT?
NOW HERE YOU GO AGAIN, YOU SAY YOU WANT YOUR FREEDOM...
OH MY GOD, I LOVE THIS SONG. YOU LIKE FLEETWOOD MAC?
THIS ALBUM IS ALL I'VE LISTENED TO SINCE I GOT OUT OF THE H--.
C'MON, COME DANCE WITH M--
*ASS*HOLE.
Dew Drop
THUNDER ONLY HAPPENS WHEN IT'S RAINING...

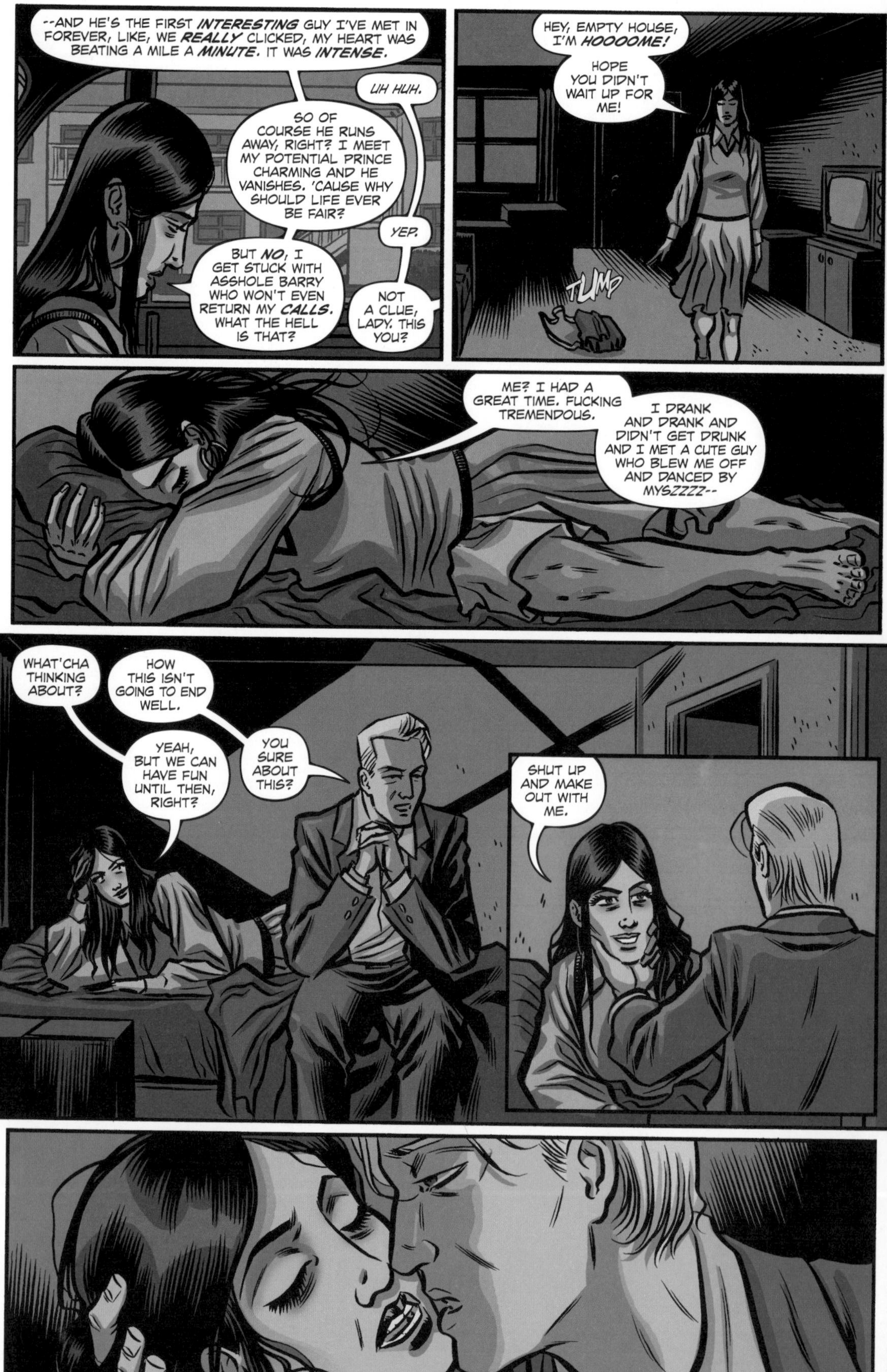
--AND HE'S THE FIRST INTERESTING GUY I'VE MET IN FOREVER, LIKE, WE REALLY CLICKED, MY HEART WAS BEATING A MILE A MINUTE. IT WAS INTENSE.
UH HUH.
SO OF COURSE HE RUNS AWAY, RIGHT? I MEET MY POTENTIAL PRINCE CHARMING AND HE VANISHES. 'CAUSE WHY SHOULD LIFE EVER BE FAIR?
YEP.
BUT NO, I GET STUCK WITH ASSHOLE BARRY WHO WON'T EVEN RETURN MY CALLS. WHAT THE HELL IS THAT?
NOT A CLUE, LADY. THIS YOU?
HEY, EMPTY HOUSE, I'M HOOOOME!
HOPE YOU DIDN'T WAIT UP FOR ME!
TUMP
ME? I HAD A GREAT TIME. FUCKING TREMENDOUS.
I DRANK AND DRANK AND DIDN'T GET DRUNK AND I MET A CUTE GUY WHO BLEW ME OFF AND DANCED BY MYSZZZZ--
WHAT'CHA THINKING ABOUT?
HOW THIS ISN'T GOING TO END WELL.
YEAH, BUT WE CAN HAVE FUN UNTIL THEN, RIGHT?
YOU SURE ABOUT THIS?
SHUT UP AND MAKE OUT WITH ME.

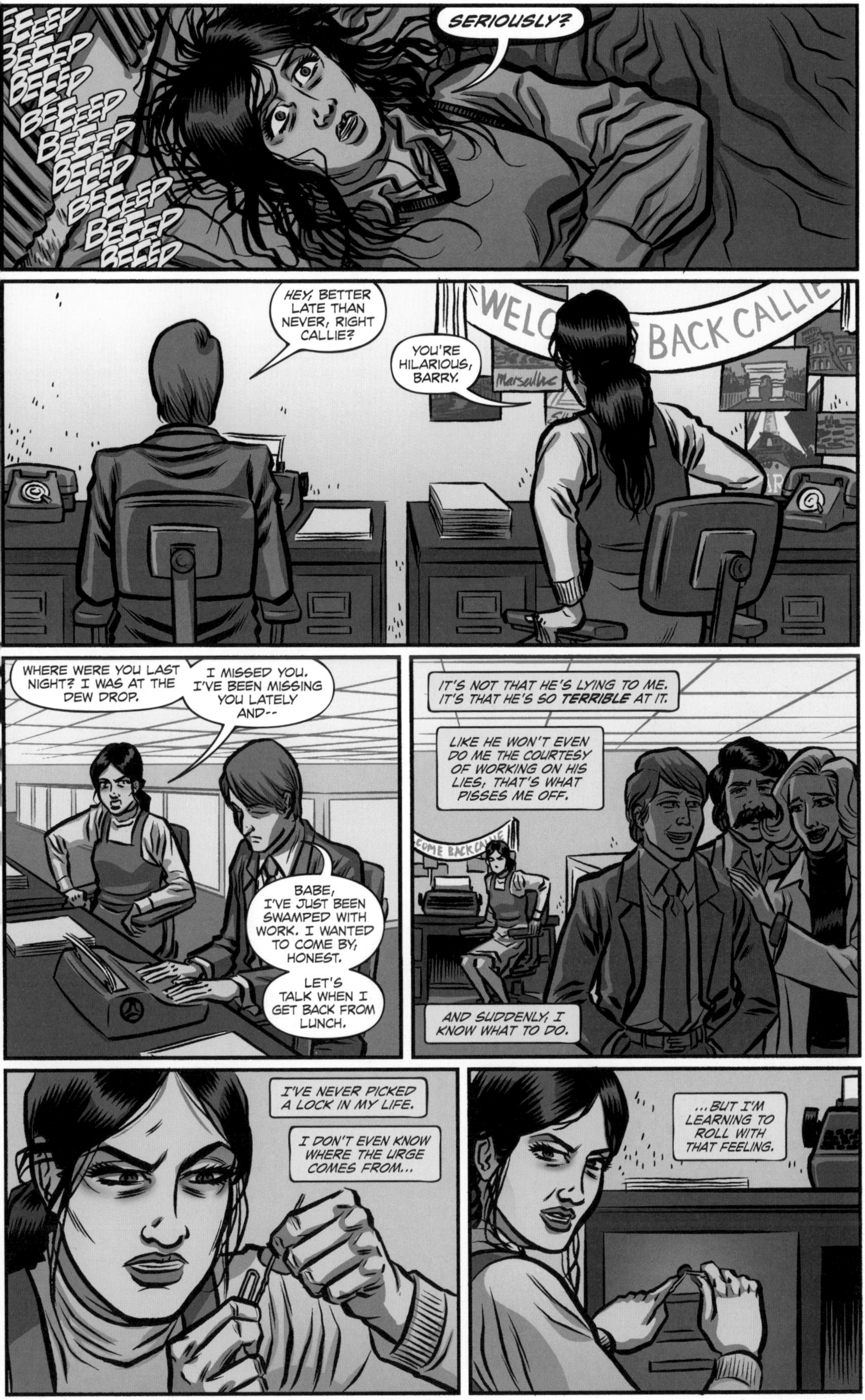
BEEEEP BEEEP BEEEP BEEEEP BEEEP BEEEP BEEEP BEEEEP BEEEP BEEEP
SERIOUSLY?
WELCOME BACK CALLIE
HEY, BETTER LATE THAN NEVER, RIGHT CALLIE?
YOU'RE HILARIOUS, BARRY.
WHERE WERE YOU LAST NIGHT? I WAS AT THE DEW DROP.
I MISSED YOU. I'VE BEEN MISSING YOU LATELY AND--
BABE, I'VE JUST BEEN SWAMPED WITH WORK. I WANTED TO COME BY, HONEST.
LET'S TALK WHEN I GET BACK FROM LUNCH.
IT'S NOT THAT HE'S LYING TO ME. IT'S THAT HE'S SO TERRIBLE AT IT.
LIKE HE WON'T EVEN DO ME THE COURTESY OF WORKING ON HIS LIES; THAT'S WHAT PISSES ME OFF.
AND SUDDENLY, I KNOW WHAT TO DO.
I'VE NEVER PICKED A LOCK IN MY LIFE.
I DON'T EVEN KNOW WHERE THE URGE COMES FROM...
...BUT I'M LEARNING TO ROLL WITH THAT FEELING.

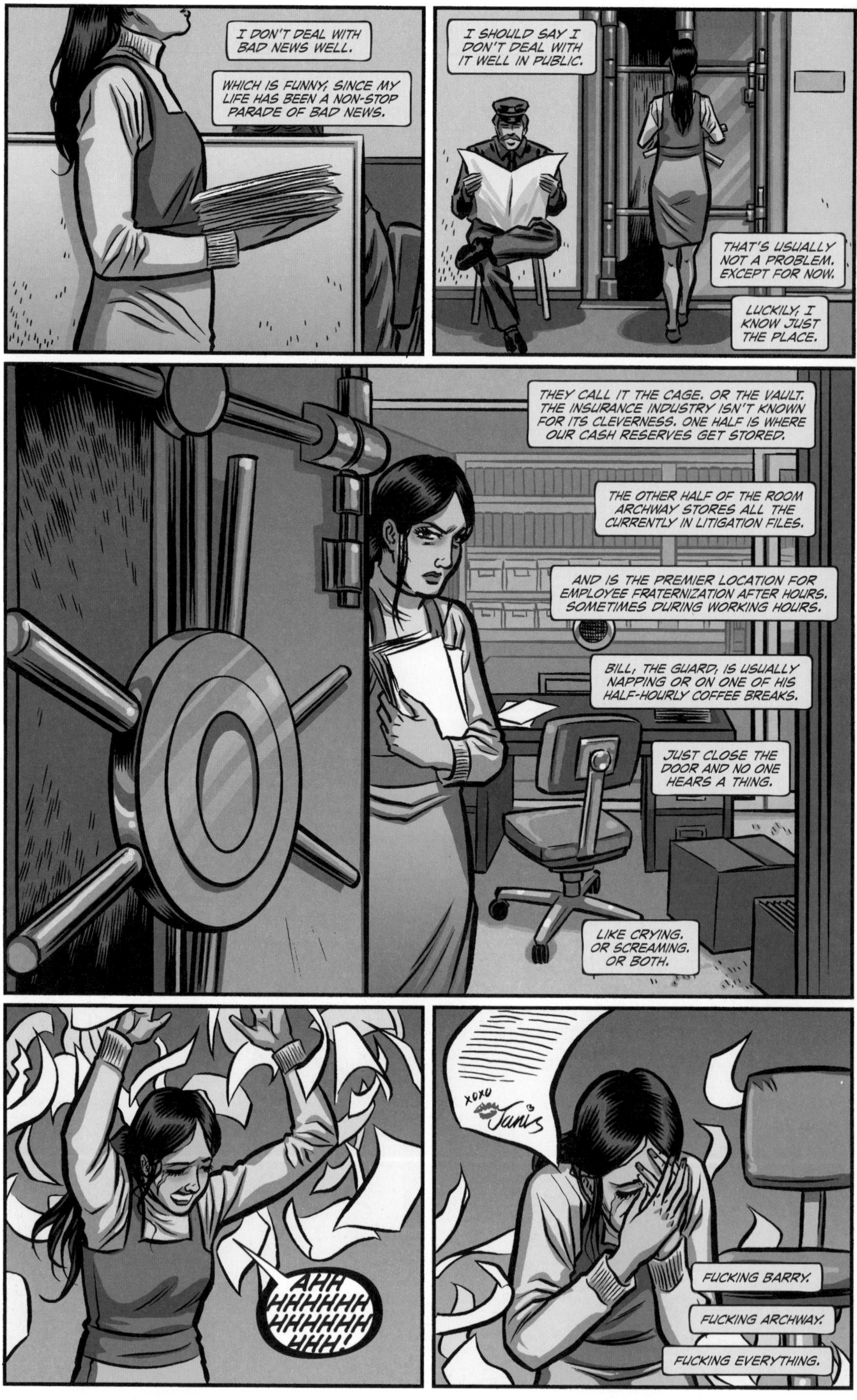

I DON'T DEAL WITH BAD NEWS WELL.
WHICH IS FUNNY, SINCE MY LIFE HAS BEEN A NON-STOP PARADE OF BAD NEWS.
I SHOULD SAY I DON'T DEAL WITH IT WELL IN PUBLIC.
THAT'S USUALLY NOT A PROBLEM. EXCEPT FOR NOW.
LUCKILY, I KNOW JUST THE PLACE.
THEY CALL IT THE CAGE. OR THE VAULT. THE INSURANCE INDUSTRY ISN'T KNOWN FOR ITS CLEVERNESS. ONE HALF IS WHERE OUR CASH RESERVES GET STORED.
THE OTHER HALF OF THE ROOM ARCHWAY STORES ALL THE CURRENTLY IN LITIGATION FILES.
AND IS THE PREMIER LOCATION FOR EMPLOYEE FRATERNIZATION AFTER HOURS. SOMETIMES DURING WORKING HOURS.
BILL, THE GUARD, IS USUALLY NAPPING OR ON ONE OF HIS HALF-HOURLY COFFEE BREAKS.
JUST CLOSE THE DOOR AND NO ONE HEARS A THING.
LIKE CRYING. OR SCREAMING. OR BOTH.
AHHHHHHHHHHHHHHHHH!
XOXO Janis
FUCKING BARRY.
FUCKING ARCHWAY.
FUCKING EVERYTHING.

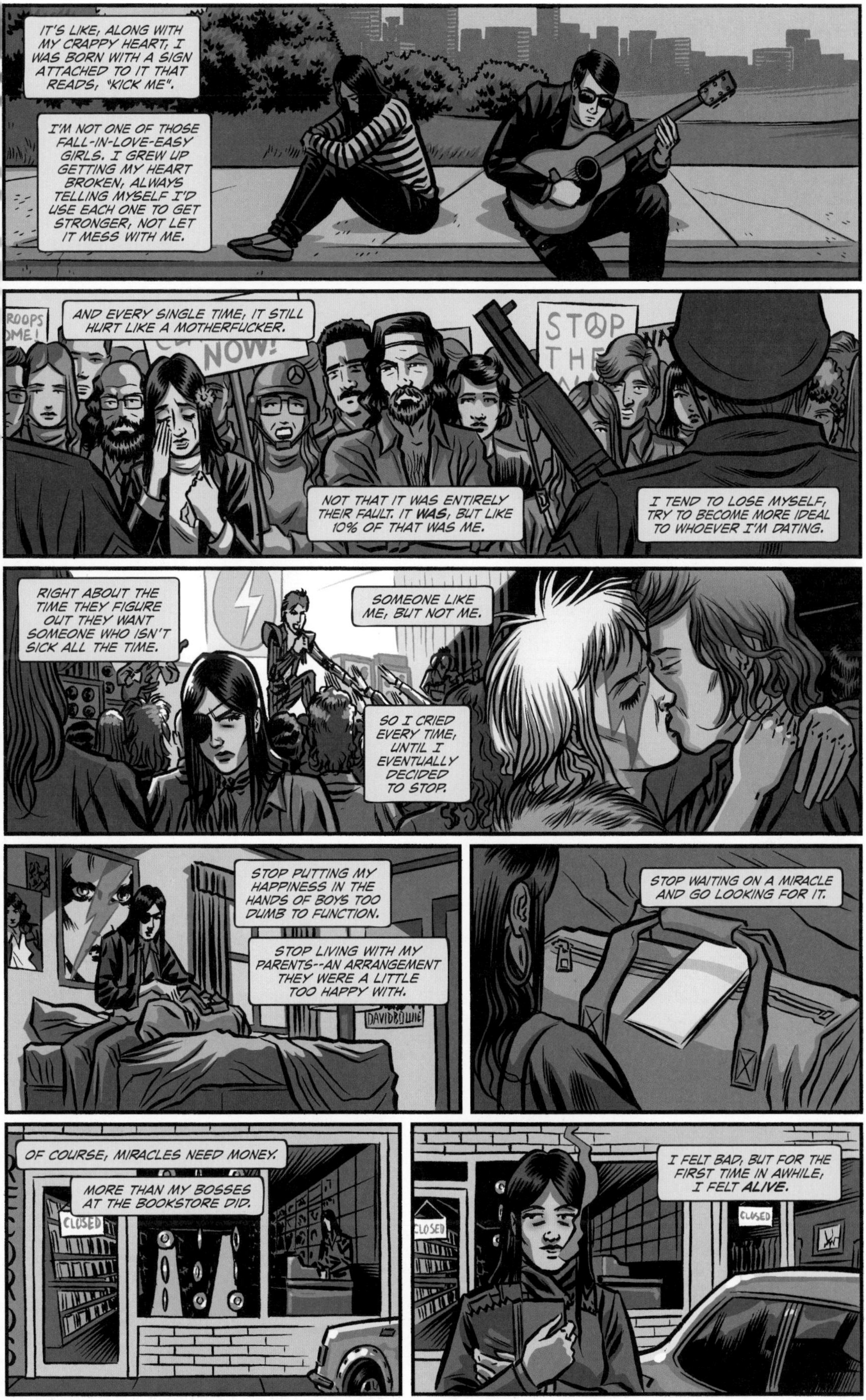
IT'S LIKE, ALONG WITH MY CRAPPY HEART, I WAS BORN WITH A SIGN ATTACHED TO IT THAT READS, "KICK ME".
I'M NOT ONE OF THOSE FALL-IN-LOVE-EASY GIRLS. I GREW UP GETTING MY HEART BROKEN, ALWAYS TELLING MYSELF I'D USE EACH ONE TO GET STRONGER, NOT LET IT MESS WITH ME.
AND EVERY SINGLE TIME, IT STILL HURT LIKE A MOTHERFUCKER.
NOW!
STOP
NOT THAT IT WAS ENTIRELY THEIR FAULT. IT WAS, BUT LIKE 10% OF THAT WAS ME.
I TEND TO LOSE MYSELF, TRY TO BECOME MORE IDEAL TO WHOEVER I'M DATING.
RIGHT ABOUT THE TIME THEY FIGURE OUT THEY WANT SOMEONE WHO ISN'T SICK ALL THE TIME.
SOMEONE LIKE ME, BUT NOT ME.
SO I CRIED EVERY TIME, UNTIL I EVENTUALLY DECIDED TO STOP.
STOP PUTTING MY HAPPINESS IN THE HANDS OF BOYS TOO DUMB TO FUNCTION.
STOP LIVING WITH MY PARENTS--AN ARRANGEMENT THEY WERE A LITTLE TOO HAPPY WITH.
DAVID BOWIE
STOP WAITING ON A MIRACLE AND GO LOOKING FOR IT.
OF COURSE, MIRACLES NEED MONEY.
MORE THAN MY BOSSES AT THE BOOKSTORE DID.
CLOSED
I FELT BAD, BUT FOR THE FIRST TIME IN AWHILE, I FELT ALIVE.
CLOSED
CLOSED

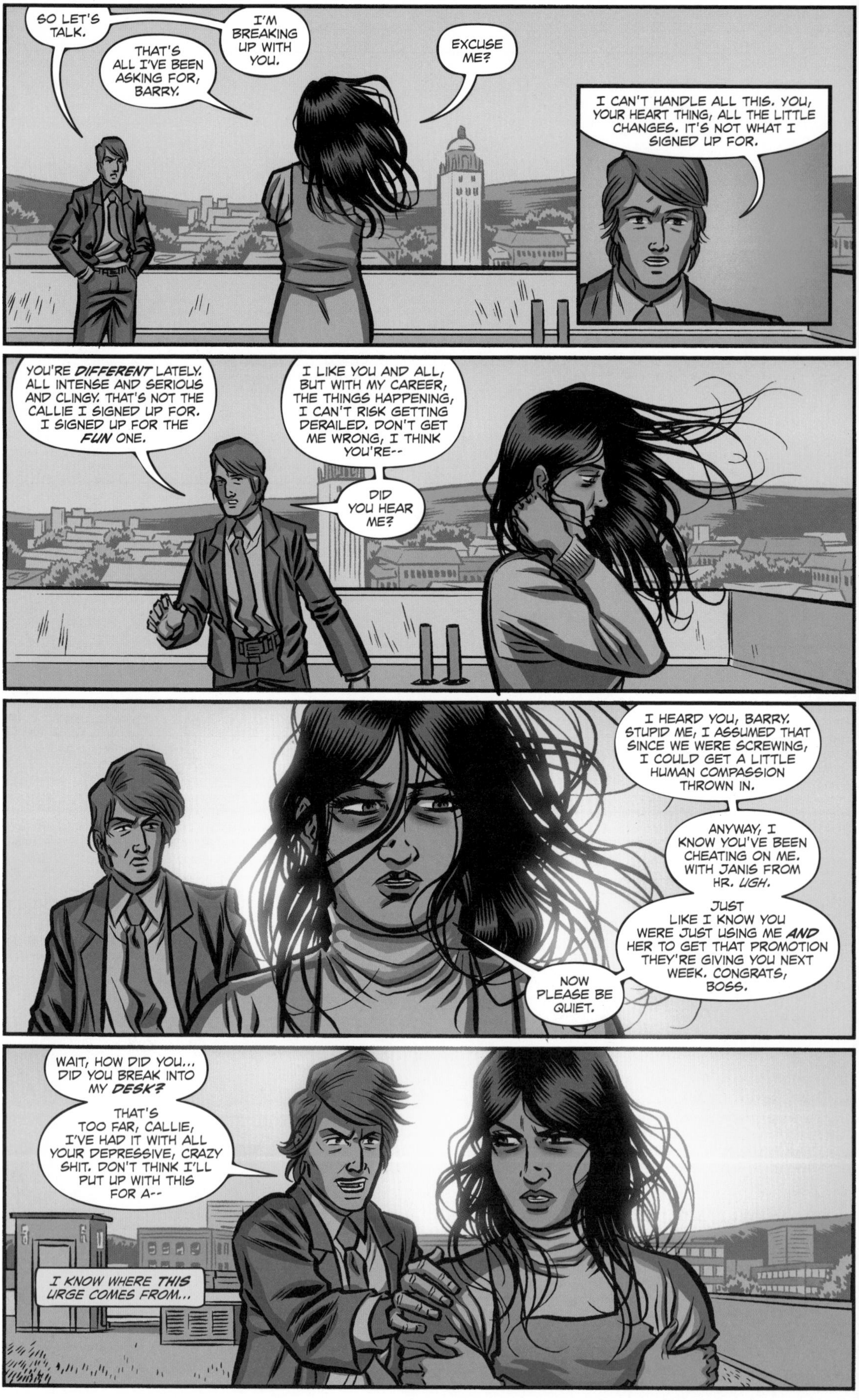
SO LET'S TALK.
THAT'S ALL I'VE BEEN ASKING FOR, BARRY.
I'M BREAKING UP WITH YOU.
EXCUSE ME?
I CAN'T HANDLE ALL THIS. YOU, YOUR HEART THING, ALL THE LITTLE CHANGES. IT'S NOT WHAT I SIGNED UP FOR.
YOU'RE DIFFERENT LATELY. ALL INTENSE AND SERIOUS AND CLINGY. THAT'S NOT THE CALLIE I SIGNED UP FOR. I SIGNED UP FOR THE FUN ONE.
I LIKE YOU AND ALL, BUT WITH MY CAREER, THE THINGS HAPPENING, I CAN'T RISK GETTING DERAILED. DON'T GET ME WRONG, I THINK YOU'RE--
DID YOU HEAR ME?
I HEARD YOU, BARRY. STUPID ME, I ASSUMED THAT SINCE WE WERE SCREWING, I COULD GET A LITTLE HUMAN COMPASSION THROWN IN.
ANYWAY, I KNOW YOU'VE BEEN CHEATING ON ME. WITH JANIS FROM HR. UGH.
JUST LIKE I KNOW YOU WERE JUST USING ME AND HER TO GET THAT PROMOTION THEY'RE GIVING YOU NEXT WEEK. CONGRATS, BOSS.
NOW PLEASE BE QUIET.
WAIT, HOW DID YOU... DID YOU BREAK INTO MY DESK?
THAT'S TOO FAR, CALLIE, I'VE HAD IT WITH ALL YOUR DEPRESSIVE, CRAZY SHIT. DON'T THINK I'LL PUT UP WITH THIS FOR A--
I KNOW WHERE THIS URGE COMES FROM...

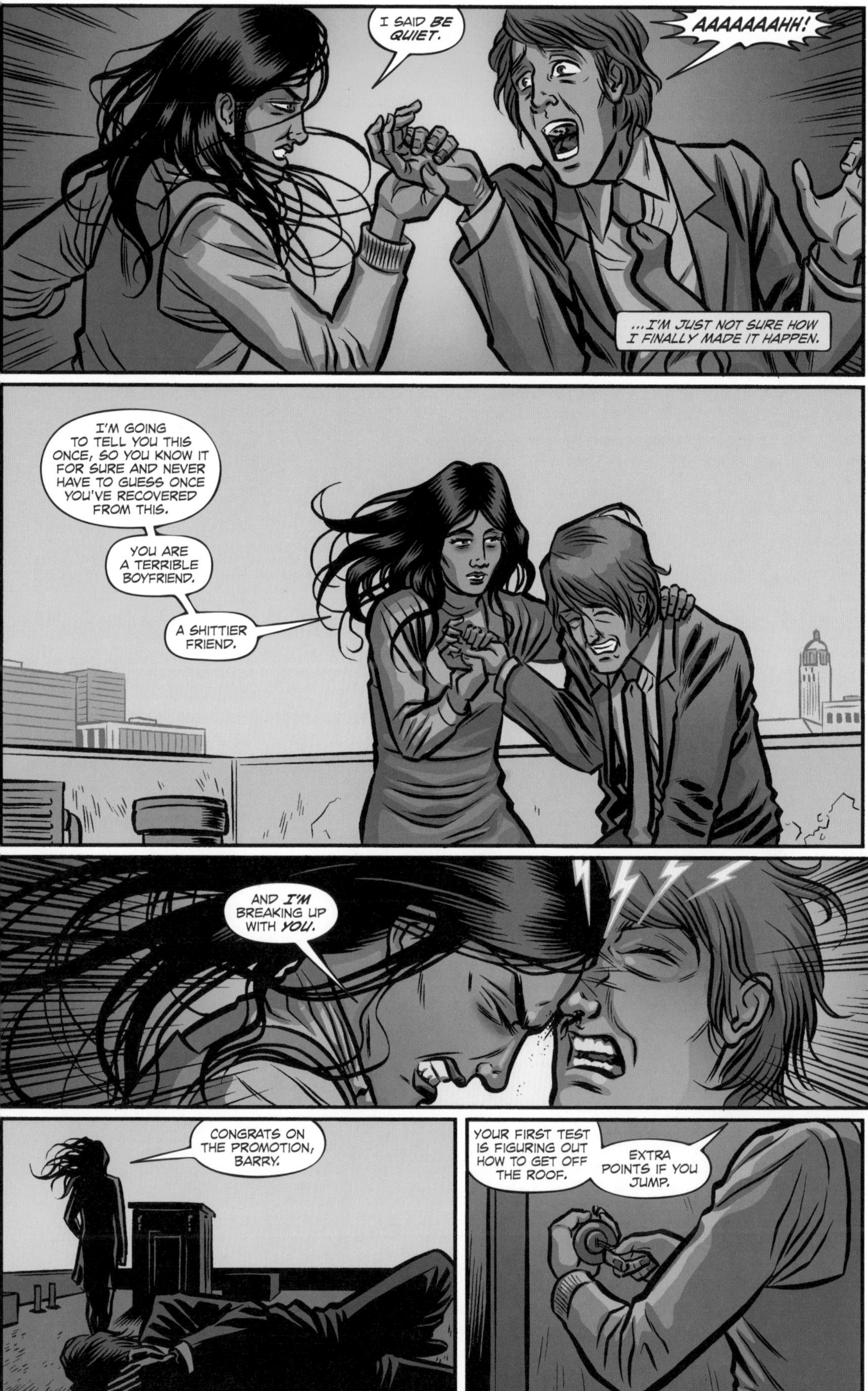
I SAID BE QUIET.
AAAAAAAHH!
...I'M JUST NOT SURE HOW I FINALLY MADE IT HAPPEN.
I'M GOING TO TELL YOU THIS ONCE, SO YOU KNOW IT FOR SURE AND NEVER HAVE TO GUESS ONCE YOU'VE RECOVERED FROM THIS.
YOU ARE A TERRIBLE BOYFRIEND.
A SHITTIER FRIEND.
AND I'M BREAKING UP WITH YOU.
CONGRATS ON THE PROMOTION, BARRY.
YOUR FIRST TEST IS FIGURING OUT HOW TO GET OFF THE ROOF.
EXTRA POINTS IF YOU JUMP.

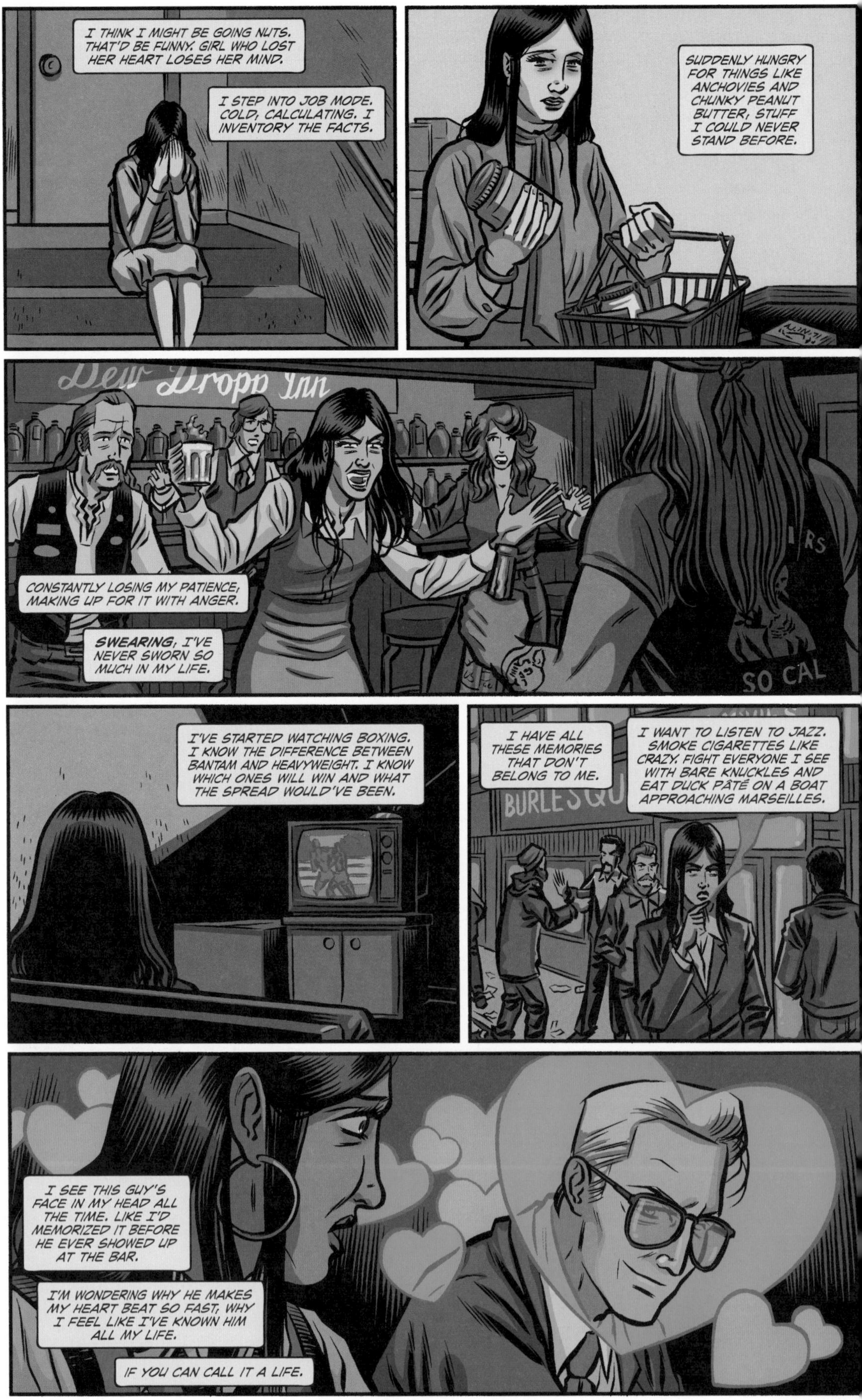
I THINK I MIGHT BE GOING NUTS. THAT'D BE FUNNY. GIRL WHO LOST HER HEART LOSES HER MIND.
I STEP INTO JOB MODE. COLD, CALCULATING. I INVENTORY THE FACTS.
SUDDENLY HUNGRY FOR THINGS LIKE ANCHOVIES AND CHUNKY PEANUT BUTTER, STUFF I COULD NEVER STAND BEFORE.
Dew Dropp Inn
CONSTANTLY LOSING MY PATIENCE, MAKING UP FOR IT WITH ANGER.
SWEARING, I'VE NEVER SWORN SO MUCH IN MY LIFE.
SO CAL
I'VE STARTED WATCHING BOXING. I KNOW THE DIFFERENCE BETWEEN BANTAM AND HEAVYWEIGHT. I KNOW WHICH ONES WILL WIN AND WHAT THE SPREAD WOULD'VE BEEN.
I HAVE ALL THESE MEMORIES THAT DON'T BELONG TO ME.
I WANT TO LISTEN TO JAZZ. SMOKE CIGARETTES LIKE CRAZY. FIGHT EVERYONE I SEE WITH BARE KNUCKLES AND EAT DUCK PÂTÉ ON A BOAT APPROACHING MARSEILLES.
BURLESQU
I SEE THIS GUY'S FACE IN MY HEAD ALL THE TIME. LIKE I'D MEMORIZED IT BEFORE HE EVER SHOWED UP AT THE BAR.
I'M WONDERING WHY HE MAKES MY HEART BEAT SO FAST, WHY I FEEL LIKE I'VE KNOWN HIM ALL MY LIFE.
IF YOU CAN CALL IT A LIFE.

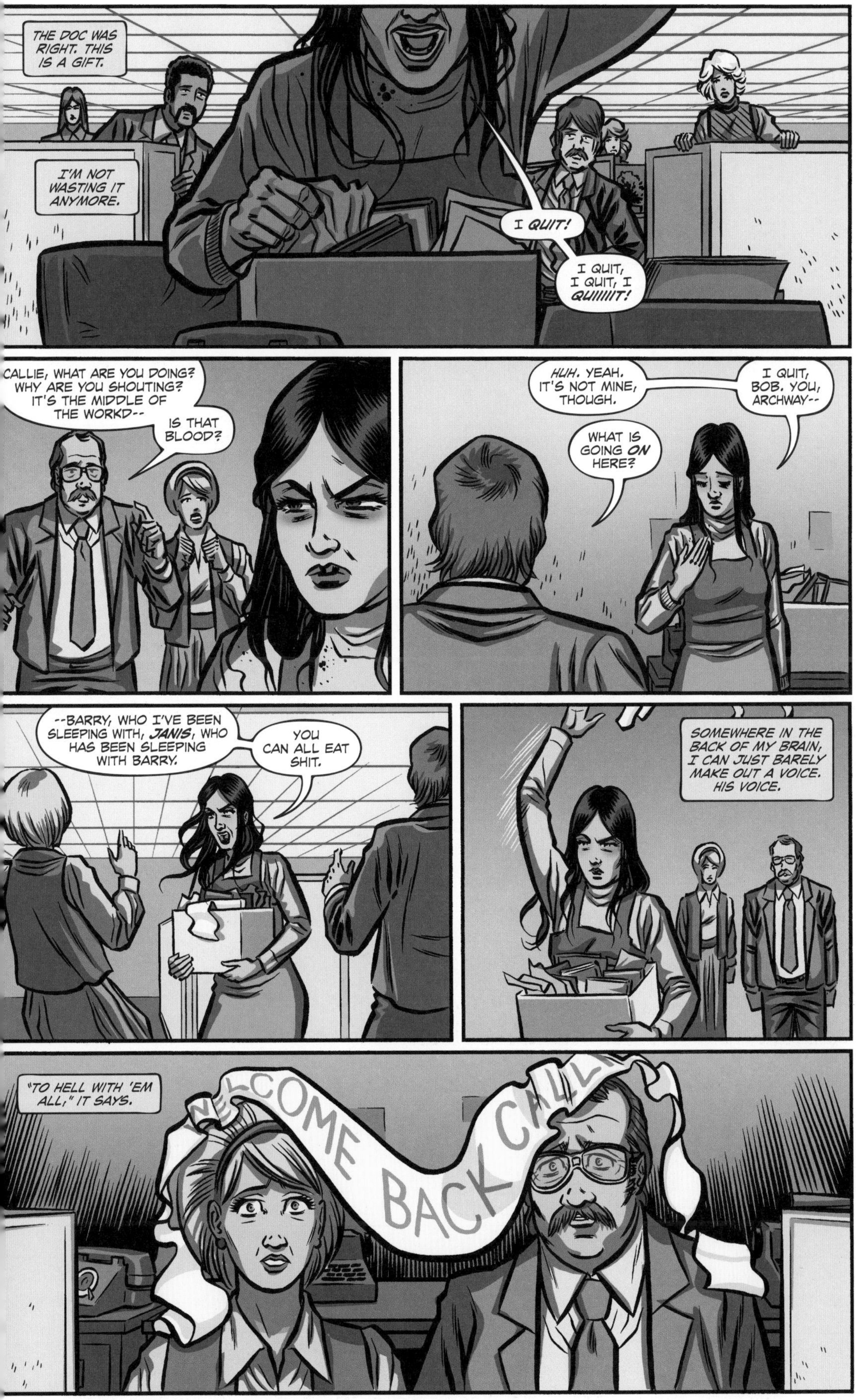

THE DOC WAS RIGHT. THIS IS A GIFT.
I'M NOT WASTING IT ANYMORE.
I QUIT!
I QUIT, I QUIT, I QUIIIIIT!
CALLIE, WHAT ARE YOU DOING? WHY ARE YOU SHOUTING? IT'S THE MIDDLE OF THE WORKD--
IS THAT BLOOD?
HUH. YEAH. IT'S NOT MINE, THOUGH.
I QUIT, BOB. YOU, ARCHWAY--
WHAT IS GOING ON HERE?
--BARRY, WHO I'VE BEEN SLEEPING WITH, JANIS, WHO HAS BEEN SLEEPING WITH BARRY.
YOU CAN ALL EAT SHIT.
SOMEWHERE IN THE BACK OF MY BRAIN, I CAN JUST BARELY MAKE OUT A VOICE. HIS VOICE.
"TO HELL WITH 'EM ALL," IT SAYS.

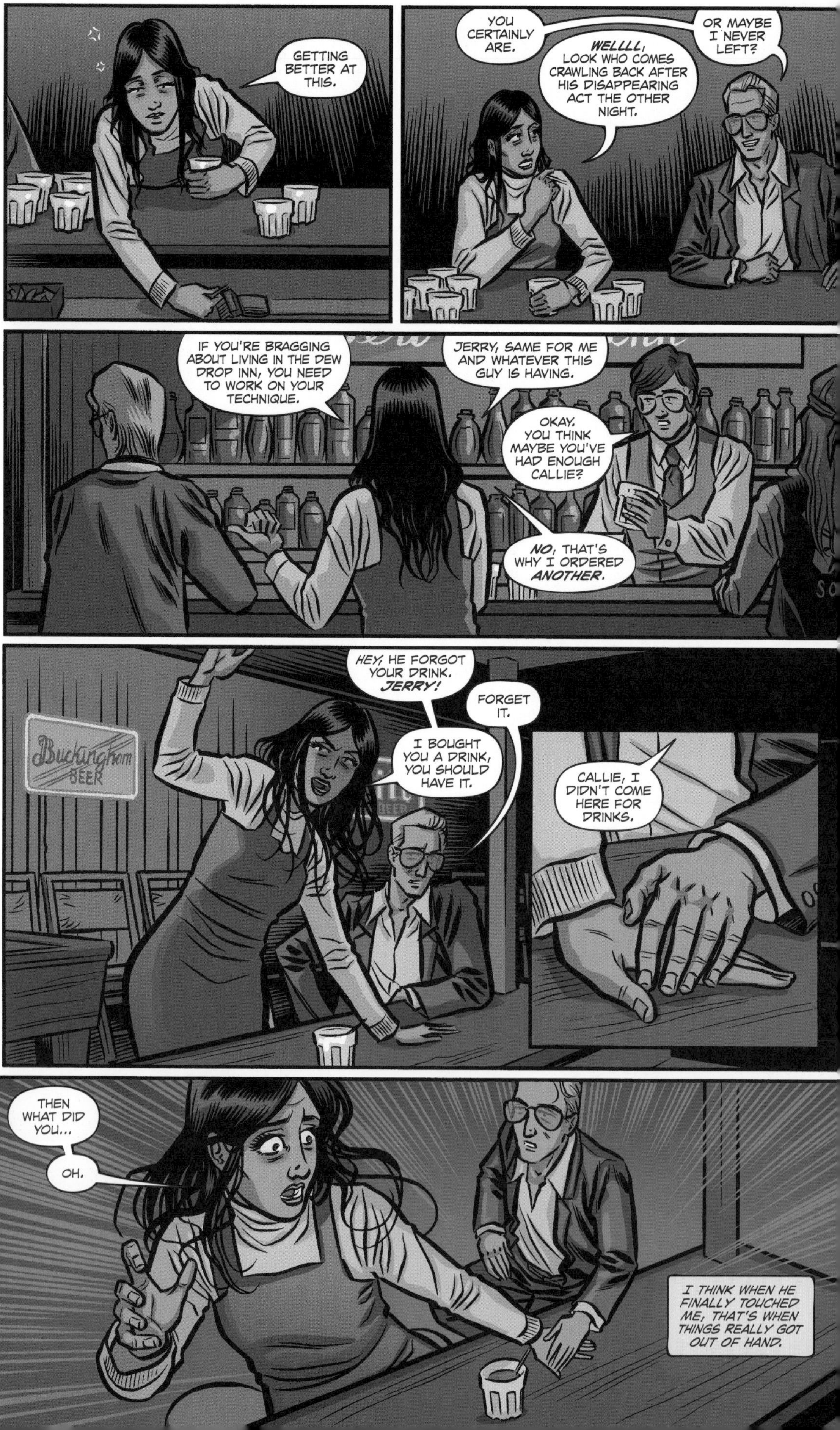

GETTING BETTER AT THIS.
YOU CERTAINLY ARE.
OR MAYBE I NEVER LEFT?
WELLLL, LOOK WHO COMES CRAWLING BACK AFTER HIS DISAPPEARING ACT THE OTHER NIGHT.
IF YOU'RE BRAGGING ABOUT LIVING IN THE DEW DROP INN, YOU NEED TO WORK ON YOUR TECHNIQUE.
JERRY, SAME FOR ME AND WHATEVER THIS GUY IS HAVING.
OKAY. YOU THINK MAYBE YOU'VE HAD ENOUGH CALLIE?
NO, THAT'S WHY I ORDERED ANOTHER.
Buckingham BEER
HEY, HE FORGOT YOUR DRINK. JERRY!
FORGET IT.
I BOUGHT YOU A DRINK, YOU SHOULD HAVE IT.
CALLIE, I DIDN'T COME HERE FOR DRINKS.
THEN WHAT DID YOU...
OH.
I THINK WHEN HE FINALLY TOUCHED ME, THAT'S WHEN THINGS REALLY GOT OUT OF HAND.

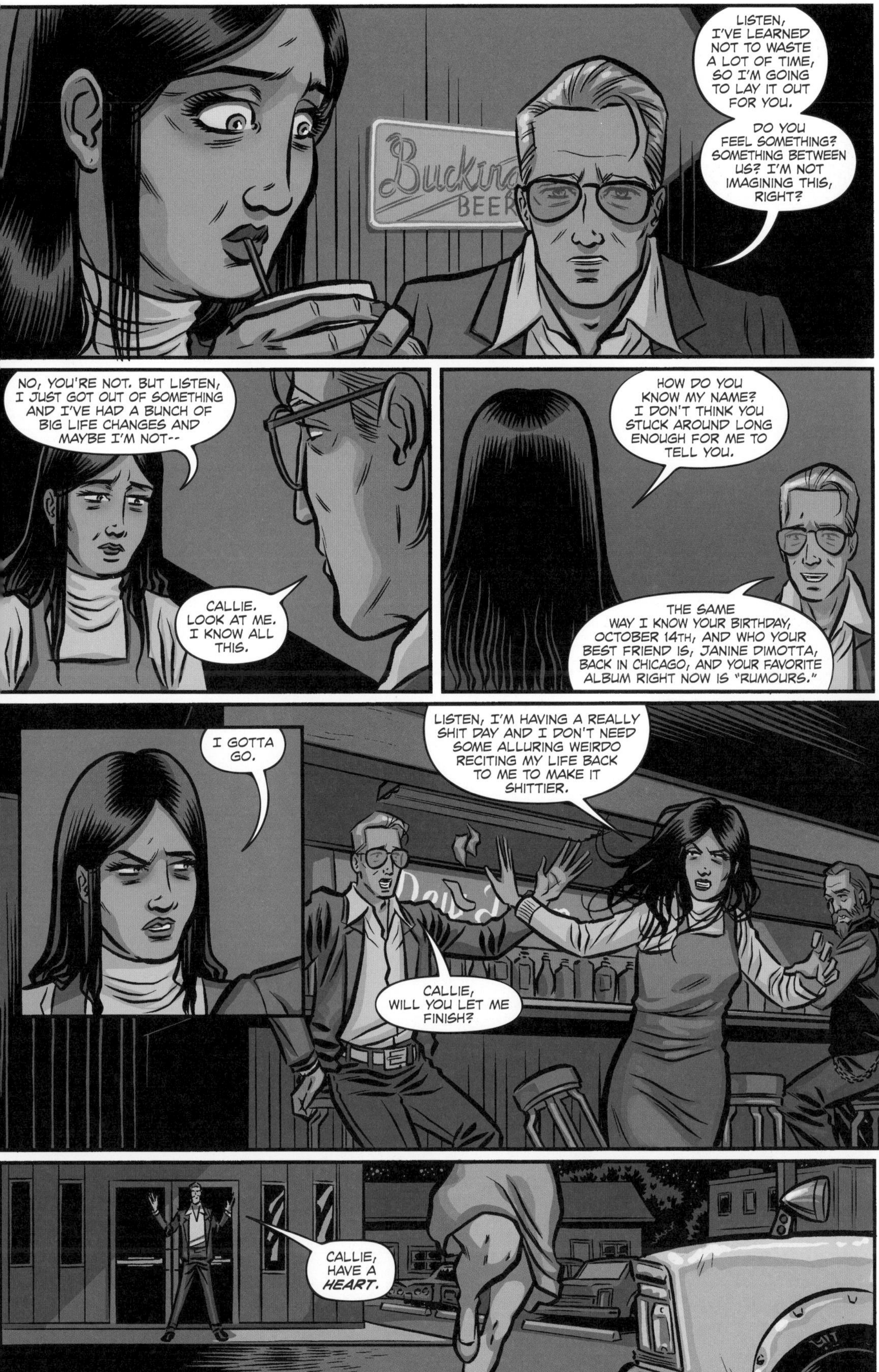
LISTEN, I'VE LEARNED NOT TO WASTE A LOT OF TIME, SO I'M GOING TO LAY IT OUT FOR YOU.
DO YOU FEEL SOMETHING? SOMETHING BETWEEN US? I'M NOT IMAGINING THIS, RIGHT?
BEER
NO, YOU'RE NOT. BUT LISTEN, I JUST GOT OUT OF SOMETHING AND I'VE HAD A BUNCH OF BIG LIFE CHANGES AND MAYBE I'M NOT--
CALLIE. LOOK AT ME. I KNOW ALL THIS.
HOW DO YOU KNOW MY NAME? I DON'T THINK YOU STUCK AROUND LONG ENOUGH FOR ME TO TELL YOU.
THE SAME WAY I KNOW YOUR BIRTHDAY, OCTOBER 14TH, AND WHO YOUR BEST FRIEND IS, JANINE DIMOTTA, BACK IN CHICAGO, AND YOUR FAVORITE ALBUM RIGHT NOW IS "RUMOURS."
I GOTTA GO.
LISTEN, I'M HAVING A REALLY SHIT DAY AND I DON'T NEED SOME ALLURING WEIRDO RECITING MY LIFE BACK TO ME TO MAKE IT SHITTIER.
CALLIE, WILL YOU LET ME FINISH?
CALLIE, HAVE A ***HEART***.

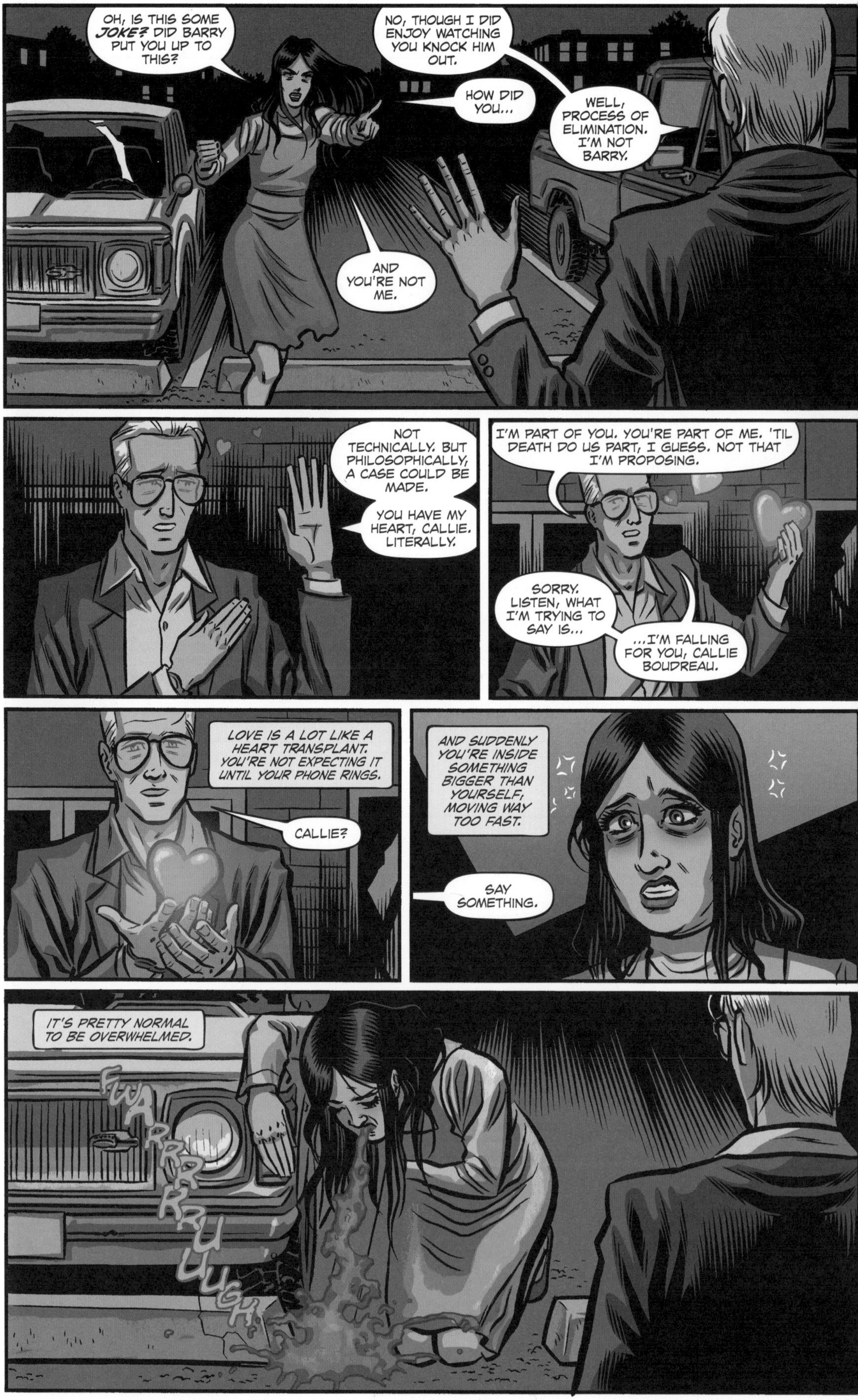

OH, IS THIS SOME JOKE? DID BARRY PUT YOU UP TO THIS?
NO, THOUGH I DID ENJOY WATCHING YOU KNOCK HIM OUT.
HOW DID YOU...
WELL, PROCESS OF ELIMINATION. I'M NOT BARRY.
AND YOU'RE NOT ME.
NOT TECHNICALLY. BUT PHILOSOPHICALLY, A CASE COULD BE MADE.
YOU HAVE MY HEART, CALLIE. LITERALLY.
I'M PART OF YOU. YOU'RE PART OF ME. 'TIL DEATH DO US PART, I GUESS. NOT THAT I'M PROPOSING.
SORRY. LISTEN, WHAT I'M TRYING TO SAY IS...
...I'M FALLING FOR YOU, CALLIE BOUDREAU.
LOVE IS A LOT LIKE A HEART TRANSPLANT. YOU'RE NOT EXPECTING IT UNTIL YOUR PHONE RINGS.
CALLIE?
AND SUDDENLY YOU'RE INSIDE SOMETHING BIGGER THAN YOURSELF, MOVING WAY TOO FAST.
SAY SOMETHING.
IT'S PRETTY NORMAL TO BE OVERWHELMED.
FWARRRRRUUUGH!

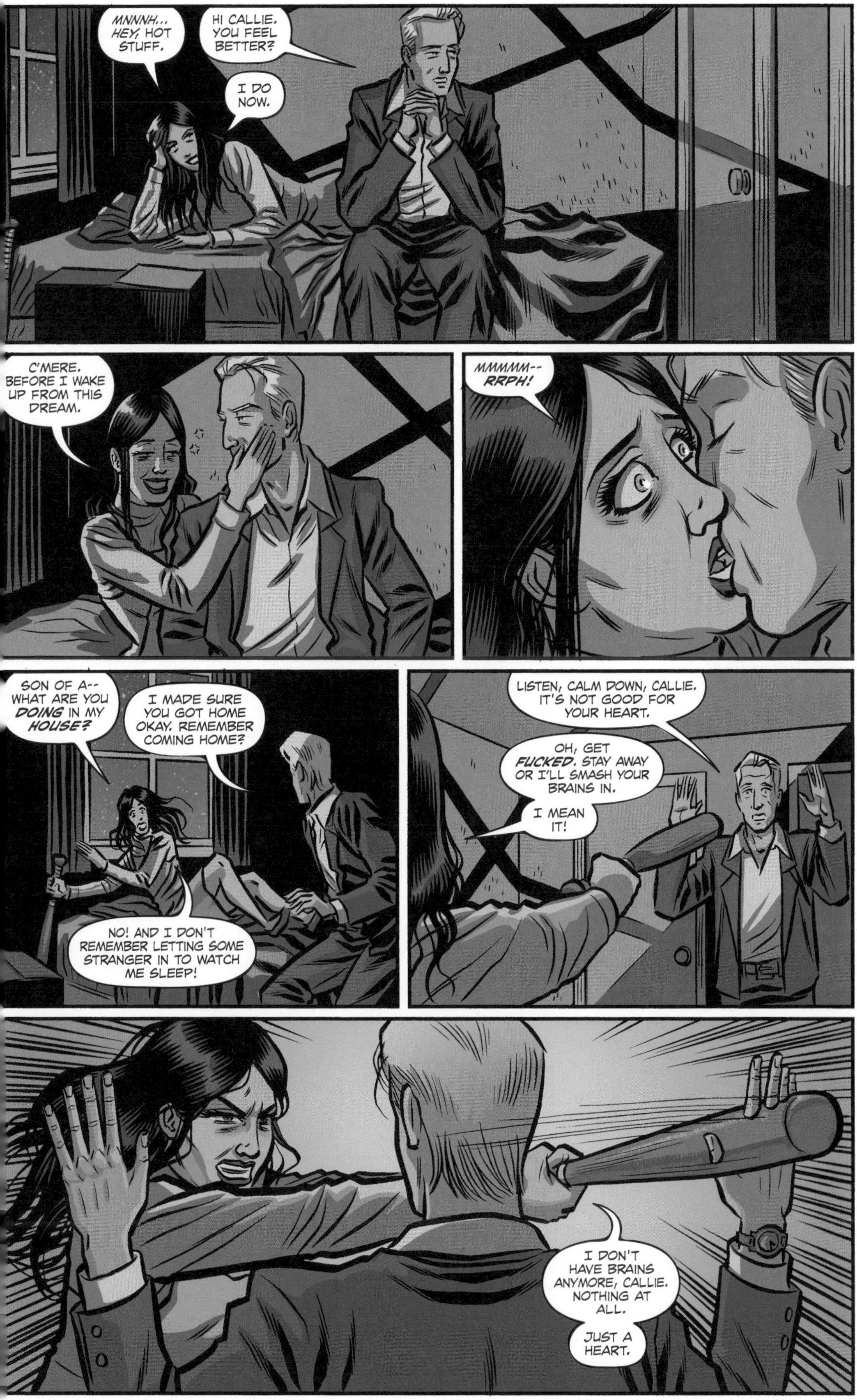
MNNNH... HEY, HOT STUFF.
HI CALLIE. YOU FEEL BETTER?
I DO NOW.
C'MERE. BEFORE I WAKE UP FROM THIS DREAM.
MMMMM--RRPH!
SON OF A-- WHAT ARE YOU DOING IN MY HOUSE?
I MADE SURE YOU GOT HOME OKAY. REMEMBER COMING HOME?
NO! AND I DON'T REMEMBER LETTING SOME STRANGER IN TO WATCH ME SLEEP!
LISTEN, CALM DOWN, CALLIE. IT'S NOT GOOD FOR YOUR HEART.
OH, GET FUCKED. STAY AWAY OR I'LL SMASH YOUR BRAINS IN.
I MEAN IT!
I DON'T HAVE BRAINS ANYMORE, CALLIE. NOTHING AT ALL.
JUST A HEART.

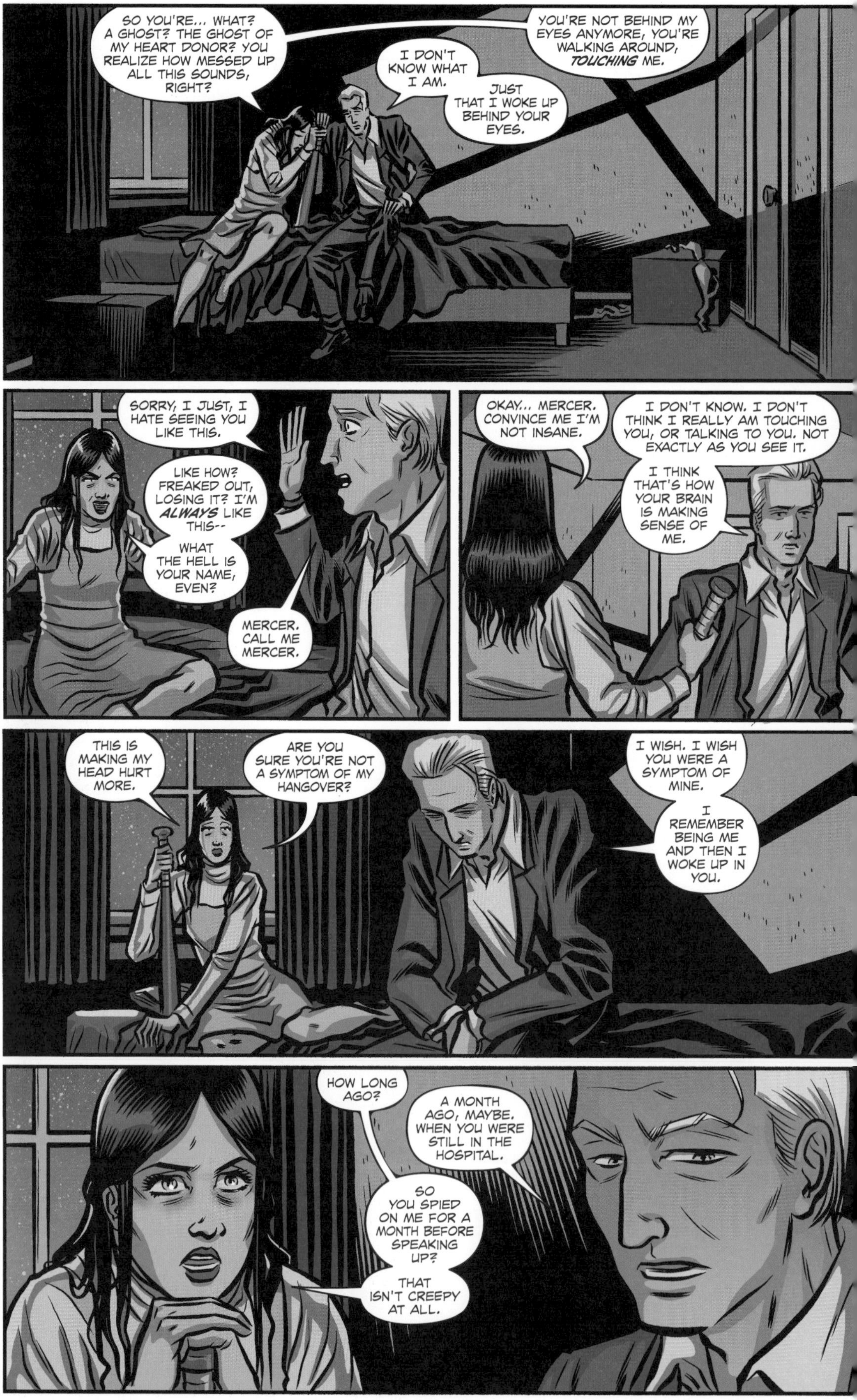
SO YOU'RE... WHAT? A GHOST? THE GHOST OF MY HEART DONOR? YOU REALIZE HOW MESSED UP ALL THIS SOUNDS, RIGHT?
I DON'T KNOW WHAT I AM.
JUST THAT I WOKE UP BEHIND YOUR EYES.
YOU'RE NOT BEHIND MY EYES ANYMORE, YOU'RE WALKING AROUND, TOUCHING ME.
SORRY, I JUST, I HATE SEEING YOU LIKE THIS.
LIKE HOW? FREAKED OUT, LOSING IT? I'M ALWAYS LIKE THIS--
WHAT THE HELL IS YOUR NAME, EVEN?
MERCER. CALL ME MERCER.
OKAY... MERCER. CONVINCE ME I'M NOT INSANE.
I DON'T KNOW. I DON'T THINK I REALLY AM TOUCHING YOU, OR TALKING TO YOU. NOT EXACTLY AS YOU SEE IT.
I THINK THAT'S HOW YOUR BRAIN IS MAKING SENSE OF ME.
THIS IS MAKING MY HEAD HURT MORE.
ARE YOU SURE YOU'RE NOT A SYMPTOM OF MY HANGOVER?
I WISH. I WISH YOU WERE A SYMPTOM OF MINE.
I REMEMBER BEING ME AND THEN I WOKE UP IN YOU.
HOW LONG AGO?
A MONTH AGO, MAYBE. WHEN YOU WERE STILL IN THE HOSPITAL.
SO YOU SPIED ON ME FOR A MONTH BEFORE SPEAKING UP?
THAT ISN'T CREEPY AT ALL.

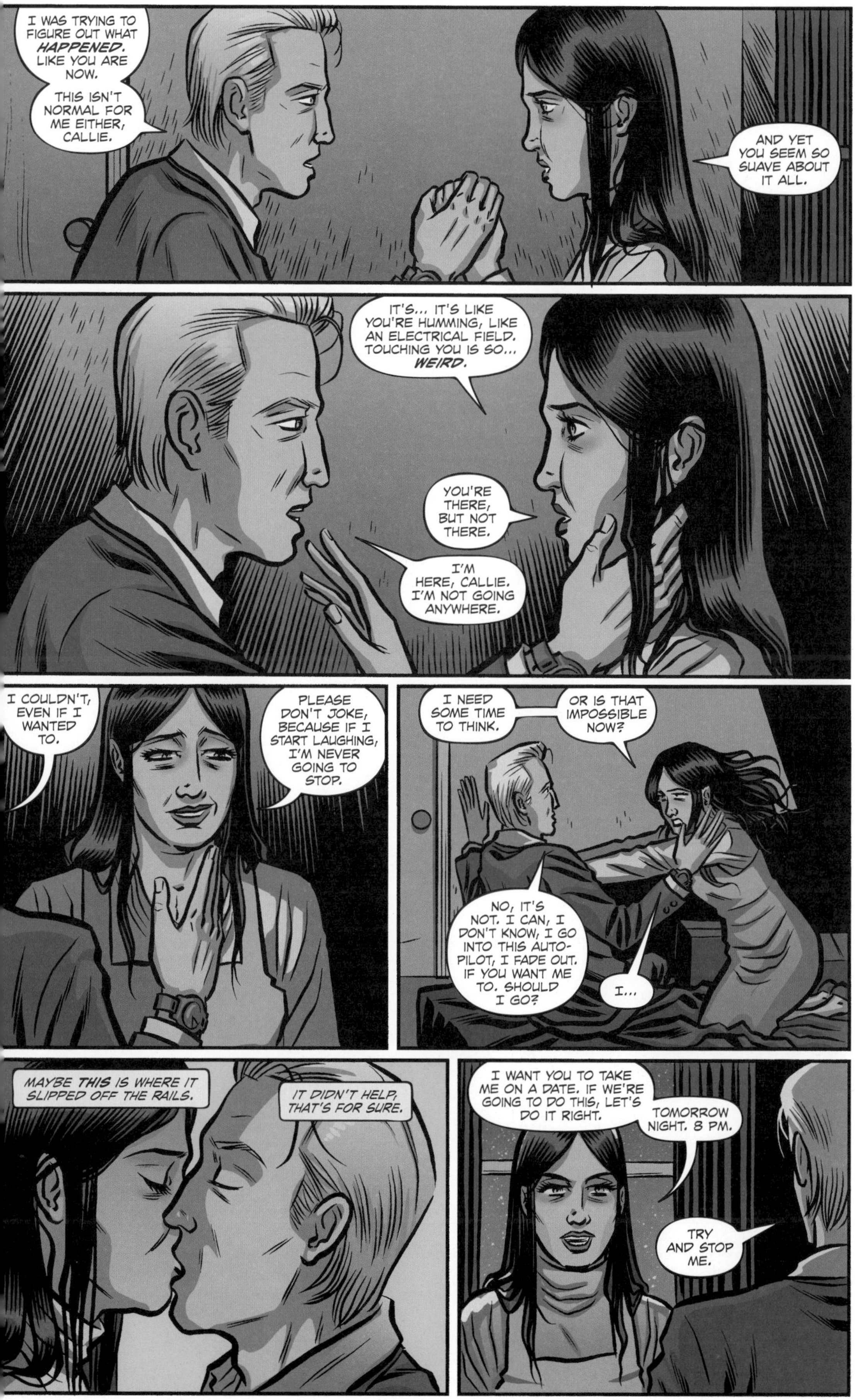
I WAS TRYING TO FIGURE OUT WHAT HAPPENED. LIKE YOU ARE NOW.
THIS ISN'T NORMAL FOR ME EITHER, CALLIE.
AND YET YOU SEEM SO SUAVE ABOUT IT ALL.
IT'S... IT'S LIKE YOU'RE HUMMING, LIKE AN ELECTRICAL FIELD. TOUCHING YOU IS SO... WEIRD.
YOU'RE THERE, BUT NOT THERE.
I'M HERE, CALLIE. I'M NOT GOING ANYWHERE.
I COULDN'T, EVEN IF I WANTED TO.
PLEASE DON'T JOKE, BECAUSE IF I START LAUGHING, I'M NEVER GOING TO STOP.
I NEED SOME TIME TO THINK.
OR IS THAT IMPOSSIBLE NOW?
NO, IT'S NOT. I CAN, I DON'T KNOW, I GO INTO THIS AUTO-PILOT, I FADE OUT. IF YOU WANT ME TO. SHOULD I GO?
I...
MAYBE THIS IS WHERE IT SLIPPED OFF THE RAILS.
IT DIDN'T HELP, THAT'S FOR SURE.
I WANT YOU TO TAKE ME ON A DATE. IF WE'RE GOING TO DO THIS, LET'S DO IT RIGHT.
TOMORROW NIGHT. 8 PM.
TRY AND STOP ME.

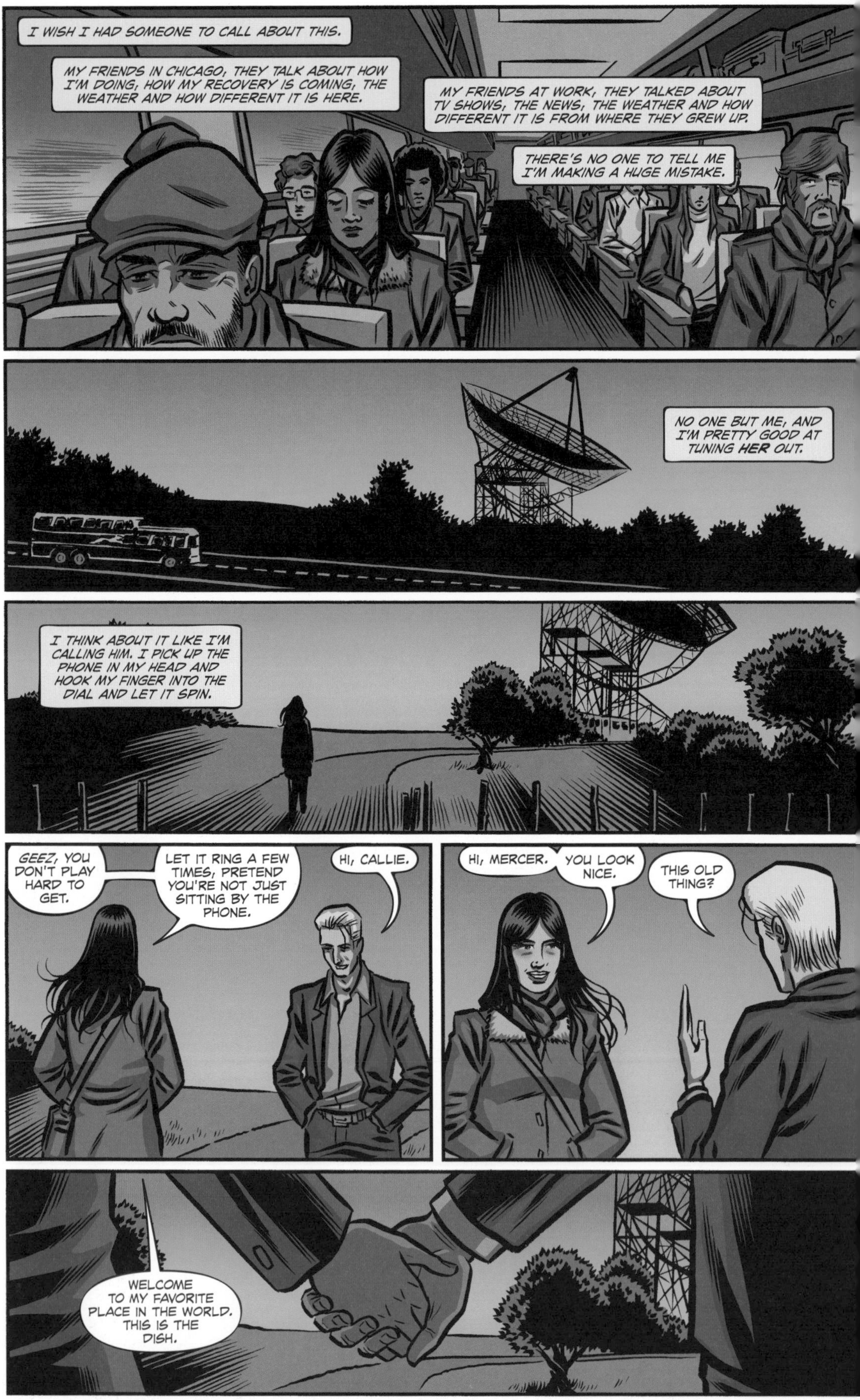
I WISH I HAD SOMEONE TO CALL ABOUT THIS.
MY FRIENDS IN CHICAGO, THEY TALK ABOUT HOW I'M DOING, HOW MY RECOVERY IS COMING, THE WEATHER AND HOW DIFFERENT IT IS HERE.
MY FRIENDS AT WORK, THEY TALKED ABOUT TV SHOWS, THE NEWS, THE WEATHER AND HOW DIFFERENT IT IS FROM WHERE THEY GREW UP.
THERE'S NO ONE TO TELL ME I'M MAKING A HUGE MISTAKE.
NO ONE BUT ME, AND I'M PRETTY GOOD AT TUNING HER OUT.
I THINK ABOUT IT LIKE I'M CALLING HIM. I PICK UP THE PHONE IN MY HEAD AND HOOK MY FINGER INTO THE DIAL AND LET IT SPIN.
GEEZ, YOU DON'T PLAY HARD TO GET.
LET IT RING A FEW TIMES, PRETEND YOU'RE NOT JUST SITTING BY THE PHONE.
HI, CALLIE.
HI, MERCER.
YOU LOOK NICE.
THIS OLD THING?
WELCOME TO MY FAVORITE PLACE IN THE WORLD. THIS IS THE DISH.

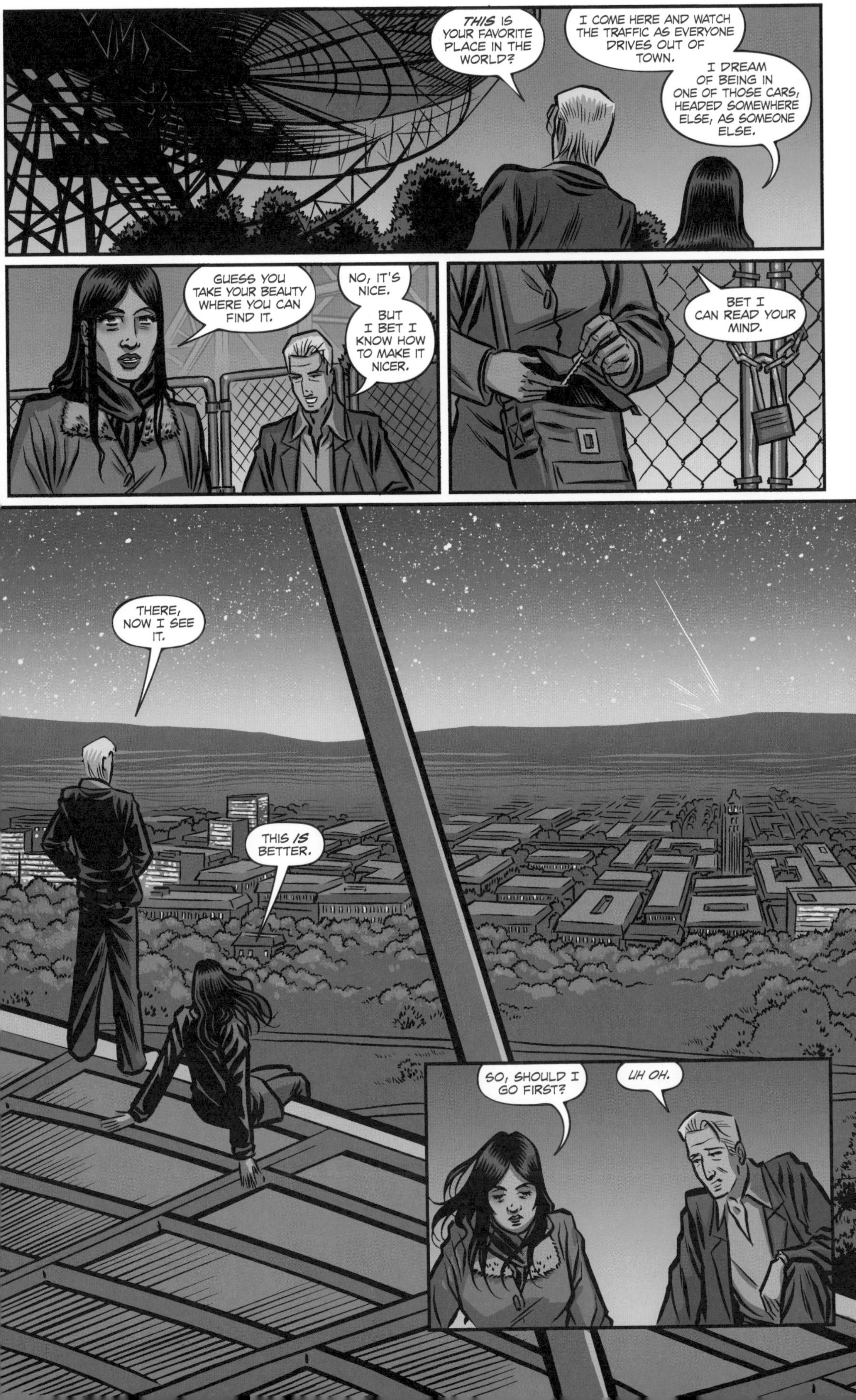
THIS IS YOUR FAVORITE PLACE IN THE WORLD?
I COME HERE AND WATCH THE TRAFFIC AS EVERYONE DRIVES OUT OF TOWN.
I DREAM OF BEING IN ONE OF THOSE CARS, HEADED SOMEWHERE ELSE, AS SOMEONE ELSE.
GUESS YOU TAKE YOUR BEAUTY WHERE YOU CAN FIND IT.
NO, IT'S NICE.
BUT I BET I KNOW HOW TO MAKE IT NICER.
BET I CAN READ YOUR MIND.
THERE, NOW I SEE IT.
THIS IS BETTER.
SO, SHOULD I GO FIRST?
UH OH.

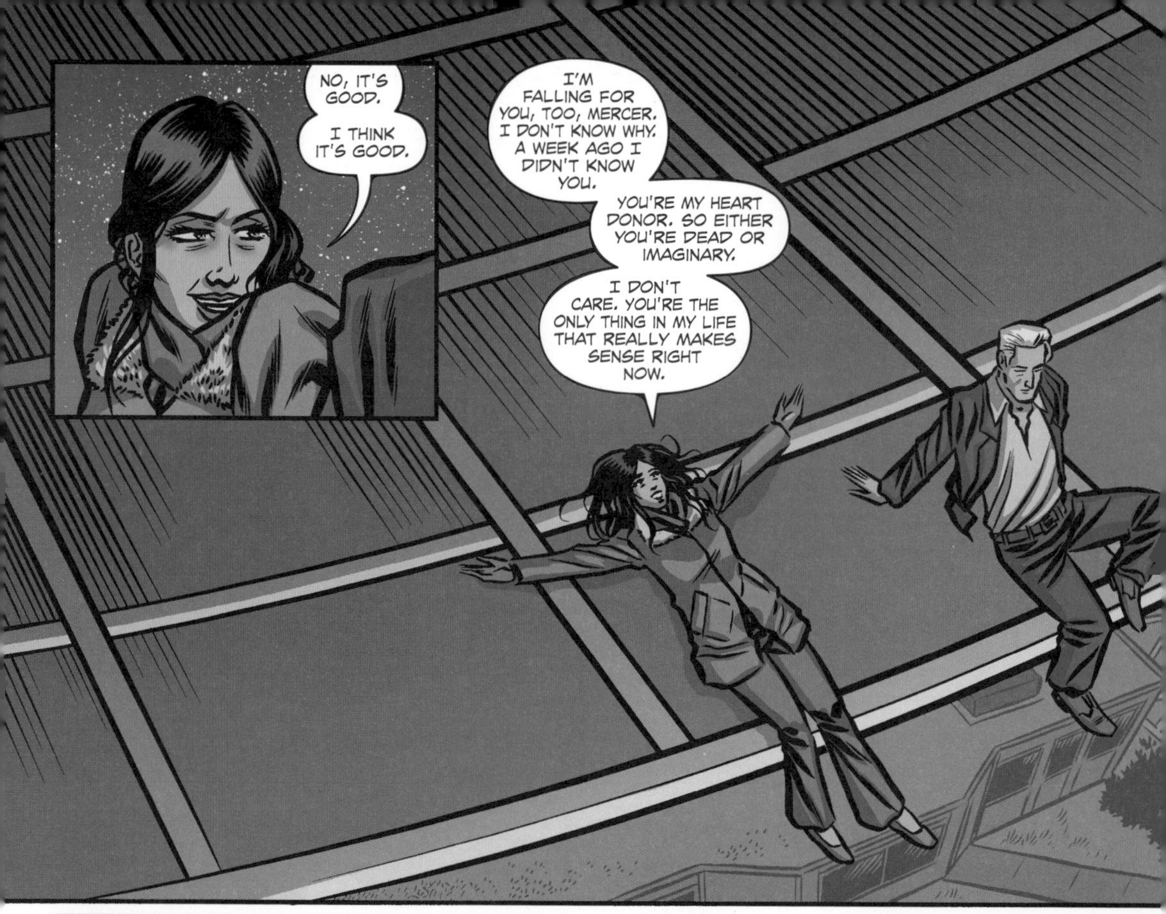
NO, IT'S GOOD.
I THINK IT'S GOOD.
I'M FALLING FOR YOU, TOO, MERCER. I DON'T KNOW WHY. A WEEK AGO I DIDN'T KNOW YOU.
YOU'RE MY HEART DONOR. SO EITHER YOU'RE DEAD OR IMAGINARY.
I DON'T CARE. YOU'RE THE ONLY THING IN MY LIFE THAT REALLY MAKES SENSE RIGHT NOW.

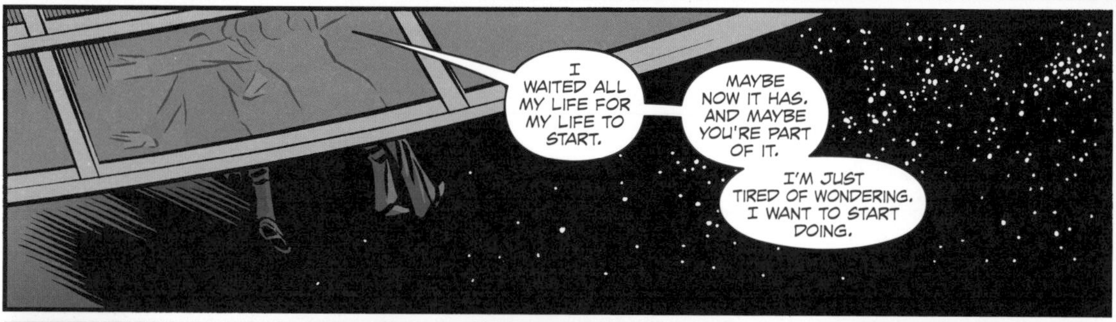
I WAITED ALL MY LIFE FOR MY LIFE TO START.
MAYBE NOW IT HAS. AND MAYBE YOU'RE PART OF IT.
I'M JUST TIRED OF WONDERING. I WANT TO START DOING.

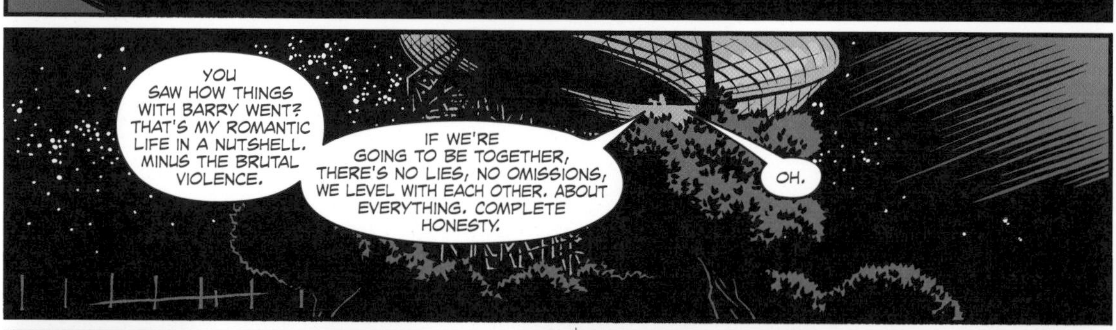
YOU SAW HOW THINGS WITH BARRY WENT? THAT'S MY ROMANTIC LIFE IN A NUTSHELL. MINUS THE BRUTAL VIOLENCE.
IF WE'RE GOING TO BE TOGETHER, THERE'S NO LIES, NO OMISSIONS, WE LEVEL WITH EACH OTHER. ABOUT EVERYTHING. COMPLETE HONESTY.
OH.

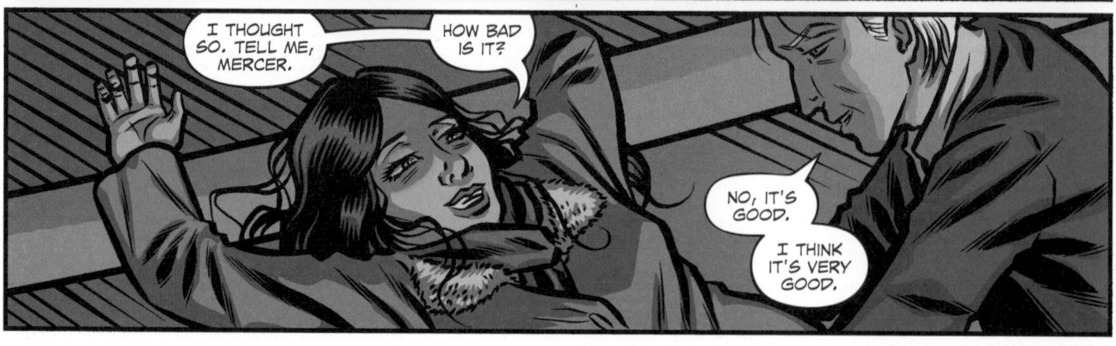
I THOUGHT SO. TELL ME, MERCER.
HOW BAD IS IT?
NO, IT'S GOOD.
I THINK IT'S VERY GOOD.

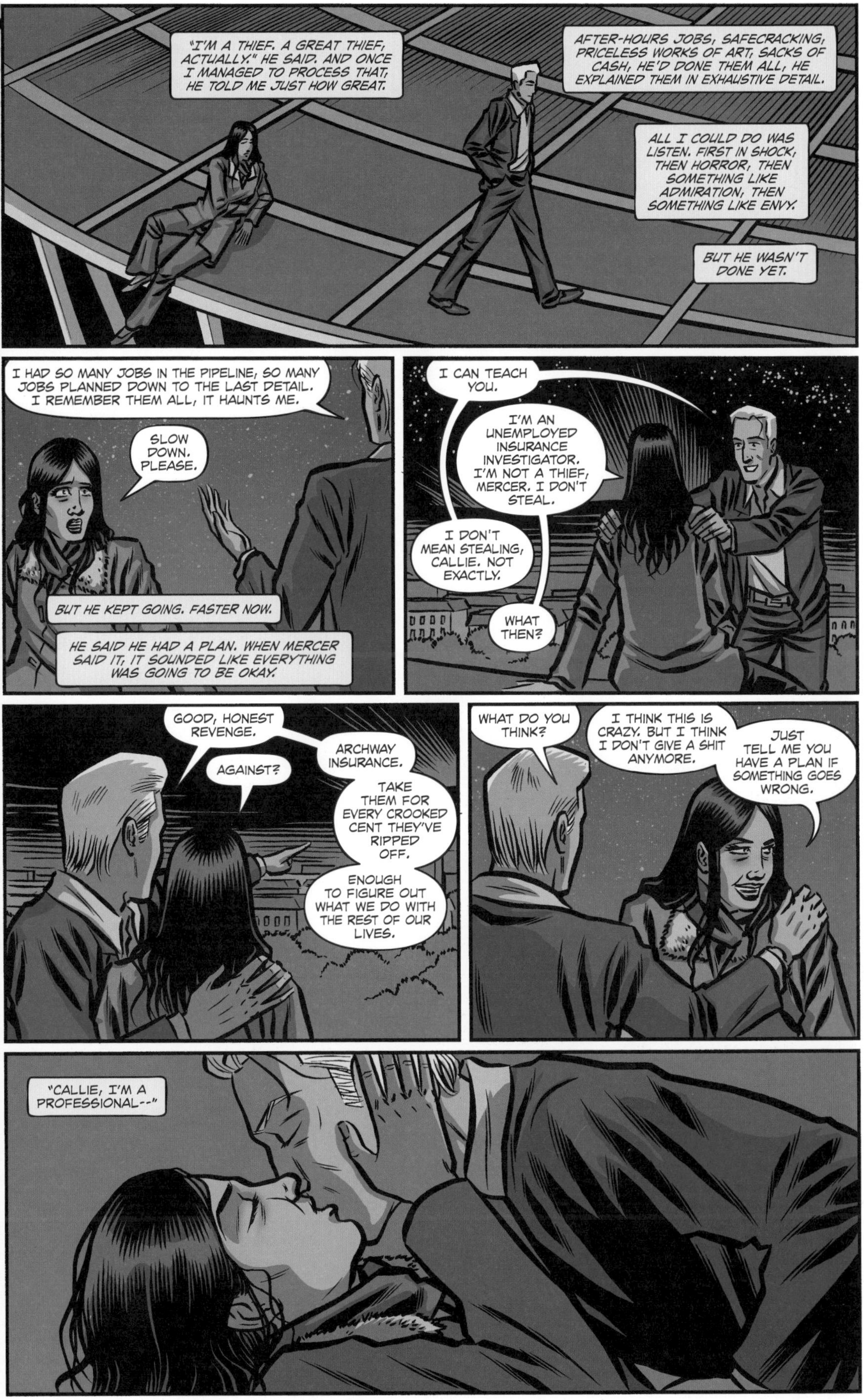
"I'M A THIEF. A GREAT THIEF, ACTUALLY." HE SAID. AND ONCE I MANAGED TO PROCESS THAT, HE TOLD ME JUST HOW GREAT.
AFTER-HOURS JOBS, SAFECRACKING, PRICELESS WORKS OF ART, SACKS OF CASH, HE'D DONE THEM ALL, HE EXPLAINED THEM IN EXHAUSTIVE DETAIL.
ALL I COULD DO WAS LISTEN. FIRST IN SHOCK, THEN HORROR, THEN SOMETHING LIKE ADMIRATION, THEN SOMETHING LIKE ENVY.
BUT HE WASN'T DONE YET.
I HAD SO MANY JOBS IN THE PIPELINE, SO MANY JOBS PLANNED DOWN TO THE LAST DETAIL. I REMEMBER THEM ALL, IT HAUNTS ME.
SLOW DOWN. PLEASE.
BUT HE KEPT GOING. FASTER NOW.
HE SAID HE HAD A PLAN. WHEN MERCER SAID IT, IT SOUNDED LIKE EVERYTHING WAS GOING TO BE OKAY.
I CAN TEACH YOU.
I'M AN UNEMPLOYED INSURANCE INVESTIGATOR. I'M NOT A THIEF, MERCER. I DON'T STEAL.
I DON'T MEAN STEALING, CALLIE. NOT EXACTLY.
WHAT THEN?
GOOD, HONEST REVENGE.
AGAINST?
ARCHWAY INSURANCE.
TAKE THEM FOR EVERY CROOKED CENT THEY'VE RIPPED OFF.
ENOUGH TO FIGURE OUT WHAT WE DO WITH THE REST OF OUR LIVES.
WHAT DO YOU THINK?
I THINK THIS IS CRAZY. BUT I THINK I DON'T GIVE A SHIT ANYMORE.
JUST TELL ME YOU HAVE A PLAN IF SOMETHING GOES WRONG.
"CALLIE, I'M A PROFESSIONAL--"

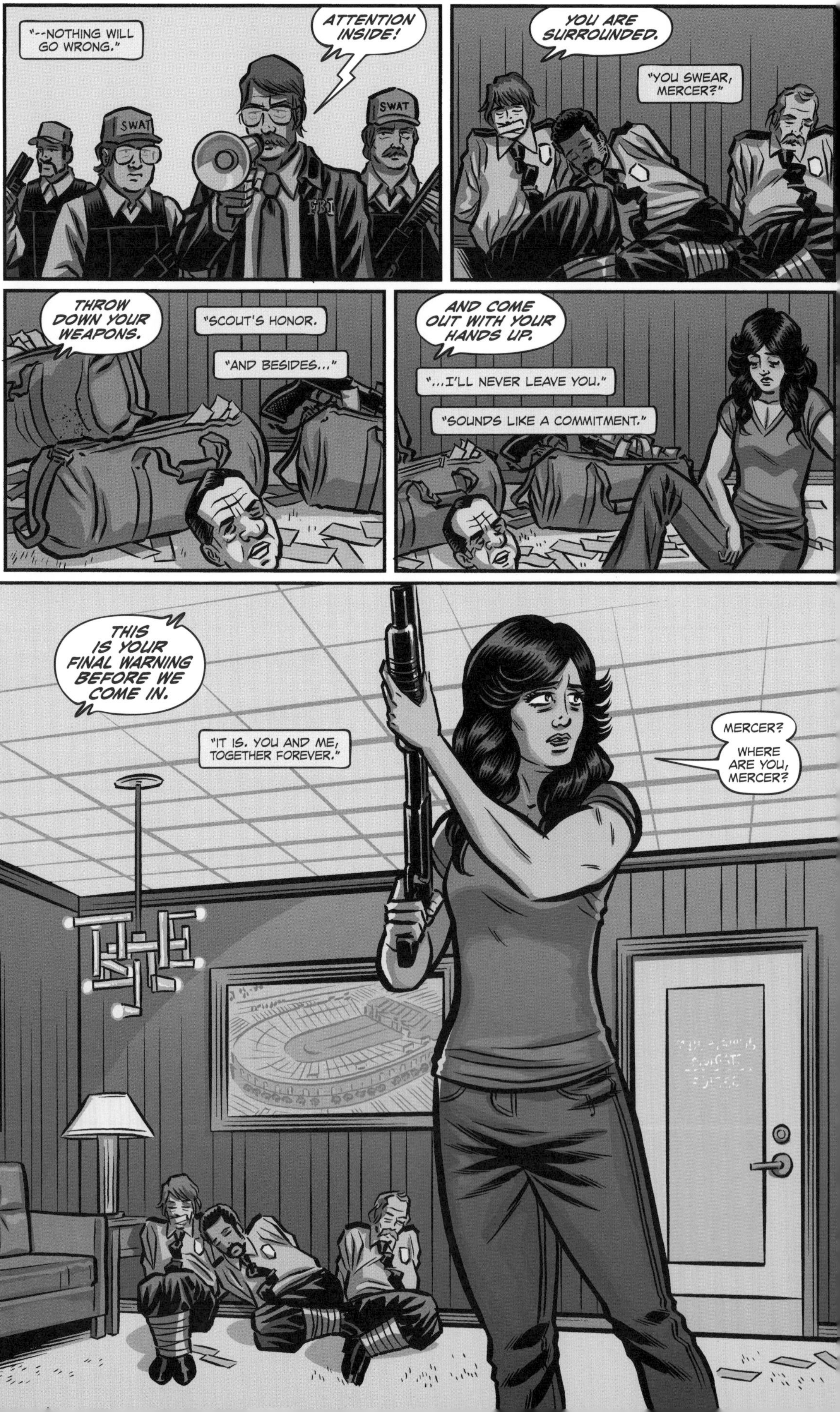
"--NOTHING WILL GO WRONG."
ATTENTION INSIDE!
SWAT
SWAT
FBI
YOU ARE SURROUNDED.
"YOU SWEAR, MERCER?"
THROW DOWN YOUR WEAPONS.
"SCOUT'S HONOR.
"AND BESIDES..."
AND COME OUT WITH YOUR HANDS UP.
"...I'LL NEVER LEAVE YOU."
"SOUNDS LIKE A COMMITMENT."
THIS IS YOUR FINAL WARNING BEFORE WE COME IN.
"IT IS. YOU AND ME, TOGETHER FOREVER."
MERCER?
WHERE ARE YOU, MERCER?

# CHAPTER 2

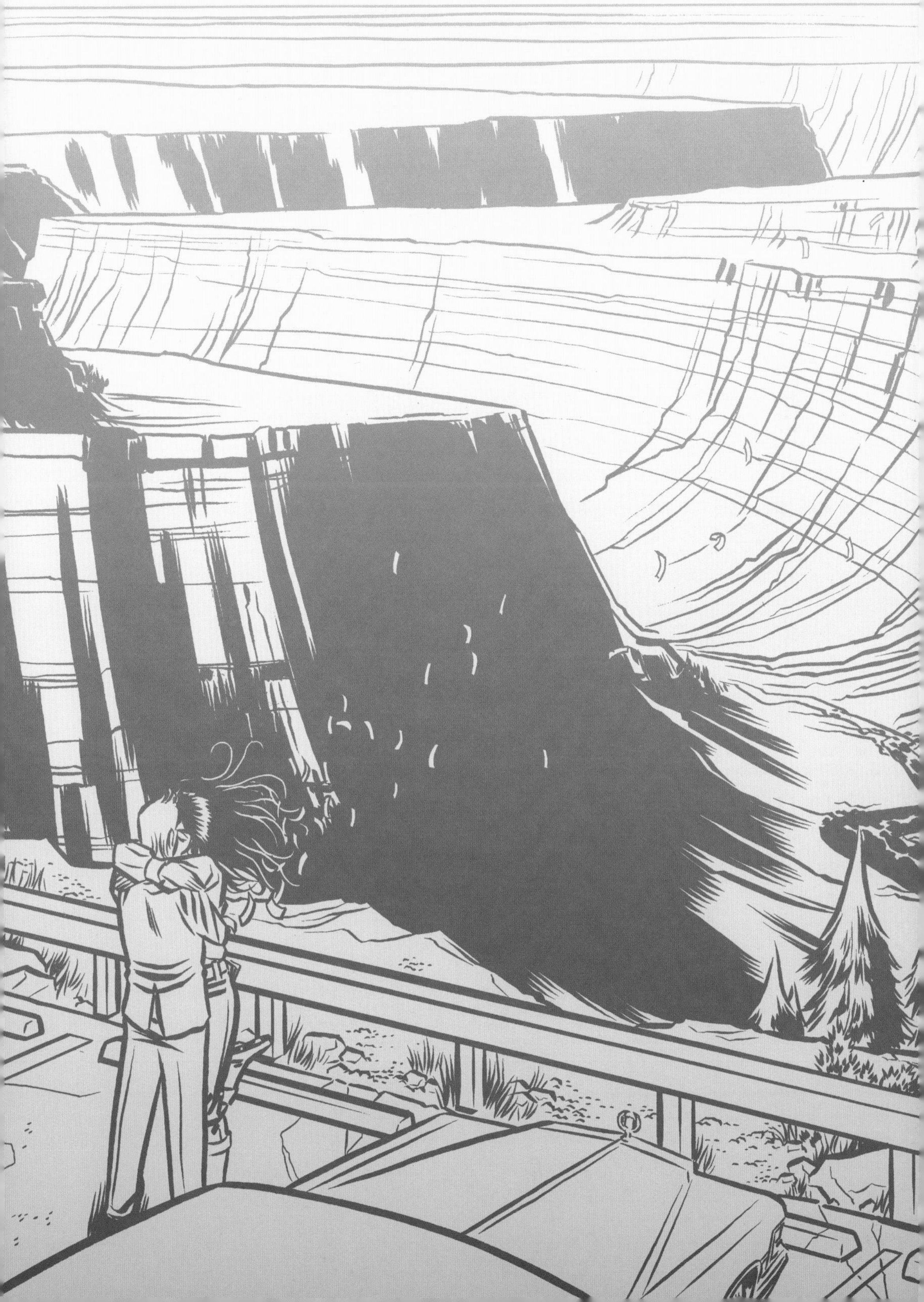

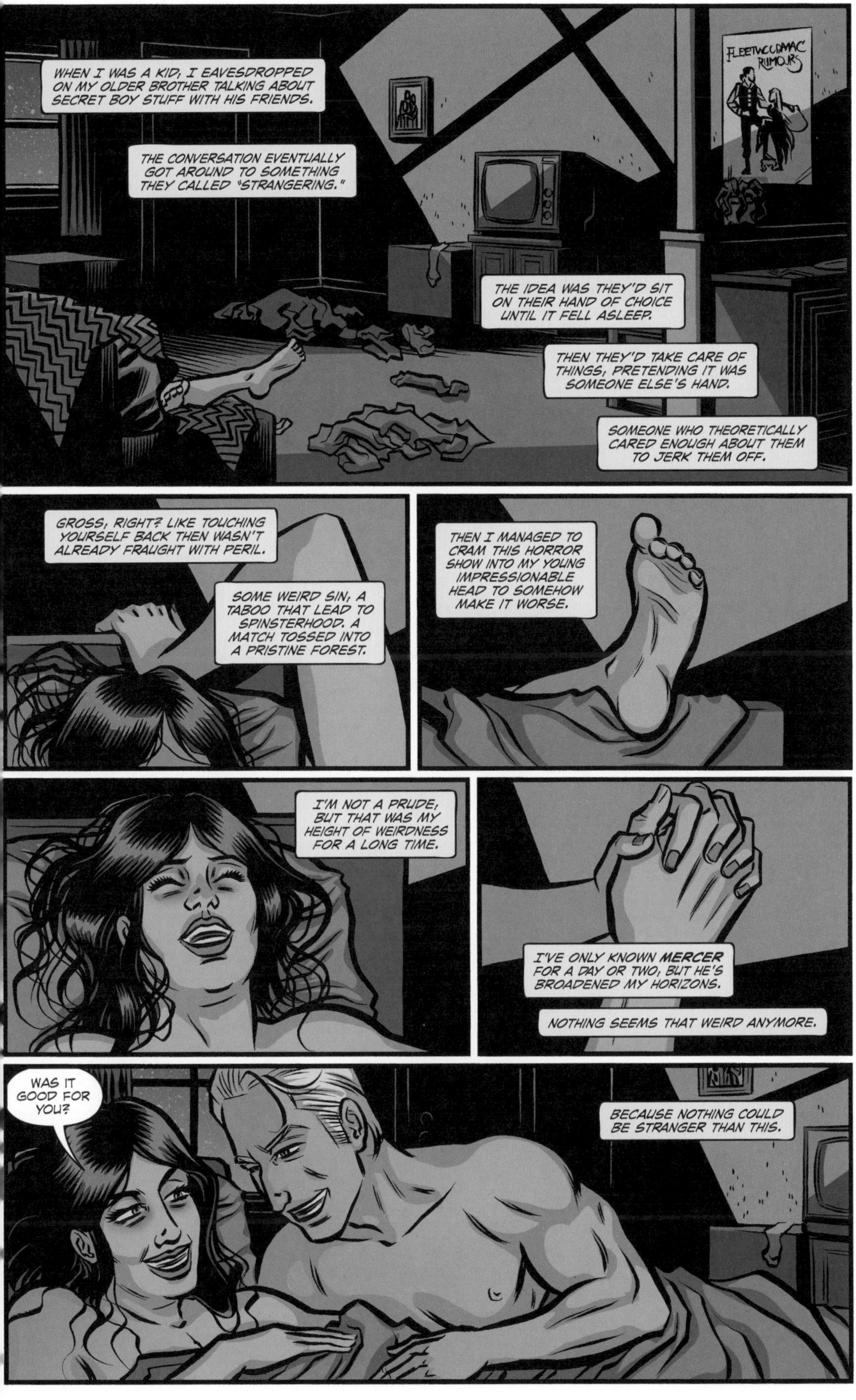
WHEN I WAS A KID, I EAVESDROPPED ON MY OLDER BROTHER TALKING ABOUT SECRET BOY STUFF WITH HIS FRIENDS.
FLEETWOOD MAC RUMOURS
THE CONVERSATION EVENTUALLY GOT AROUND TO SOMETHING THEY CALLED "STRANGERING."
THE IDEA WAS THEY'D SIT ON THEIR HAND OF CHOICE UNTIL IT FELL ASLEEP.
THEN THEY'D TAKE CARE OF THINGS, PRETENDING IT WAS SOMEONE ELSE'S HAND.
SOMEONE WHO THEORETICALLY CARED ENOUGH ABOUT THEM TO JERK THEM OFF.
GROSS, RIGHT? LIKE TOUCHING YOURSELF BACK THEN WASN'T ALREADY FRAUGHT WITH PERIL.
SOME WEIRD SIN, A TABOO THAT LEAD TO SPINSTERHOOD. A MATCH TOSSED INTO A PRISTINE FOREST.
THEN I MANAGED TO CRAM THIS HORROR SHOW INTO MY YOUNG IMPRESSIONABLE HEAD TO SOMEHOW MAKE IT WORSE.
I'M NOT A PRUDE, BUT THAT WAS MY HEIGHT OF WEIRDNESS FOR A LONG TIME.
I'VE ONLY KNOWN MERCER FOR A DAY OR TWO, BUT HE'S BROADENED MY HORIZONS.
NOTHING SEEMS THAT WEIRD ANYMORE.
WAS IT GOOD FOR YOU?
BECAUSE NOTHING COULD BE STRANGER THAN THIS.

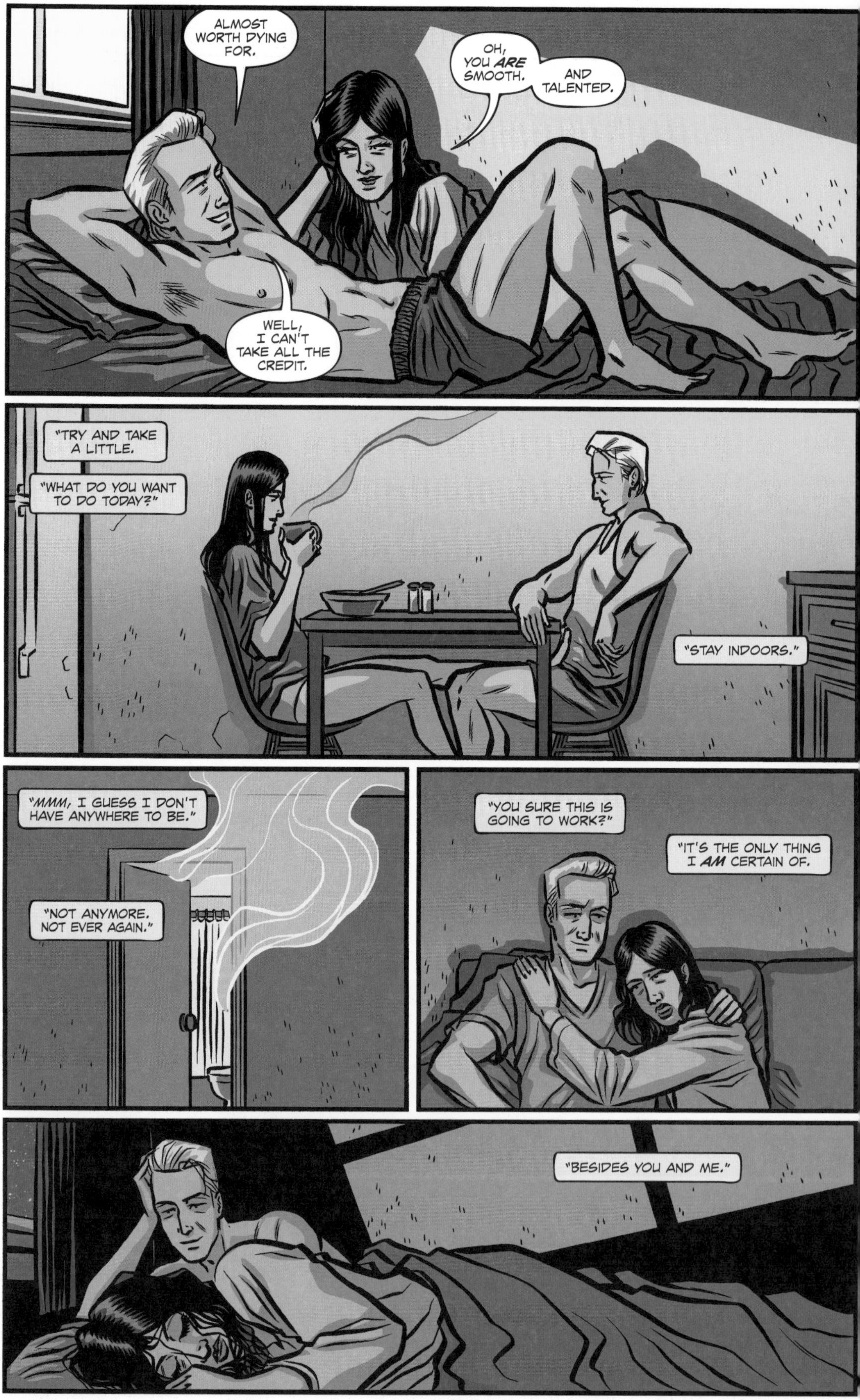
ALMOST WORTH DYING FOR.
OH, YOU *ARE* SMOOTH.
AND TALENTED.
WELL, I CAN'T TAKE ALL THE CREDIT.
"TRY AND TAKE A LITTLE.
"WHAT DO YOU WANT TO DO TODAY?"
"STAY INDOORS."
"*MMM*, I GUESS I DON'T HAVE ANYWHERE TO BE."
"NOT ANYMORE. NOT EVER AGAIN."
"YOU SURE THIS IS GOING TO WORK?"
"IT'S THE ONLY THING I *AM* CERTAIN OF.
"BESIDES YOU AND ME."

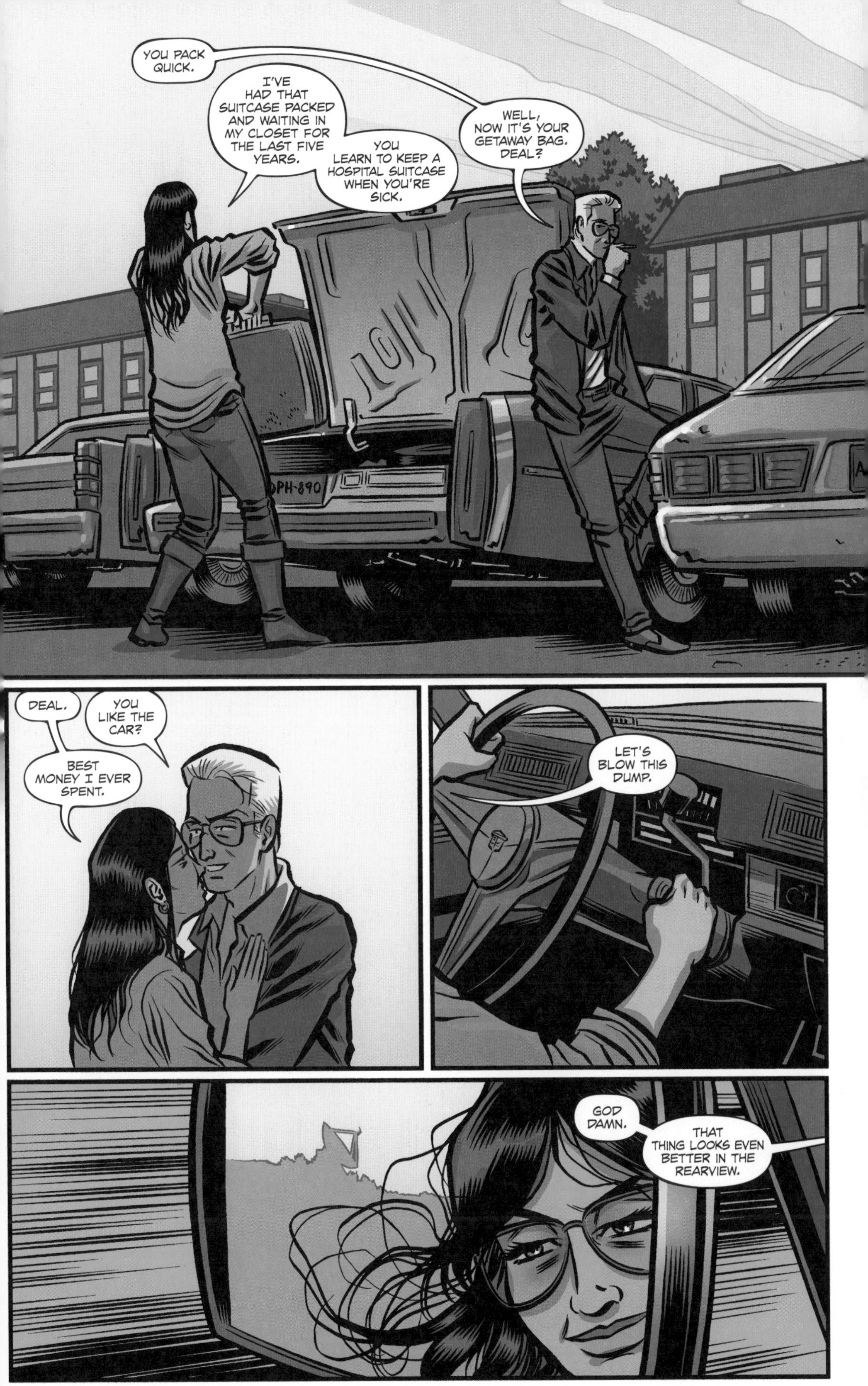
YOU PACK QUICK.
I'VE HAD THAT SUITCASE PACKED AND WAITING IN MY CLOSET FOR THE LAST FIVE YEARS.
YOU LEARN TO KEEP A HOSPITAL SUITCASE WHEN YOU'RE SICK.
WELL, NOW IT'S YOUR GETAWAY BAG. DEAL?
DEAL.
YOU LIKE THE CAR?
BEST MONEY I EVER SPENT.
LET'S BLOW THIS DUMP.
GOD DAMN.
THAT THING LOOKS EVEN BETTER IN THE REARVIEW.

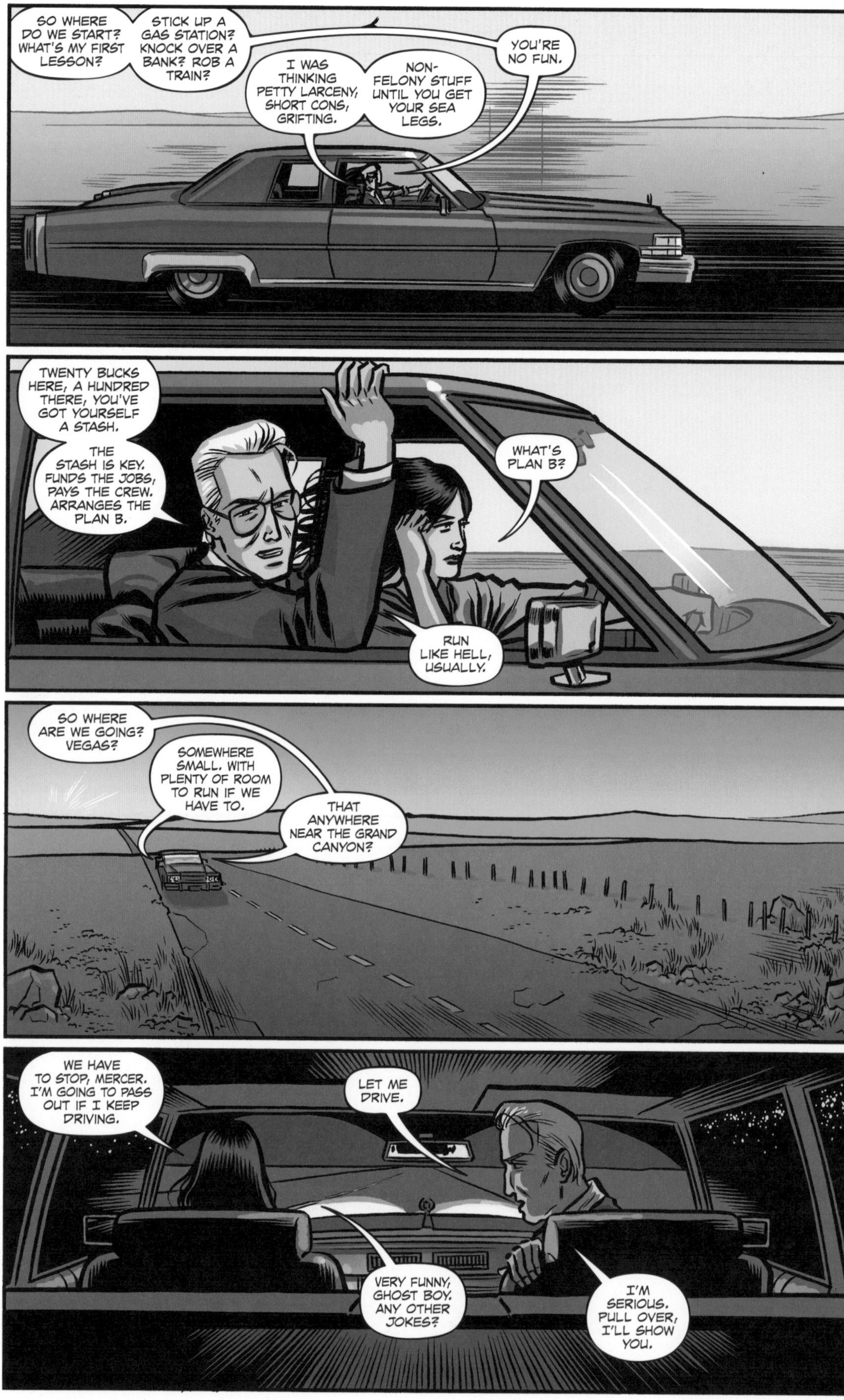
SO WHERE DO WE START? WHAT'S MY FIRST LESSON?
STICK UP A GAS STATION? KNOCK OVER A BANK? ROB A TRAIN?
I WAS THINKING PETTY LARCENY, SHORT CONS, GRIFTING.
NON-FELONY STUFF UNTIL YOU GET YOUR SEA LEGS.
YOU'RE NO FUN.
TWENTY BUCKS HERE, A HUNDRED THERE, YOU'VE GOT YOURSELF A STASH.
THE STASH IS KEY. FUNDS THE JOBS, PAYS THE CREW. ARRANGES THE PLAN B.
WHAT'S PLAN B?
RUN LIKE HELL, USUALLY.
SO WHERE ARE WE GOING? VEGAS?
SOMEWHERE SMALL. WITH PLENTY OF ROOM TO RUN IF WE HAVE TO.
THAT ANYWHERE NEAR THE GRAND CANYON?
WE HAVE TO STOP, MERCER. I'M GOING TO PASS OUT IF I KEEP DRIVING.
LET ME DRIVE.
VERY FUNNY, GHOST BOY. ANY OTHER JOKES?
I'M SERIOUS. PULL OVER, I'LL SHOW YOU.

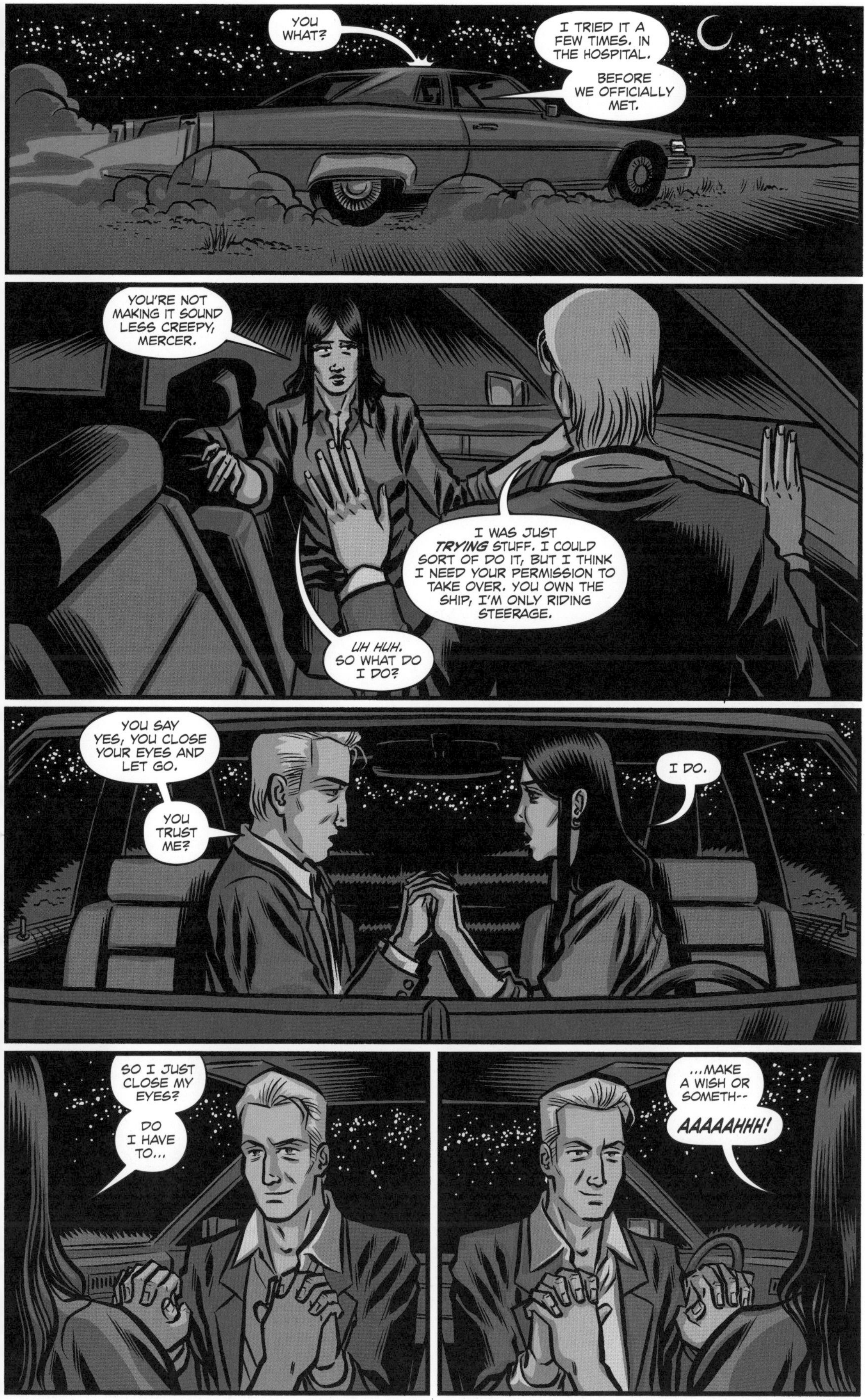
YOU WHAT?
I TRIED IT A FEW TIMES. IN THE HOSPITAL.
BEFORE WE OFFICIALLY MET.
YOU'RE NOT MAKING IT SOUND LESS CREEPY, MERCER.
I WAS JUST *TRYING* STUFF. I COULD SORT OF DO IT, BUT I THINK I NEED YOUR PERMISSION TO TAKE OVER. YOU OWN THE SHIP, I'M ONLY RIDING STEERAGE.
*UH HUH.* SO WHAT DO I DO?
YOU SAY YES, YOU CLOSE YOUR EYES AND LET GO.
YOU TRUST ME?
I DO.
SO I JUST CLOSE MY EYES?
DO I HAVE TO...
...MAKE A WISH OR SOMETH--
AAAAAHHH!

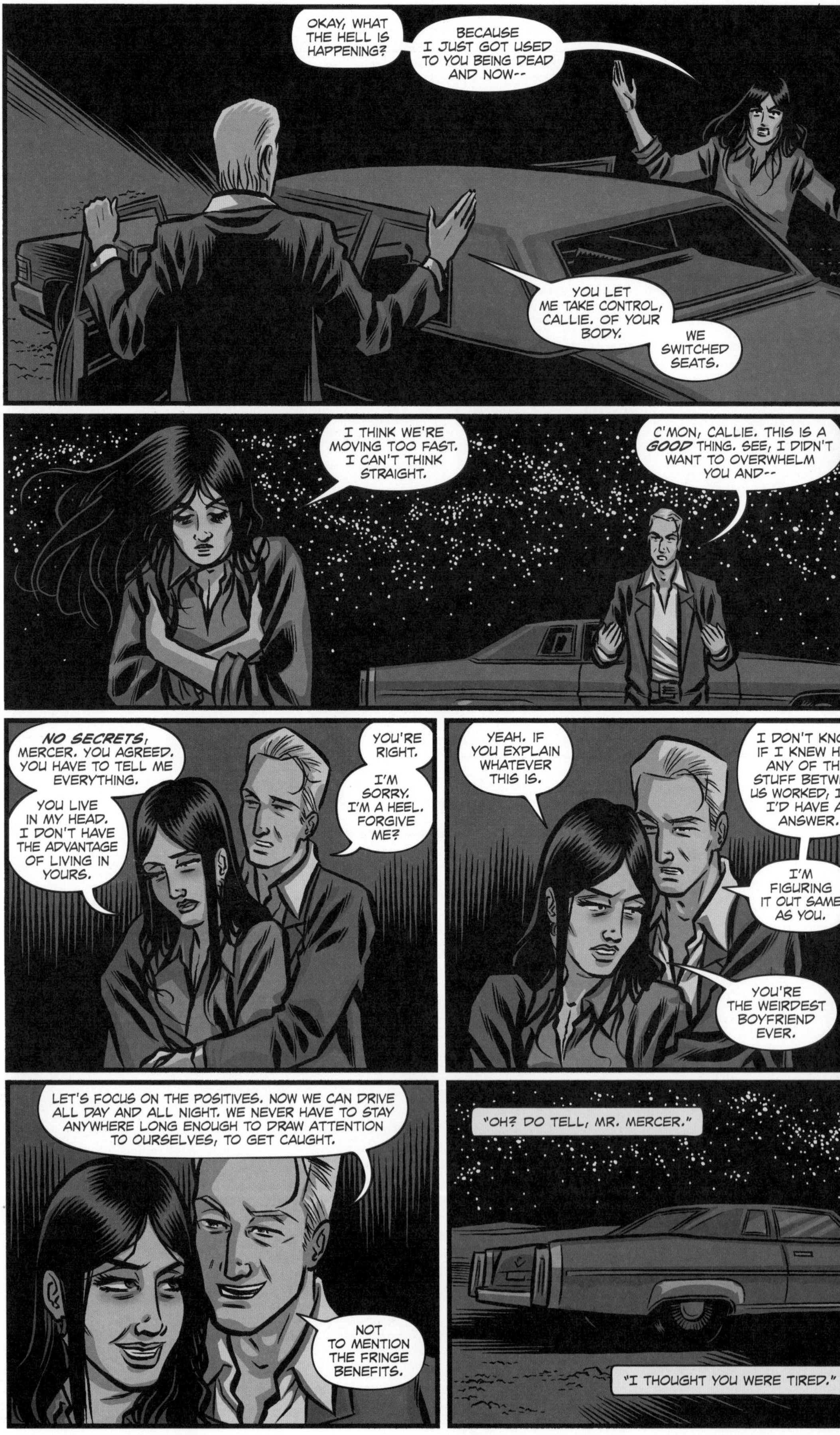
OKAY, WHAT THE HELL IS HAPPENING?
BECAUSE I JUST GOT USED TO YOU BEING DEAD AND NOW--
YOU LET ME TAKE CONTROL, CALLIE. OF YOUR BODY.
WE SWITCHED SEATS.
I THINK WE'RE MOVING TOO FAST. I CAN'T THINK STRAIGHT.
C'MON, CALLIE. THIS IS A *GOOD* THING. SEE, I DIDN'T WANT TO OVERWHELM YOU AND--
***NO SECRETS***, MERCER. YOU AGREED. YOU HAVE TO TELL ME EVERYTHING.
YOU LIVE IN MY HEAD. I DON'T HAVE THE ADVANTAGE OF LIVING IN YOURS.
YOU'RE RIGHT.
I'M SORRY. I'M A HEEL. FORGIVE ME?
YEAH. IF YOU EXPLAIN WHATEVER THIS IS.
I DON'T KNOW. IF I KNEW HOW ANY OF THIS STUFF BETWEEN US WORKED, I'D... I'D HAVE AN ANSWER.
I'M FIGURING IT OUT SAME AS YOU.
YOU'RE THE WEIRDEST BOYFRIEND EVER.
LET'S FOCUS ON THE POSITIVES. NOW WE CAN DRIVE ALL DAY AND ALL NIGHT. WE NEVER HAVE TO STAY ANYWHERE LONG ENOUGH TO DRAW ATTENTION TO OURSELVES, TO GET CAUGHT.
NOT TO MENTION THE FRINGE BENEFITS.
"OH? DO TELL, MR. MERCER."
"I THOUGHT YOU WERE TIRED."

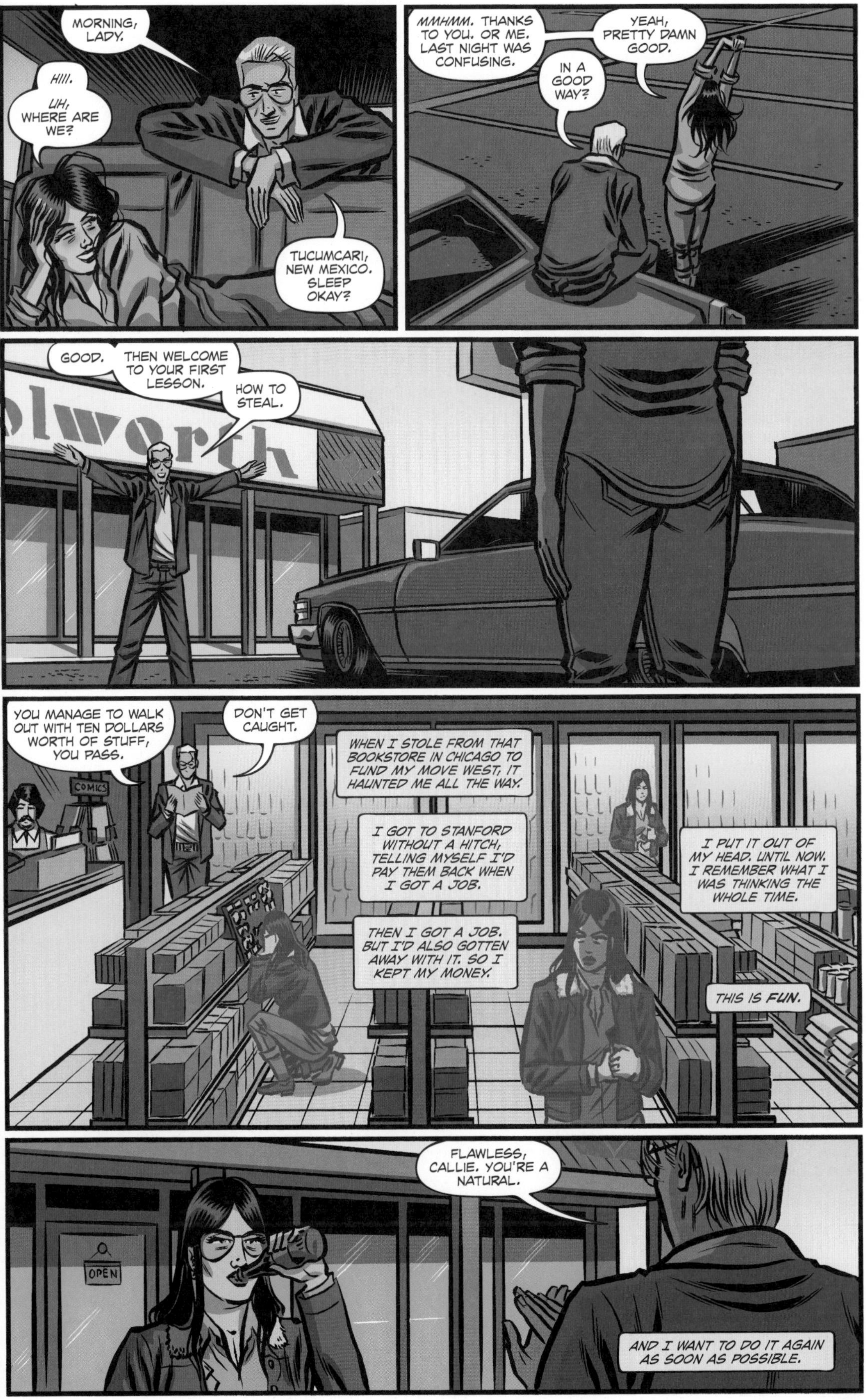

MORNING, LADY.
HIII.
UH, WHERE ARE WE?
TUCUMCARI, NEW MEXICO. SLEEP OKAY?
MMHMM. THANKS TO YOU. OR ME. LAST NIGHT WAS CONFUSING.
YEAH, PRETTY DAMN GOOD.
IN A GOOD WAY?
GOOD.
THEN WELCOME TO YOUR FIRST LESSON.
HOW TO STEAL.
olworth
YOU MANAGE TO WALK OUT WITH TEN DOLLARS WORTH OF STUFF, YOU PASS.
DON'T GET CAUGHT.
COMICS
WHEN I STOLE FROM THAT BOOKSTORE IN CHICAGO TO FUND MY MOVE WEST, IT HAUNTED ME ALL THE WAY.
I GOT TO STANFORD WITHOUT A HITCH, TELLING MYSELF I'D PAY THEM BACK WHEN I GOT A JOB.
THEN I GOT A JOB. BUT I'D ALSO GOTTEN AWAY WITH IT. SO I KEPT MY MONEY.
I PUT IT OUT OF MY HEAD. UNTIL NOW. I REMEMBER WHAT I WAS THINKING THE WHOLE TIME.
THIS IS FUN.
FLAWLESS, CALLIE. YOU'RE A NATURAL.
OPEN
AND I WANT TO DO IT AGAIN AS SOON AS POSSIBLE.

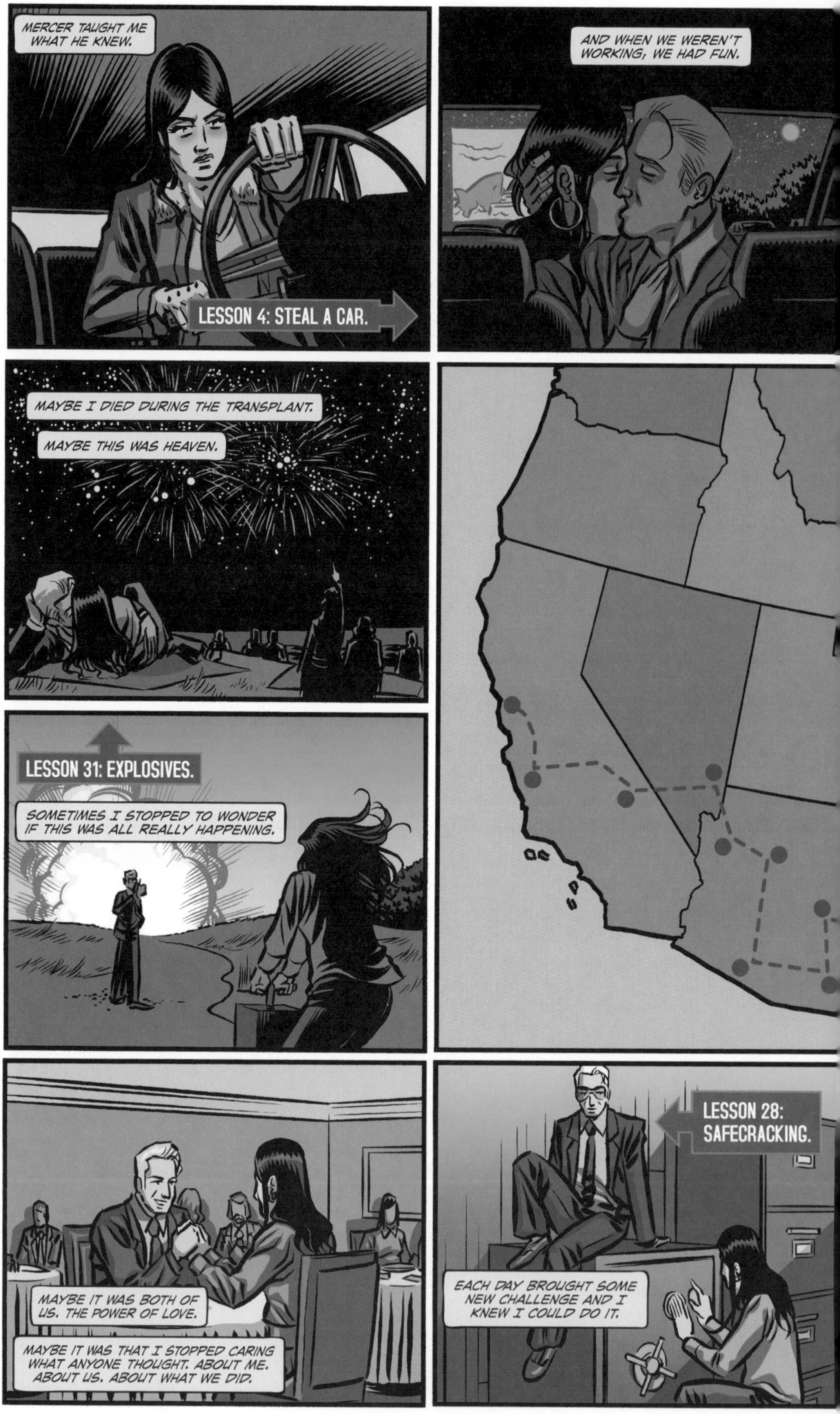
MERCER TAUGHT ME WHAT HE KNEW.
LESSON 4: STEAL A CAR.
AND WHEN WE WEREN'T WORKING, WE HAD FUN.
MAYBE I DIED DURING THE TRANSPLANT.
MAYBE THIS WAS HEAVEN.
LESSON 31: EXPLOSIVES.
SOMETIMES I STOPPED TO WONDER IF THIS WAS ALL REALLY HAPPENING.
MAYBE IT WAS BOTH OF US. THE POWER OF LOVE.
MAYBE IT WAS THAT I STOPPED CARING WHAT ANYONE THOUGHT. ABOUT ME. ABOUT US. ABOUT WHAT WE DID.
LESSON 28: SAFECRACKING.
EACH DAY BROUGHT SOME NEW CHALLENGE AND I KNEW I COULD DO IT.

WE WERE LIKE KIDS. OR WHAT I IMAGINED KIDS WERE SUPPOSED TO BE LIKE.

WE DID WHAT WE WANTED, WHEN WE WANTED.

MY SUMMER AS AN OUTLAW.

LESSON 7: BREAKING & ENTERING (BRUTE FORCE VERSION)

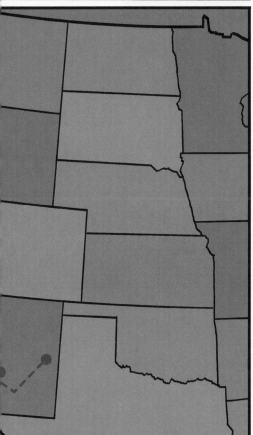

WE STOLE JUST ENOUGH TO PAY FOR GAS AND FOOD.

AND A FEW OTHER THINGS.

IT TURNS OUT I'M A NATURAL.

MERCER SAID I WAS THE BEST THIEF HE'D MET IN YEARS.

LESSON 12: PICKPOCKETING.

AND I FELT LOVED. FOR THE FIRST TIME MAYBE EVER.

I FELT SAFE.

I FELT USEFUL FOR THE FIRST TIME MAYBE EVER.

I FELT LIKE I WAS CAPABLE OF ANYTHING.

LESSON 19: FIREARMS.

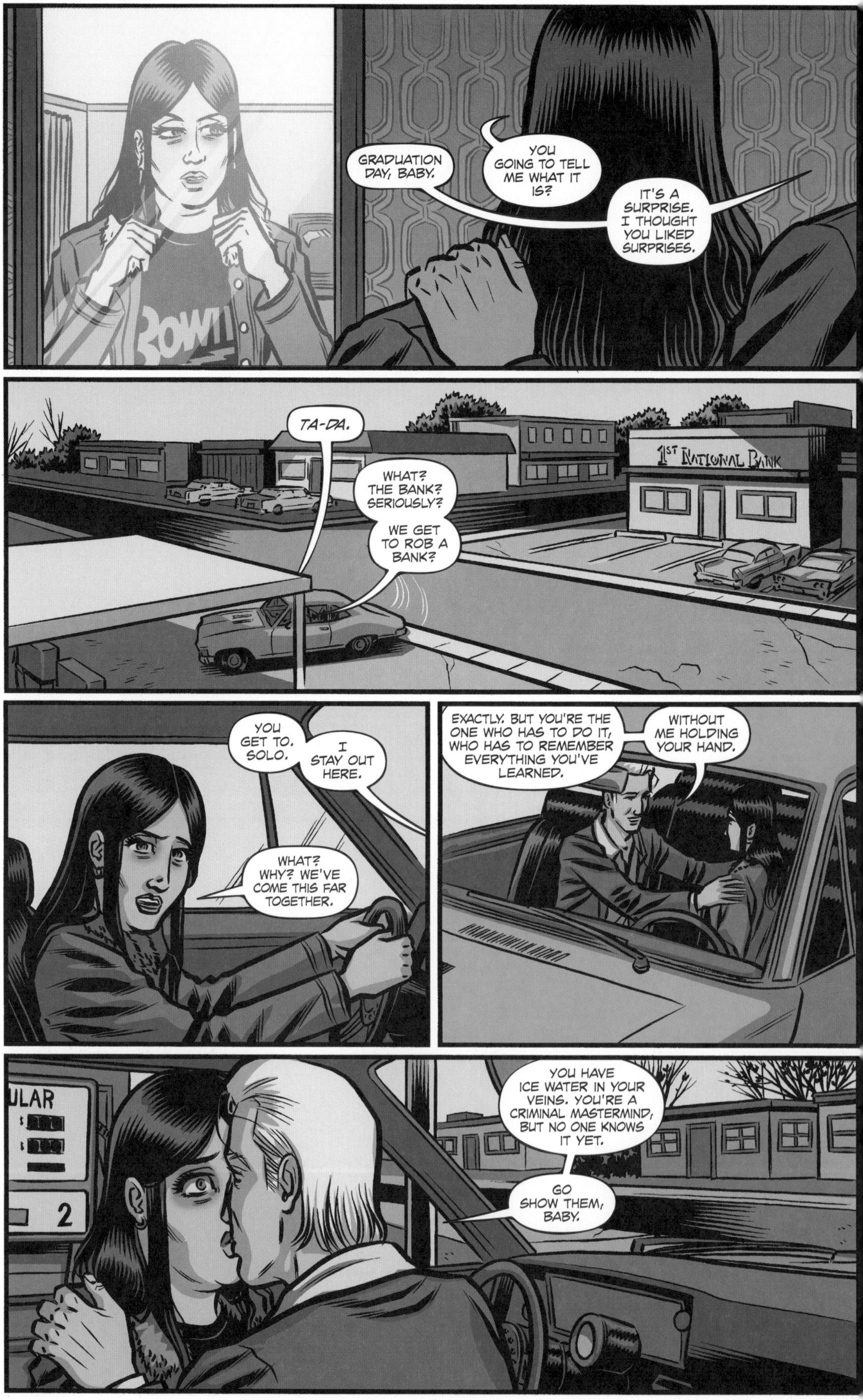
GRADUATION DAY, BABY.
YOU GOING TO TELL ME WHAT IT IS?
IT'S A SURPRISE. I THOUGHT YOU LIKED SURPRISES.
1ST NATIONAL BANK
TA-DA.
WHAT? THE BANK? SERIOUSLY?
WE GET TO ROB A BANK?
YOU GET TO. SOLO.
I STAY OUT HERE.
WHAT? WHY? WE'VE COME THIS FAR TOGETHER.
EXACTLY. BUT YOU'RE THE ONE WHO HAS TO DO IT, WHO HAS TO REMEMBER EVERYTHING YOU'VE LEARNED.
WITHOUT ME HOLDING YOUR HAND.
ULAR
2
YOU HAVE ICE WATER IN YOUR VEINS. YOU'RE A CRIMINAL MASTERMIND, BUT NO ONE KNOWS IT YET.
GO SHOW THEM, BABY.

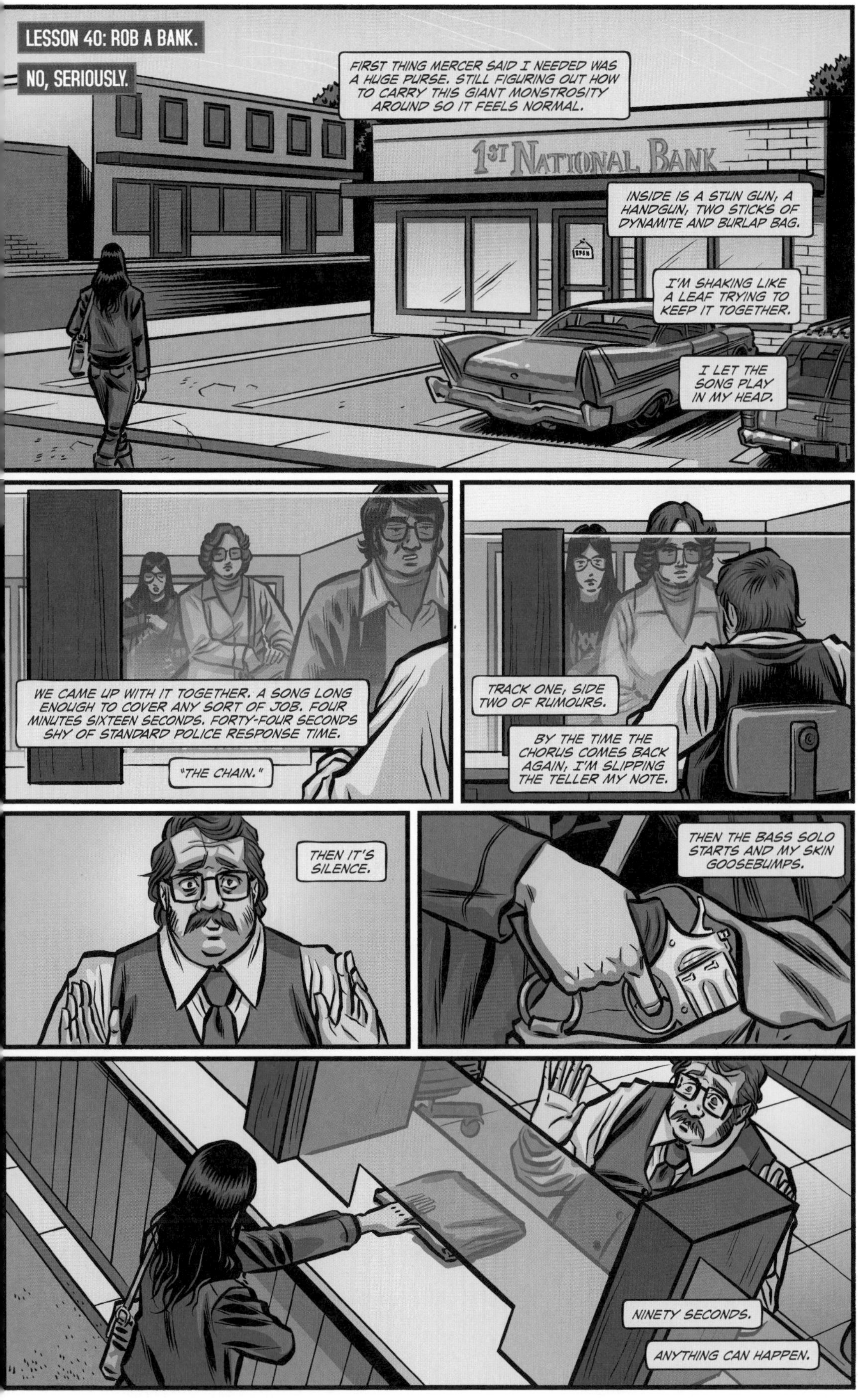
LESSON 40: ROB A BANK.
NO, SERIOUSLY.
FIRST THING MERCER SAID I NEEDED WAS A HUGE PURSE. STILL FIGURING OUT HOW TO CARRY THIS GIANT MONSTROSITY AROUND SO IT FEELS NORMAL.
1ST NATIONAL BANK
INSIDE IS A STUN GUN, A HANDGUN, TWO STICKS OF DYNAMITE AND BURLAP BAG.
I'M SHAKING LIKE A LEAF TRYING TO KEEP IT TOGETHER.
I LET THE SONG PLAY IN MY HEAD.
WE CAME UP WITH IT TOGETHER. A SONG LONG ENOUGH TO COVER ANY SORT OF JOB. FOUR MINUTES SIXTEEN SECONDS. FORTY-FOUR SECONDS SHY OF STANDARD POLICE RESPONSE TIME.
"THE CHAIN."
TRACK ONE, SIDE TWO OF RUMOURS.
BY THE TIME THE CHORUS COMES BACK AGAIN, I'M SLIPPING THE TELLER MY NOTE.
THEN IT'S SILENCE.
THEN THE BASS SOLO STARTS AND MY SKIN GOOSEBUMPS.
NINETY SECONDS.
ANYTHING CAN HAPPEN.

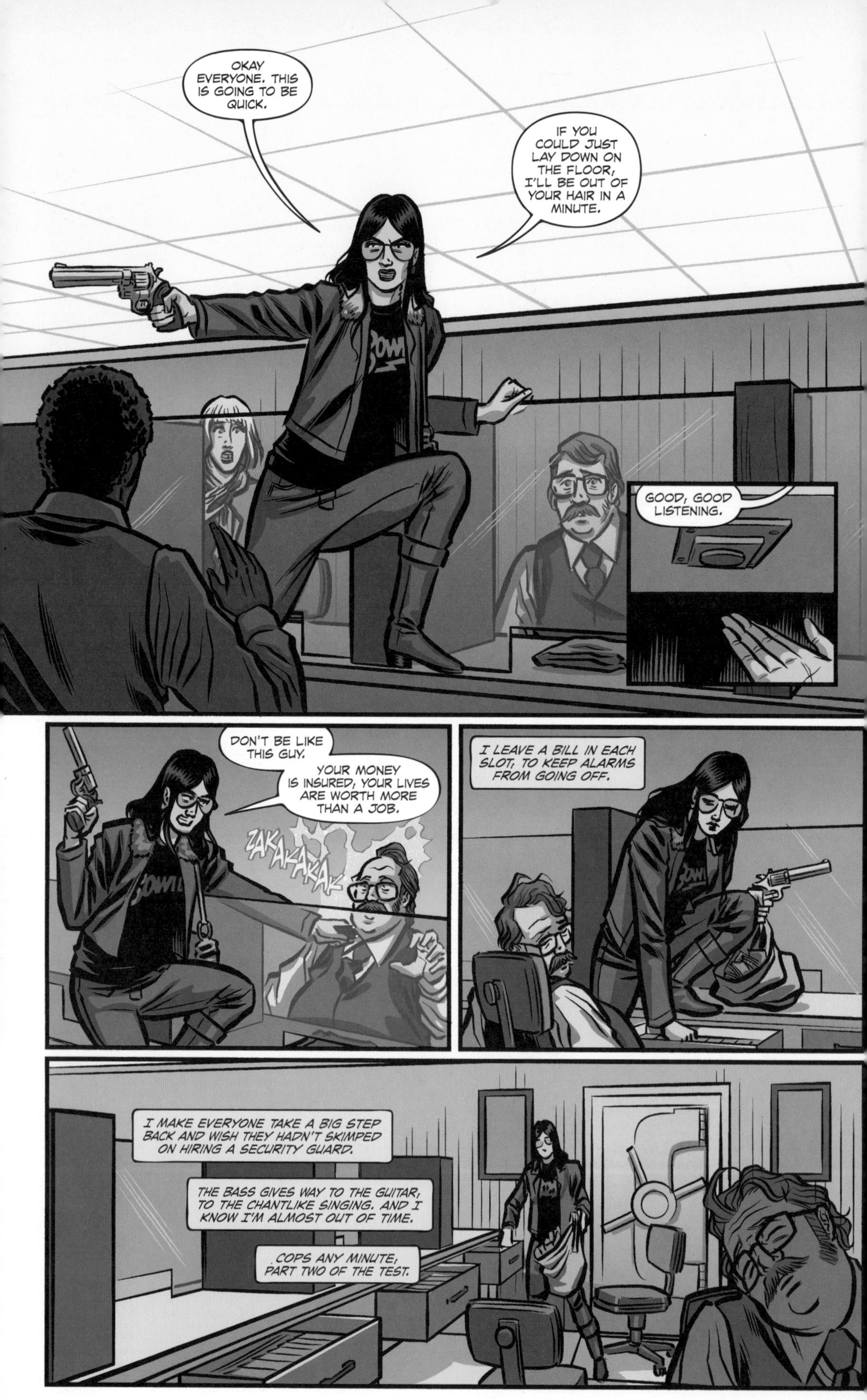

OKAY EVERYONE. THIS IS GOING TO BE QUICK.
IF YOU COULD JUST LAY DOWN ON THE FLOOR, I'LL BE OUT OF YOUR HAIR IN A MINUTE.
GOOD, GOOD LISTENING.
DON'T BE LIKE THIS GUY.
YOUR MONEY IS INSURED, YOUR LIVES ARE WORTH MORE THAN A JOB.
ZAKAKAKAKAK
I LEAVE A BILL IN EACH SLOT, TO KEEP ALARMS FROM GOING OFF.
I MAKE EVERYONE TAKE A BIG STEP BACK AND WISH THEY HADN'T SKIMPED ON HIRING A SECURITY GUARD.
THE BASS GIVES WAY TO THE GUITAR, TO THE CHANTLIKE SINGING. AND I KNOW I'M ALMOST OUT OF TIME.
COPS ANY MINUTE, PART TWO OF THE TEST.

THE SONG FADES OUT AND I KNOW I'M FREE. I FEEL LIKE I'M MORE ALIVE THAN I EVER HAVE BEEN.

THEN IT HITS ME.

HOLY CRAP, I JUST ROBBED A BANK.

BNGBNGBNGBNGBNGBNG

GOT YOU SOMETHING, SWEETIE.

I HOPE IT FITS.

JACKPOT! I TOLD YOU YOU COULD DO THIS.

ANY PROBLEMS?

NO, HAD TO STUN A GUY, ALARM'S GOING OFF, COPS ARE COMING.

BUT OTHERWISE SMOOTH AS SILK.

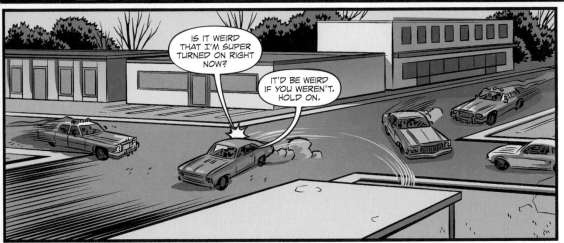

IS IT WEIRD THAT I'M SUPER TURNED ON RIGHT NOW?

IT'D BE WEIRD IF YOU WEREN'T. HOLD ON.

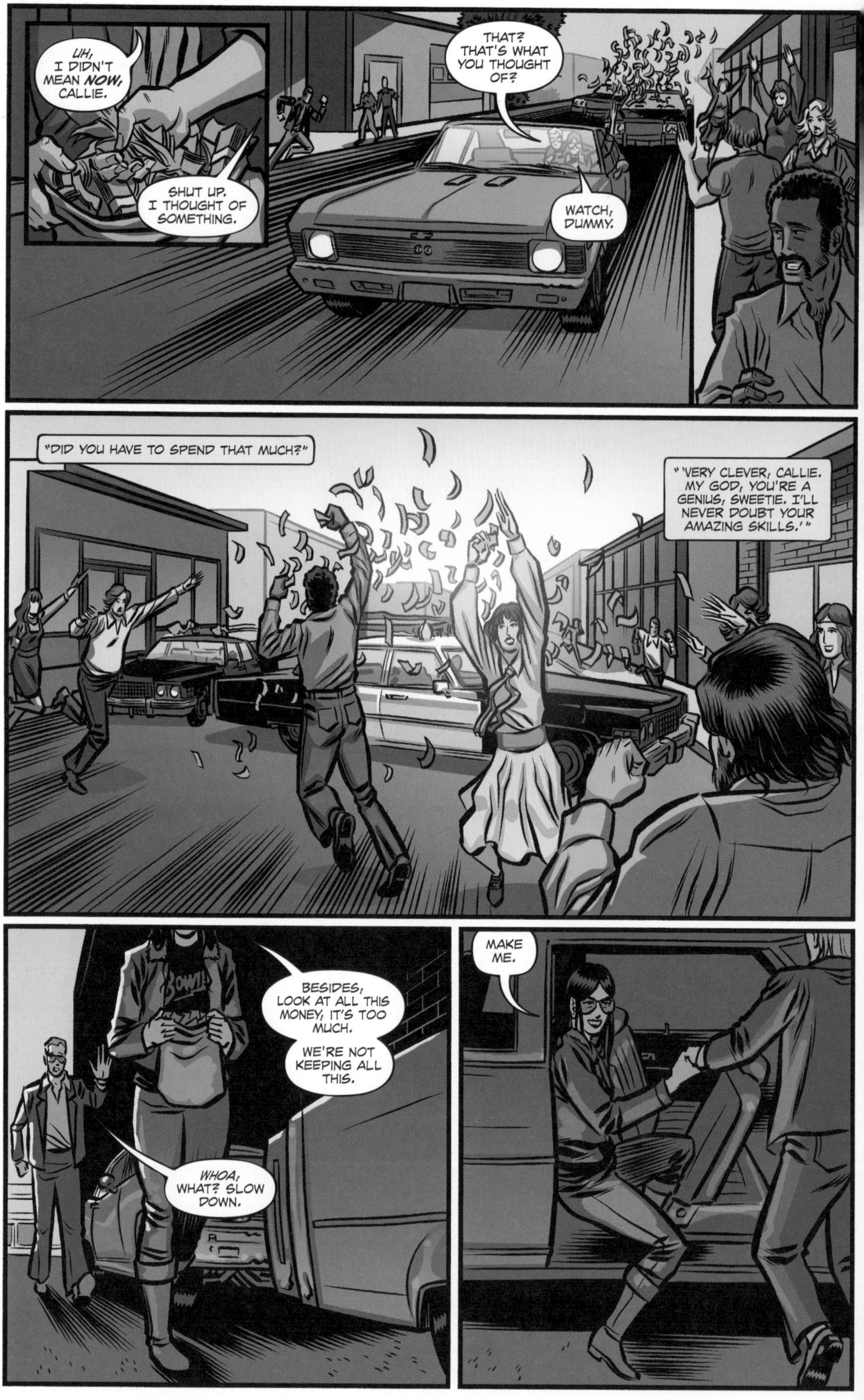

UH, I DIDN'T MEAN NOW, CALLIE.
SHUT UP. I THOUGHT OF SOMETHING.
THAT? THAT'S WHAT YOU THOUGHT OF?
WATCH, DUMMY.
"DID YOU HAVE TO SPEND THAT MUCH?"
"'VERY CLEVER, CALLIE. MY GOD, YOU'RE A GENIUS, SWEETIE. I'LL NEVER DOUBT YOUR AMAZING SKILLS.'"
BESIDES, LOOK AT ALL THIS MONEY, IT'S TOO MUCH.
WE'RE NOT KEEPING ALL THIS.
WHOA, WHAT? SLOW DOWN.
MAKE ME.

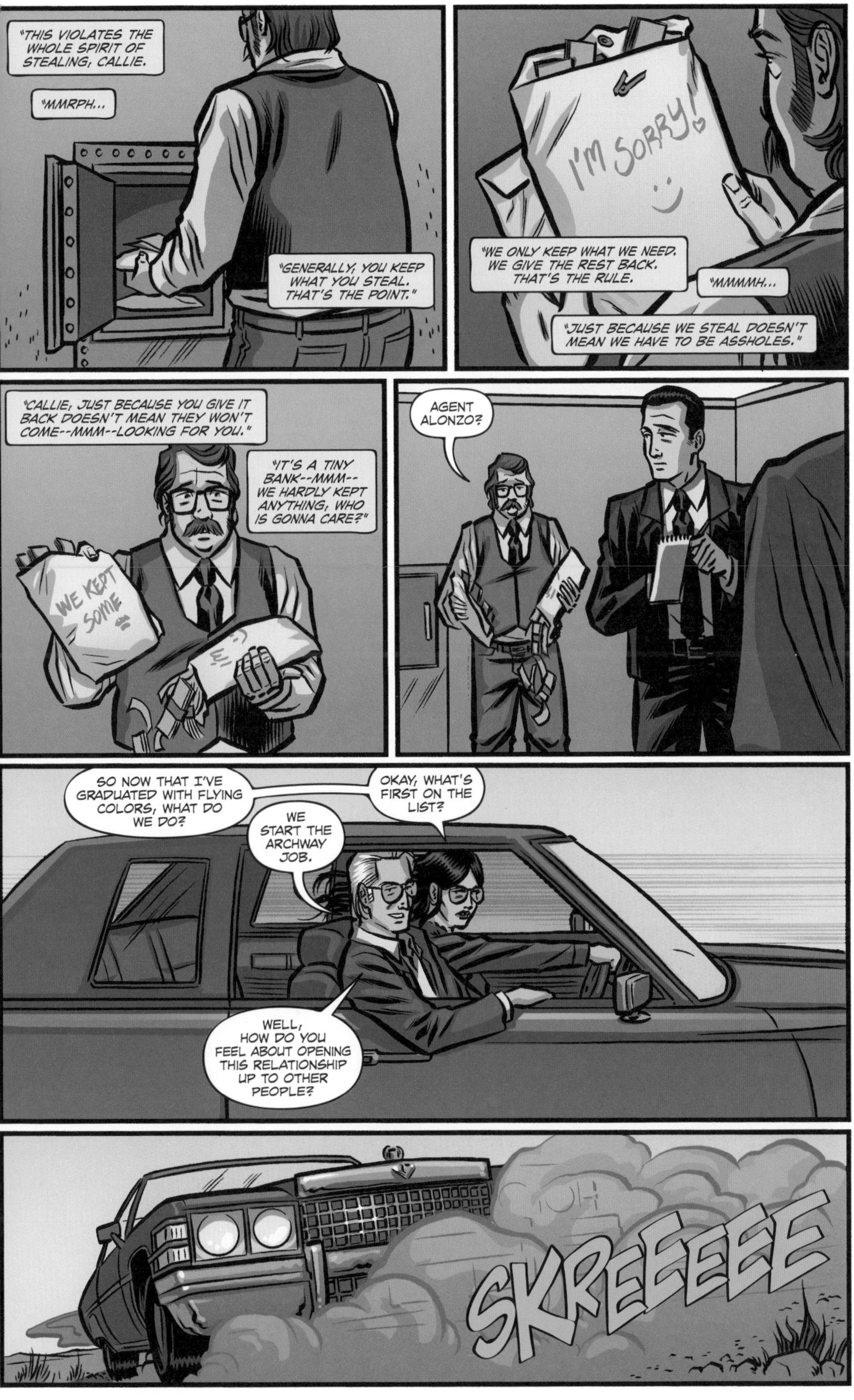
"THIS VIOLATES THE WHOLE SPIRIT OF STEALING, CALLIE.
"MMRPH...
"GENERALLY, YOU KEEP WHAT YOU STEAL. THAT'S THE POINT."
I'M SORRY!
"WE ONLY KEEP WHAT WE NEED. WE GIVE THE REST BACK. THAT'S THE RULE.
"MMMMH...
"JUST BECAUSE WE STEAL DOESN'T MEAN WE HAVE TO BE ASSHOLES."
"CALLIE, JUST BECAUSE YOU GIVE IT BACK DOESN'T MEAN THEY WON'T COME--MMM--LOOKING FOR YOU."
"IT'S A TINY BANK--MMM--WE HARDLY KEPT ANYTHING, WHO IS GONNA CARE?"
WE KEPT SOME
AGENT ALONZO?
SO NOW THAT I'VE GRADUATED WITH FLYING COLORS, WHAT DO WE DO?
WE START THE ARCHWAY JOB.
OKAY, WHAT'S FIRST ON THE LIST?
WELL, HOW DO YOU FEEL ABOUT OPENING THIS RELATIONSHIP UP TO OTHER PEOPLE?
SKREEEEE

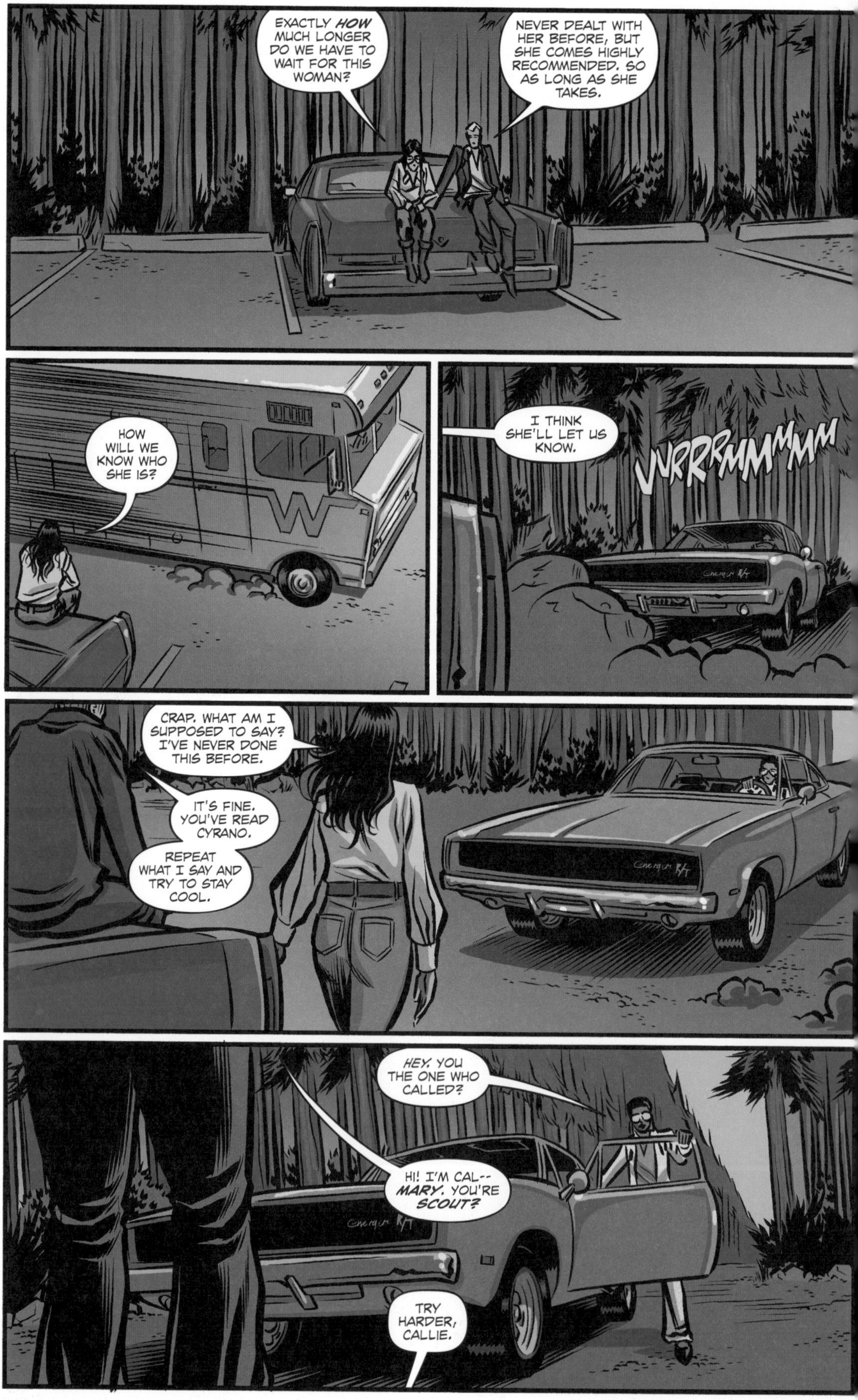

EXACTLY *HOW* MUCH LONGER DO WE HAVE TO WAIT FOR THIS WOMAN?
NEVER DEALT WITH HER BEFORE, BUT SHE COMES HIGHLY RECOMMENDED. SO AS LONG AS SHE TAKES.
HOW WILL WE KNOW WHO SHE IS?
I THINK SHE'LL LET US KNOW.
VVRRRMMMMMM
CRAP. WHAT AM I SUPPOSED TO SAY? I'VE NEVER DONE THIS BEFORE.
IT'S FINE. YOU'VE READ CYRANO.
REPEAT WHAT I SAY AND TRY TO STAY COOL.
*HEY.* YOU THE ONE WHO CALLED?
HI! I'M CAL-- *MARY.* YOU'RE *SCOUT?*
TRY HARDER, CALLIE.

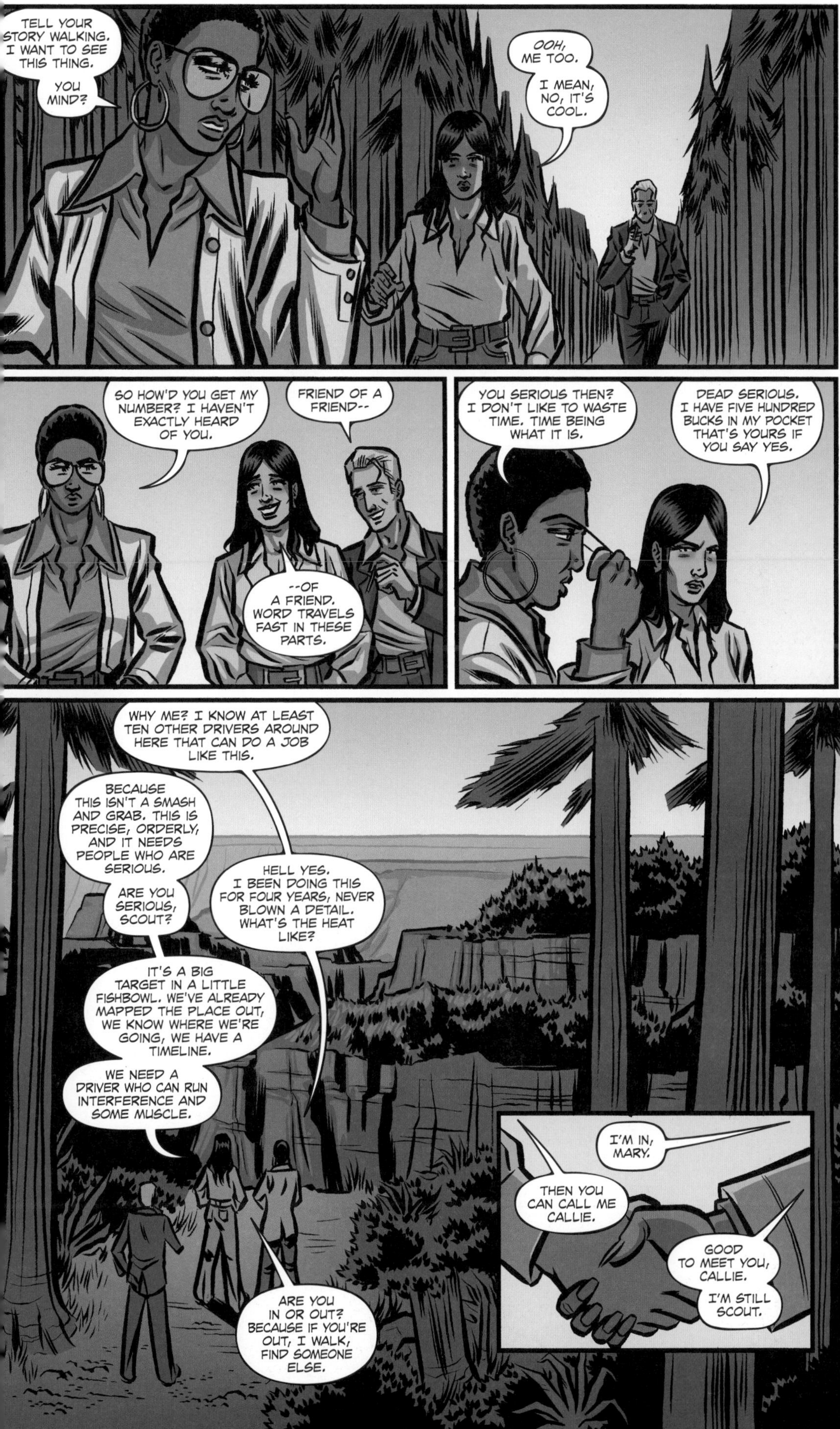
TELL YOUR STORY WALKING. I WANT TO SEE THIS THING.
YOU MIND?
OOH, ME TOO.
I MEAN, NO, IT'S COOL.
SO HOW'D YOU GET MY NUMBER? I HAVEN'T EXACTLY HEARD OF YOU.
FRIEND OF A FRIEND--
--OF A FRIEND. WORD TRAVELS FAST IN THESE PARTS.
YOU SERIOUS THEN? I DON'T LIKE TO WASTE TIME. TIME BEING WHAT IT IS.
DEAD SERIOUS. I HAVE FIVE HUNDRED BUCKS IN MY POCKET THAT'S YOURS IF YOU SAY YES.
WHY ME? I KNOW AT LEAST TEN OTHER DRIVERS AROUND HERE THAT CAN DO A JOB LIKE THIS.
BECAUSE THIS ISN'T A SMASH AND GRAB. THIS IS PRECISE, ORDERLY, AND IT NEEDS PEOPLE WHO ARE SERIOUS.
ARE YOU SERIOUS, SCOUT?
HELL YES. I BEEN DOING THIS FOR FOUR YEARS, NEVER BLOWN A DETAIL. WHAT'S THE HEAT LIKE?
IT'S A BIG TARGET IN A LITTLE FISHBOWL. WE'VE ALREADY MAPPED THE PLACE OUT, WE KNOW WHERE WE'RE GOING, WE HAVE A TIMELINE.
WE NEED A DRIVER WHO CAN RUN INTERFERENCE AND SOME MUSCLE.
ARE YOU IN OR OUT? BECAUSE IF YOU'RE OUT, I WALK, FIND SOMEONE ELSE.
I'M IN, MARY.
THEN YOU CAN CALL ME CALLIE.
GOOD TO MEET YOU, CALLIE.
I'M STILL SCOUT.

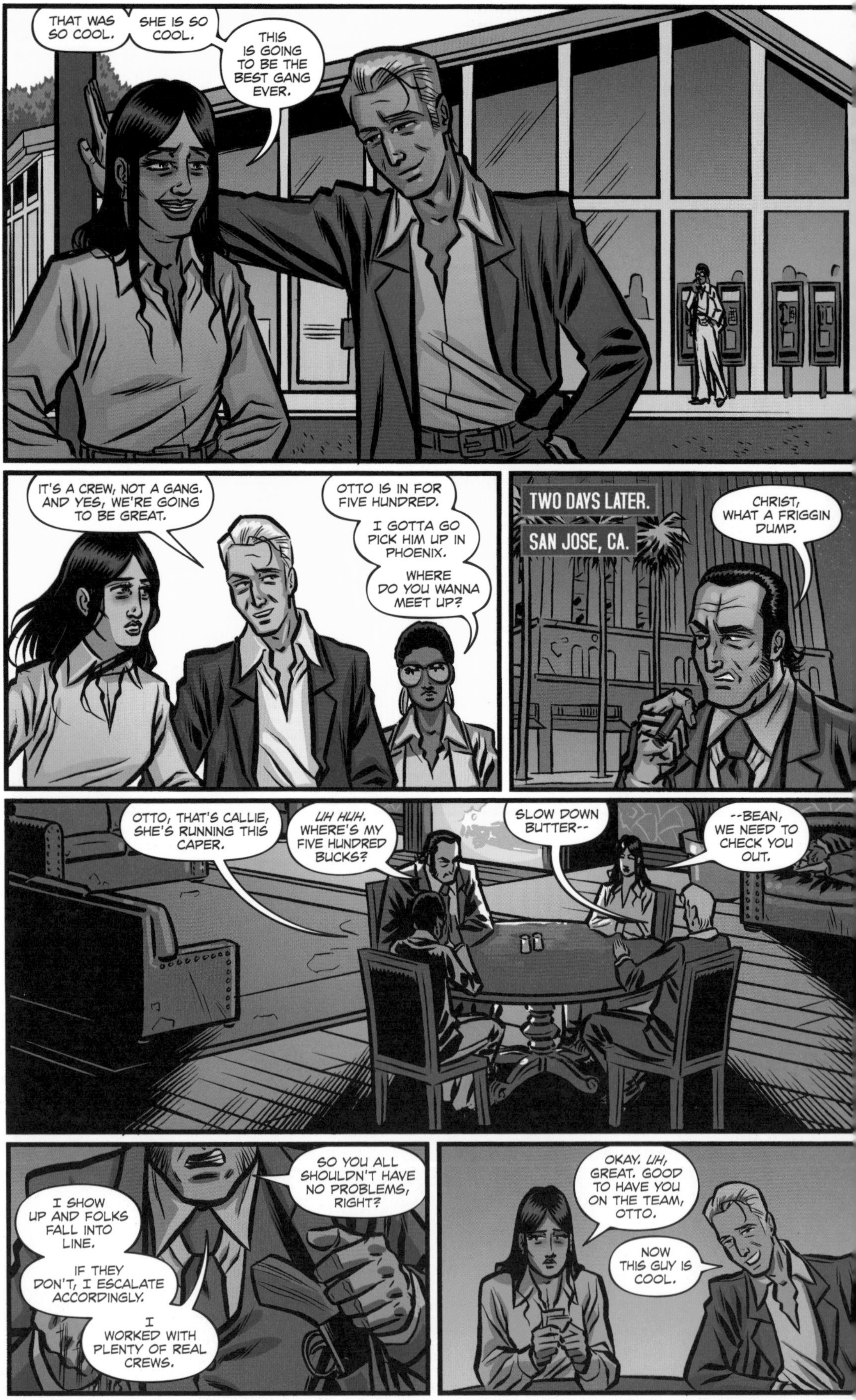

THAT WAS SO COOL.
SHE IS SO COOL.
THIS IS GOING TO BE THE BEST GANG EVER.
IT'S A CREW, NOT A GANG. AND YES, WE'RE GOING TO BE GREAT.
OTTO IS IN FOR FIVE HUNDRED.
I GOTTA GO PICK HIM UP IN PHOENIX.
WHERE DO YOU WANNA MEET UP?
TWO DAYS LATER.
SAN JOSE, CA.
CHRIST, WHAT A FRIGGIN DUMP.
OTTO, THAT'S CALLIE, SHE'S RUNNING THIS CAPER.
*UH HUH.* WHERE'S MY FIVE HUNDRED BUCKS?
SLOW DOWN BUTTER--
--BEAN, WE NEED TO CHECK YOU OUT.
I WORKED WITH PLENTY OF REAL CREWS.
I SHOW UP AND FOLKS FALL INTO LINE.
IF THEY DON'T, I ESCALATE ACCORDINGLY.
SO YOU ALL SHOULDN'T HAVE NO PROBLEMS, RIGHT?
OKAY. *UH,* GREAT. GOOD TO HAVE YOU ON THE TEAM, OTTO.
NOW THIS GUY IS COOL.

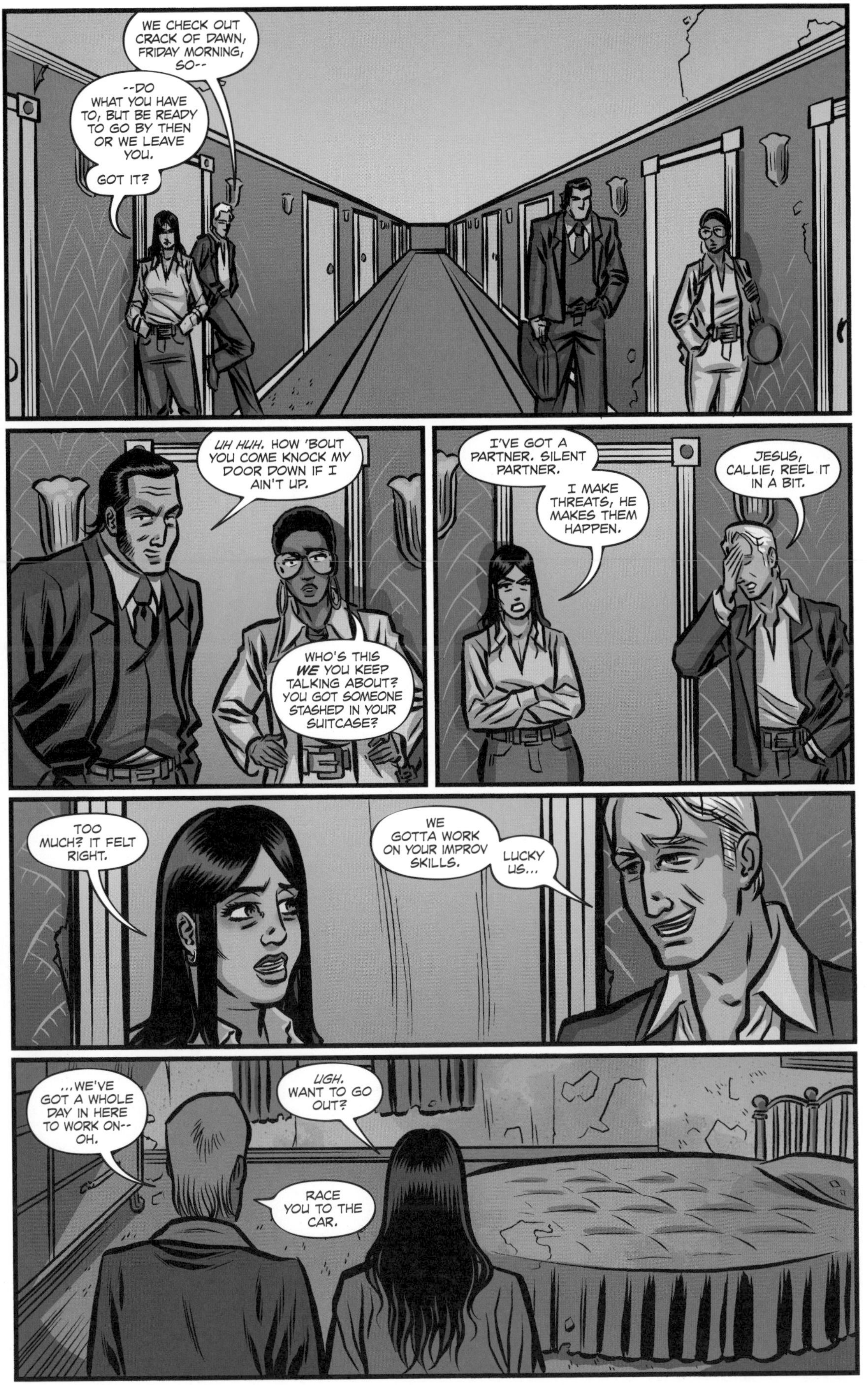
WE CHECK OUT CRACK OF DAWN, FRIDAY MORNING, SO--
--DO WHAT YOU HAVE TO, BUT BE READY TO GO BY THEN OR WE LEAVE YOU.
GOT IT?
UH HUH. HOW 'BOUT YOU COME KNOCK MY DOOR DOWN IF I AIN'T UP.
WHO'S THIS WE YOU KEEP TALKING ABOUT? YOU GOT SOMEONE STASHED IN YOUR SUITCASE?
I'VE GOT A PARTNER. SILENT PARTNER.
I MAKE THREATS, HE MAKES THEM HAPPEN.
JESUS, CALLIE, REEL IT IN A BIT.
TOO MUCH? IT FELT RIGHT.
WE GOTTA WORK ON YOUR IMPROV SKILLS.
LUCKY US...
...WE'VE GOT A WHOLE DAY IN HERE TO WORK ON-- OH.
UGH. WANT TO GO OUT?
RACE YOU TO THE CAR.

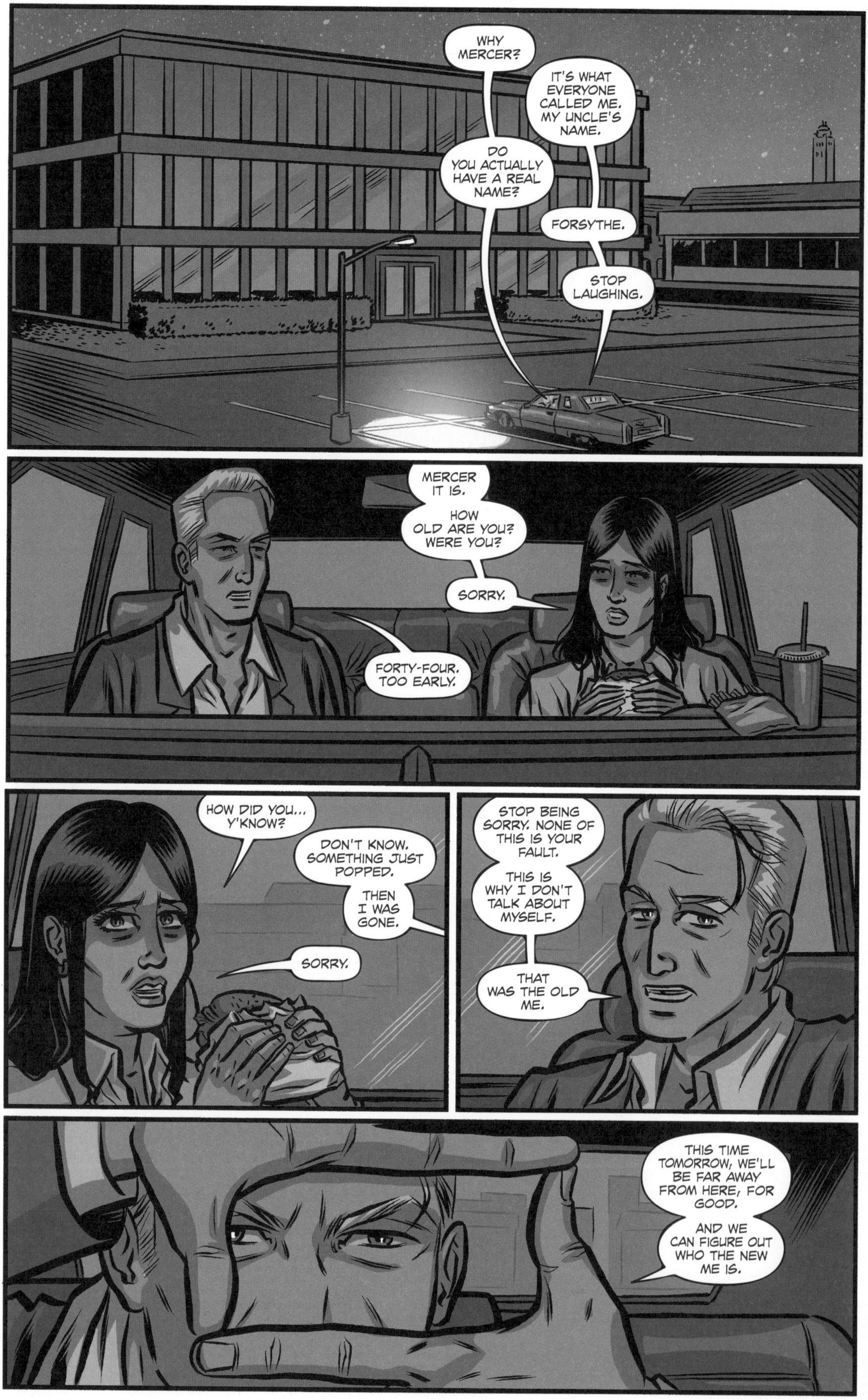
WHY MERCER?
IT'S WHAT EVERYONE CALLED ME. MY UNCLE'S NAME.
DO YOU ACTUALLY HAVE A REAL NAME?
FORSYTHE.
STOP LAUGHING.
MERCER IT IS.
HOW OLD ARE YOU? WERE YOU?
SORRY.
FORTY-FOUR. TOO EARLY.
HOW DID YOU... Y'KNOW?
DON'T KNOW. SOMETHING JUST POPPED.
THEN I WAS GONE.
SORRY.
STOP BEING SORRY. NONE OF THIS IS YOUR FAULT.
THIS IS WHY I DON'T TALK ABOUT MYSELF.
THAT WAS THE OLD ME.
THIS TIME TOMORROW, WE'LL BE FAR AWAY FROM HERE, FOR GOOD.
AND WE CAN FIGURE OUT WHO THE NEW ME IS.

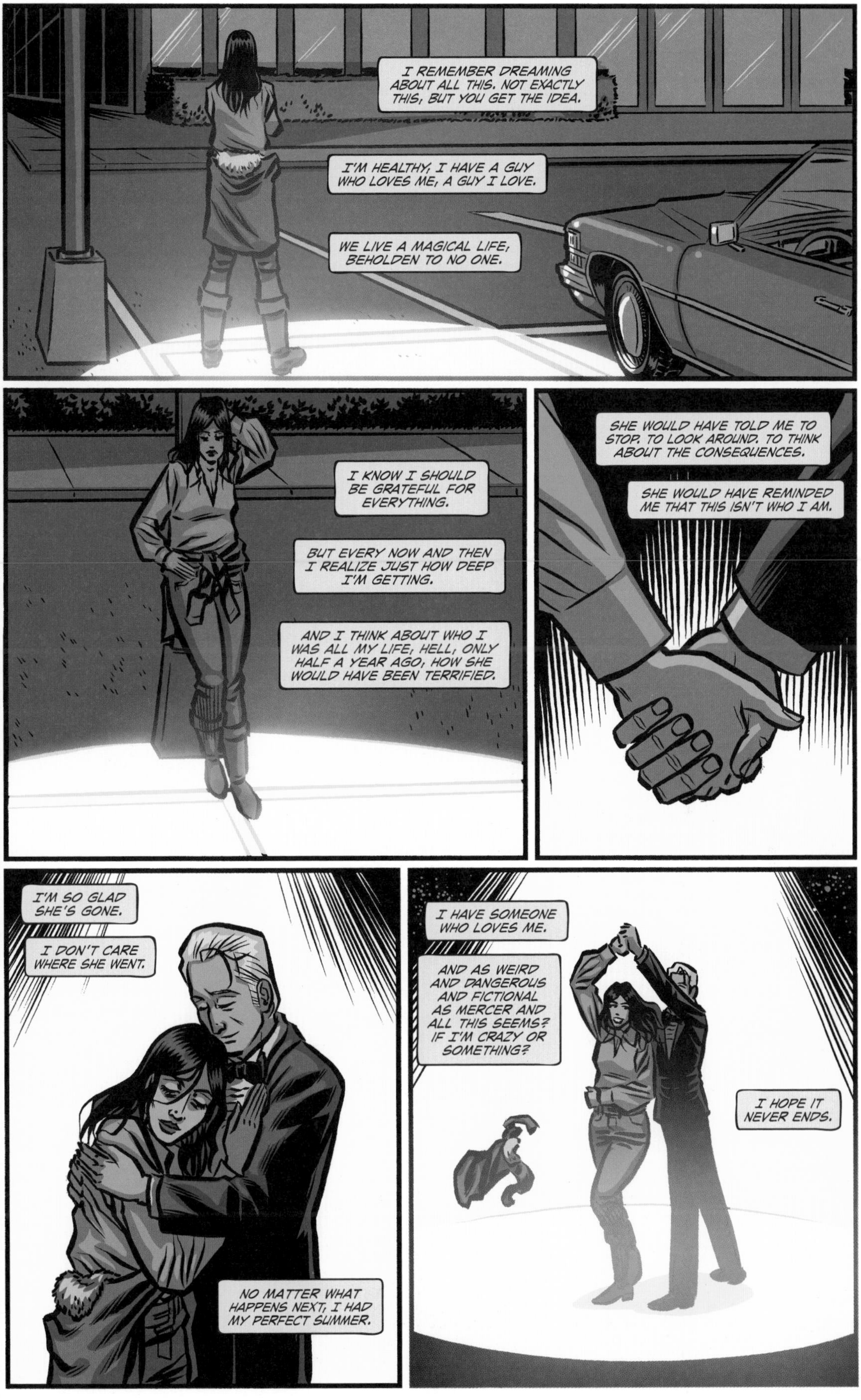
I REMEMBER DREAMING ABOUT ALL THIS. NOT EXACTLY THIS, BUT YOU GET THE IDEA.
I'M HEALTHY; I HAVE A GUY WHO LOVES ME, A GUY I LOVE.
WE LIVE A MAGICAL LIFE, BEHOLDEN TO NO ONE.
I KNOW I SHOULD BE GRATEFUL FOR EVERYTHING.
BUT EVERY NOW AND THEN I REALIZE JUST HOW DEEP I'M GETTING.
AND I THINK ABOUT WHO I WAS ALL MY LIFE; HELL, ONLY HALF A YEAR AGO, HOW SHE WOULD HAVE BEEN TERRIFIED.
SHE WOULD HAVE TOLD ME TO STOP. TO LOOK AROUND. TO THINK ABOUT THE CONSEQUENCES.
SHE WOULD HAVE REMINDED ME THAT THIS ISN'T WHO I AM.
I'M SO GLAD SHE'S GONE.
I DON'T CARE WHERE SHE WENT.
NO MATTER WHAT HAPPENS NEXT, I HAD MY PERFECT SUMMER.
I HAVE SOMEONE WHO LOVES ME.
AND AS WEIRD AND DANGEROUS AND FICTIONAL AS MERCER AND ALL THIS SEEMS? IF I'M CRAZY OR SOMETHING?
I HOPE IT NEVER ENDS.

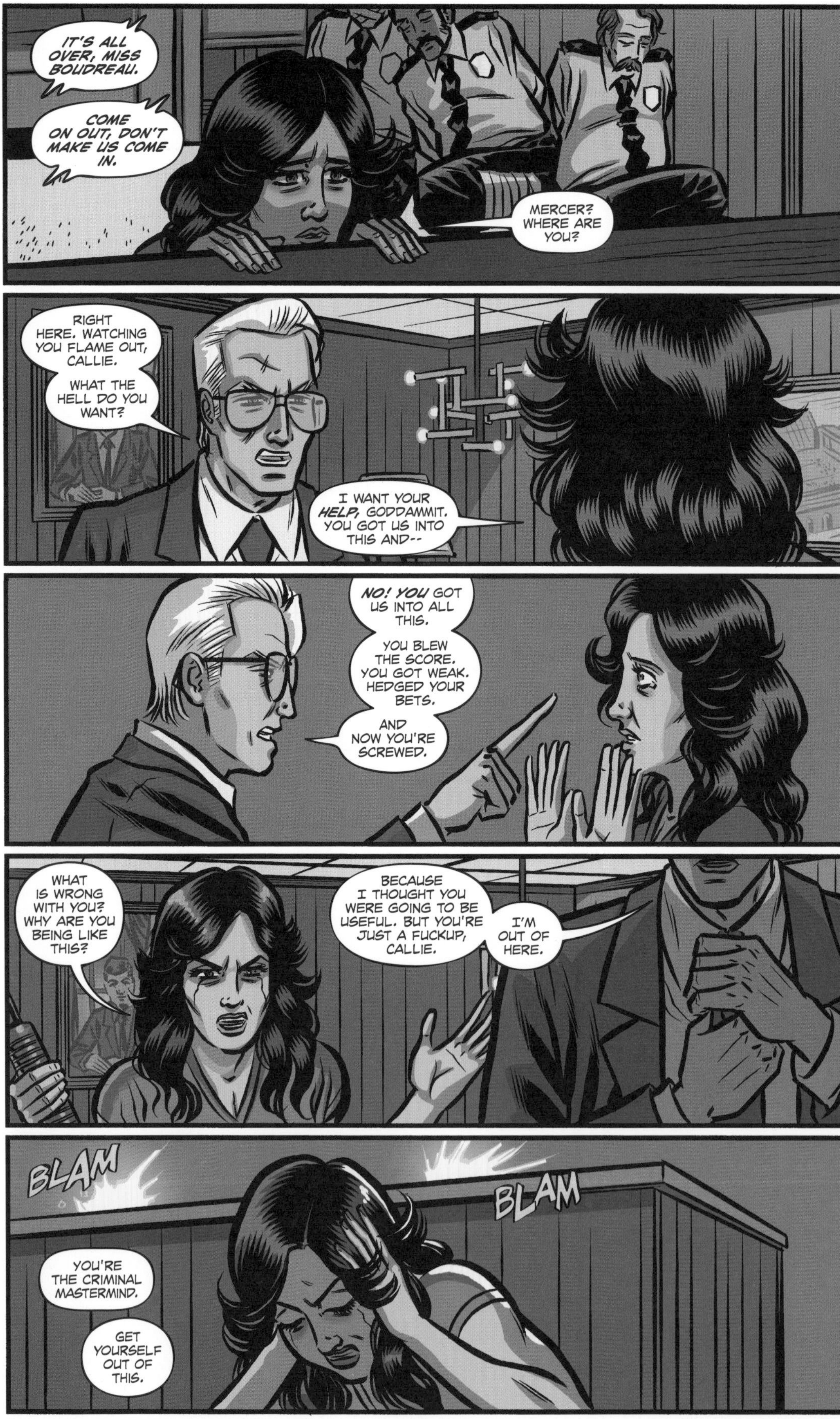

IT'S ALL OVER, MISS BOUDREAU.
COME ON OUT, DON'T MAKE US COME IN.
MERCER? WHERE ARE YOU?
RIGHT HERE. WATCHING YOU FLAME OUT, CALLIE.
WHAT THE HELL DO YOU WANT?
I WANT YOUR HELP, GODDAMMIT. YOU GOT US INTO THIS AND--
NO! YOU GOT US INTO ALL THIS.
YOU BLEW THE SCORE. YOU GOT WEAK. HEDGED YOUR BETS.
AND NOW YOU'RE SCREWED.
WHAT IS WRONG WITH YOU? WHY ARE YOU BEING LIKE THIS?
BECAUSE I THOUGHT YOU WERE GOING TO BE USEFUL. BUT YOU'RE JUST A FUCKUP, CALLIE.
I'M OUT OF HERE.
BLAM
BLAM
YOU'RE THE CRIMINAL MASTERMIND.
GET YOURSELF OUT OF THIS.

# CHAPTER 3

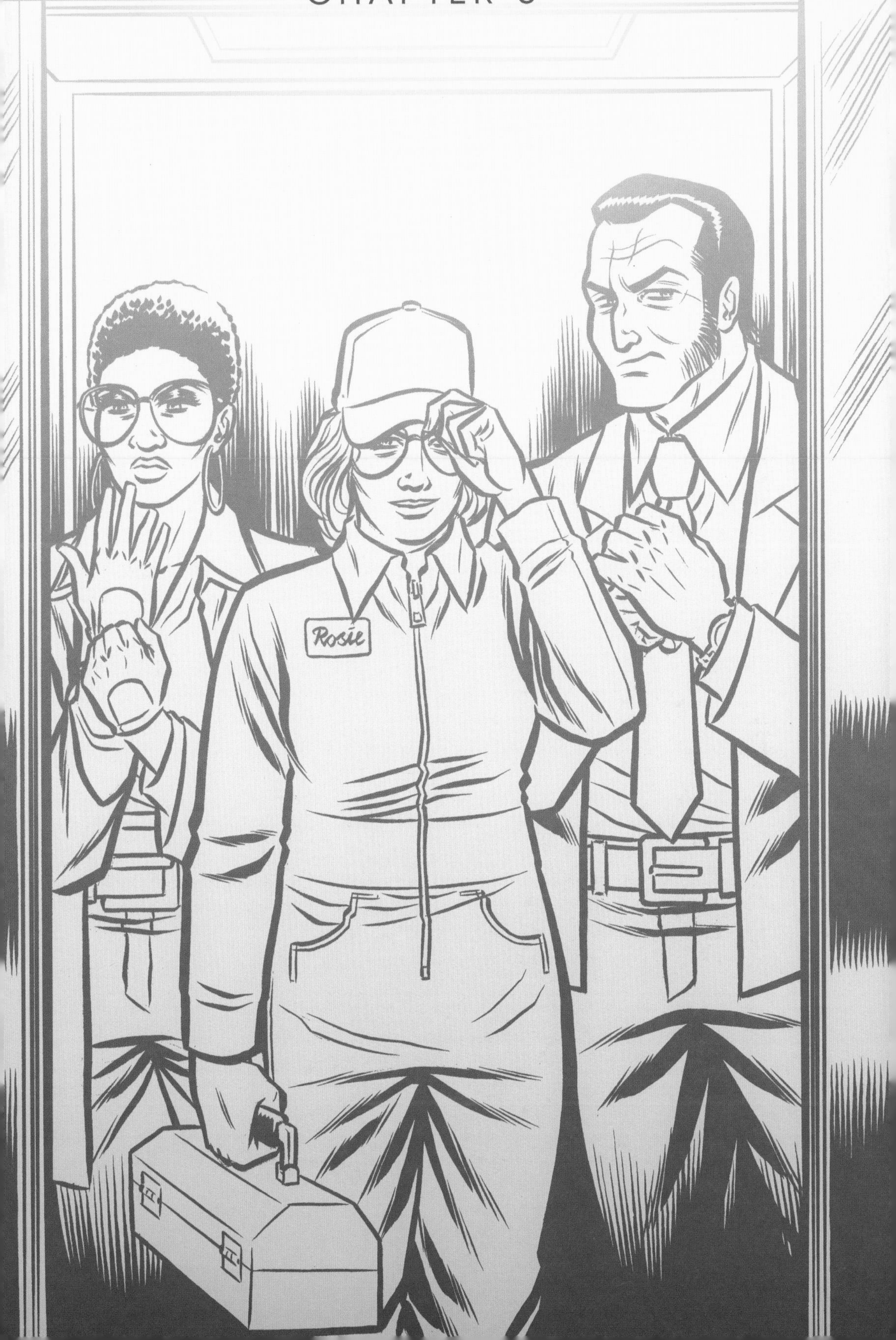
Rosie

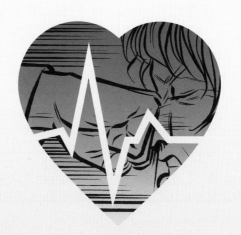

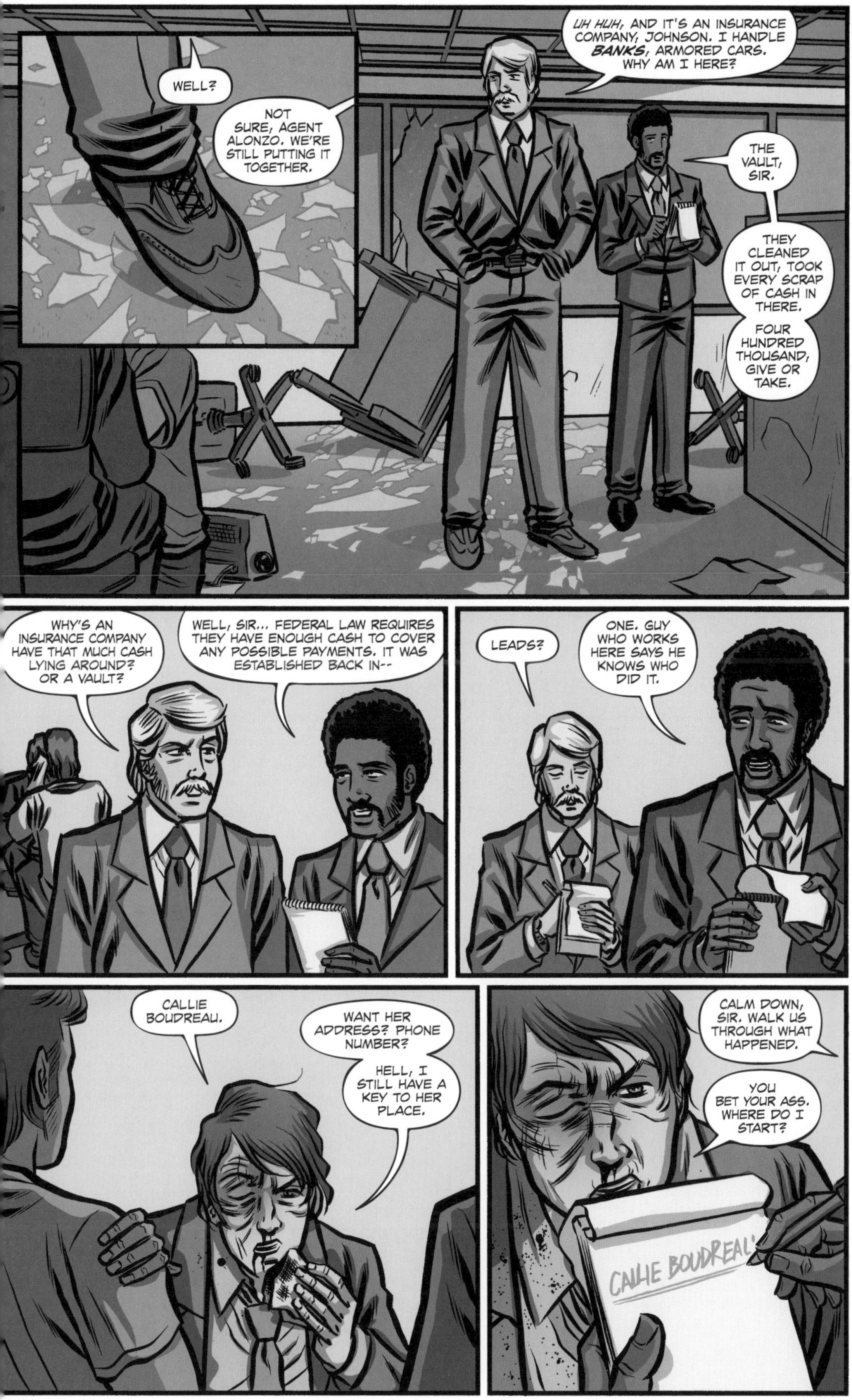
WELL?
NOT SURE, AGENT ALONZO. WE'RE STILL PUTTING IT TOGETHER.
UH HUH, AND IT'S AN INSURANCE COMPANY, JOHNSON. I HANDLE BANKS, ARMORED CARS. WHY AM I HERE?
THE VAULT, SIR.
THEY CLEANED IT OUT, TOOK EVERY SCRAP OF CASH IN THERE.
FOUR HUNDRED THOUSAND, GIVE OR TAKE.
WHY'S AN INSURANCE COMPANY HAVE THAT MUCH CASH LYING AROUND? OR A VAULT?
WELL, SIR... FEDERAL LAW REQUIRES THEY HAVE ENOUGH CASH TO COVER ANY POSSIBLE PAYMENTS. IT WAS ESTABLISHED BACK IN--
LEADS?
ONE. GUY WHO WORKS HERE SAYS HE KNOWS WHO DID IT.
CALLIE BOUDREAU.
WANT HER ADDRESS? PHONE NUMBER?
HELL, I STILL HAVE A KEY TO HER PLACE.
CALM DOWN, SIR. WALK US THROUGH WHAT HAPPENED.
YOU BET YOUR ASS. WHERE DO I START?
CALLIE BOUDREAU

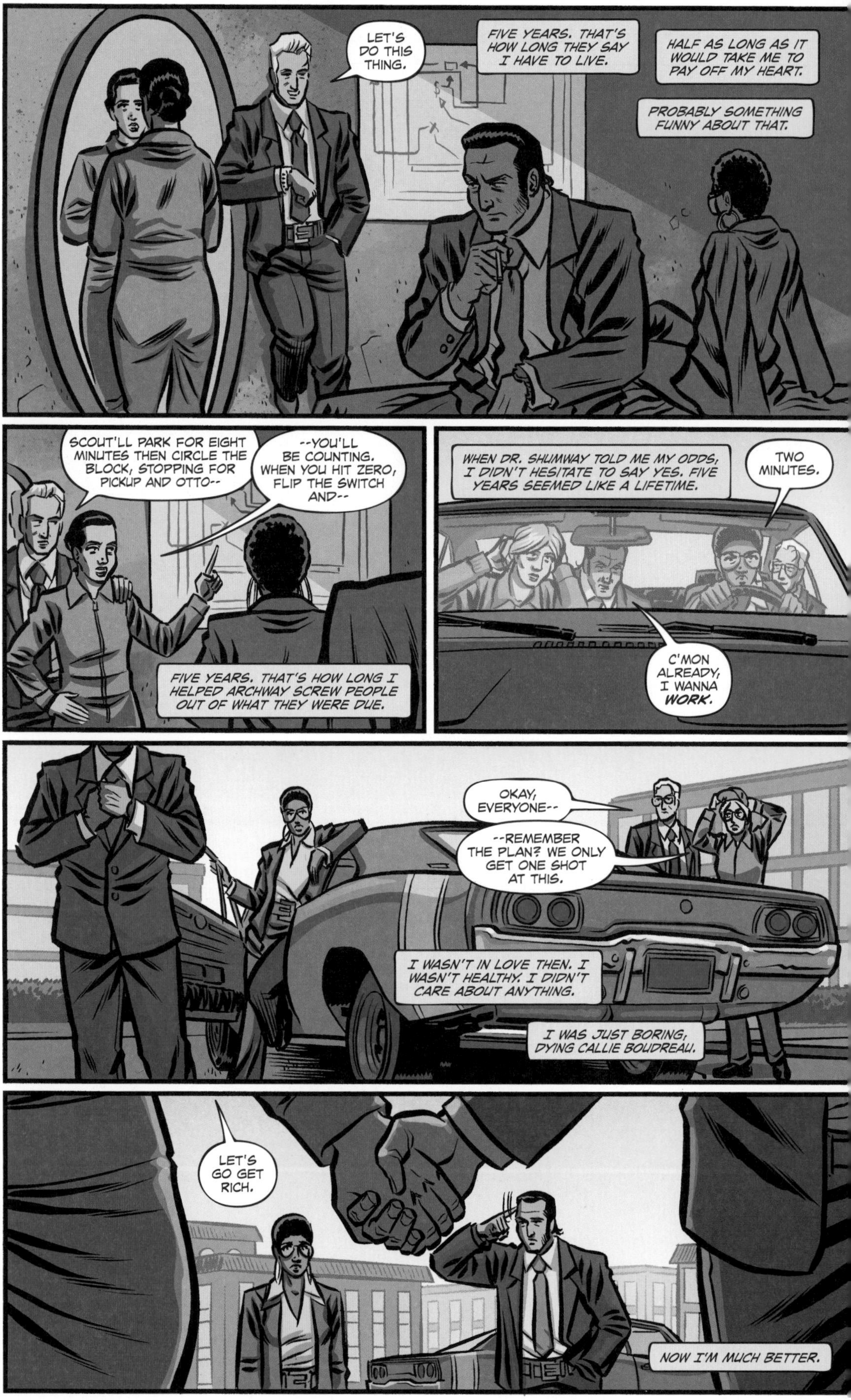
LET'S DO THIS THING.
FIVE YEARS. THAT'S HOW LONG THEY SAY I HAVE TO LIVE.
HALF AS LONG AS IT WOULD TAKE ME TO PAY OFF MY HEART.
PROBABLY SOMETHING FUNNY ABOUT THAT.
SCOUT'LL PARK FOR EIGHT MINUTES THEN CIRCLE THE BLOCK, STOPPING FOR PICKUP AND OTTO--
--YOU'LL BE COUNTING. WHEN YOU HIT ZERO, FLIP THE SWITCH AND--
FIVE YEARS. THAT'S HOW LONG I HELPED ARCHWAY SCREW PEOPLE OUT OF WHAT THEY WERE DUE.
WHEN DR. SHUMWAY TOLD ME MY ODDS, I DIDN'T HESITATE TO SAY YES. FIVE YEARS SEEMED LIKE A LIFETIME.
TWO MINUTES.
C'MON ALREADY, I WANNA **WORK**.
OKAY, EVERYONE--
--REMEMBER THE PLAN? WE ONLY GET ONE SHOT AT THIS.
I WASN'T IN LOVE THEN. I WASN'T HEALTHY. I DIDN'T CARE ABOUT ANYTHING.
I WAS JUST BORING, DYING CALLIE BOUDREAU.
LET'S GO GET RICH.
NOW I'M MUCH BETTER.

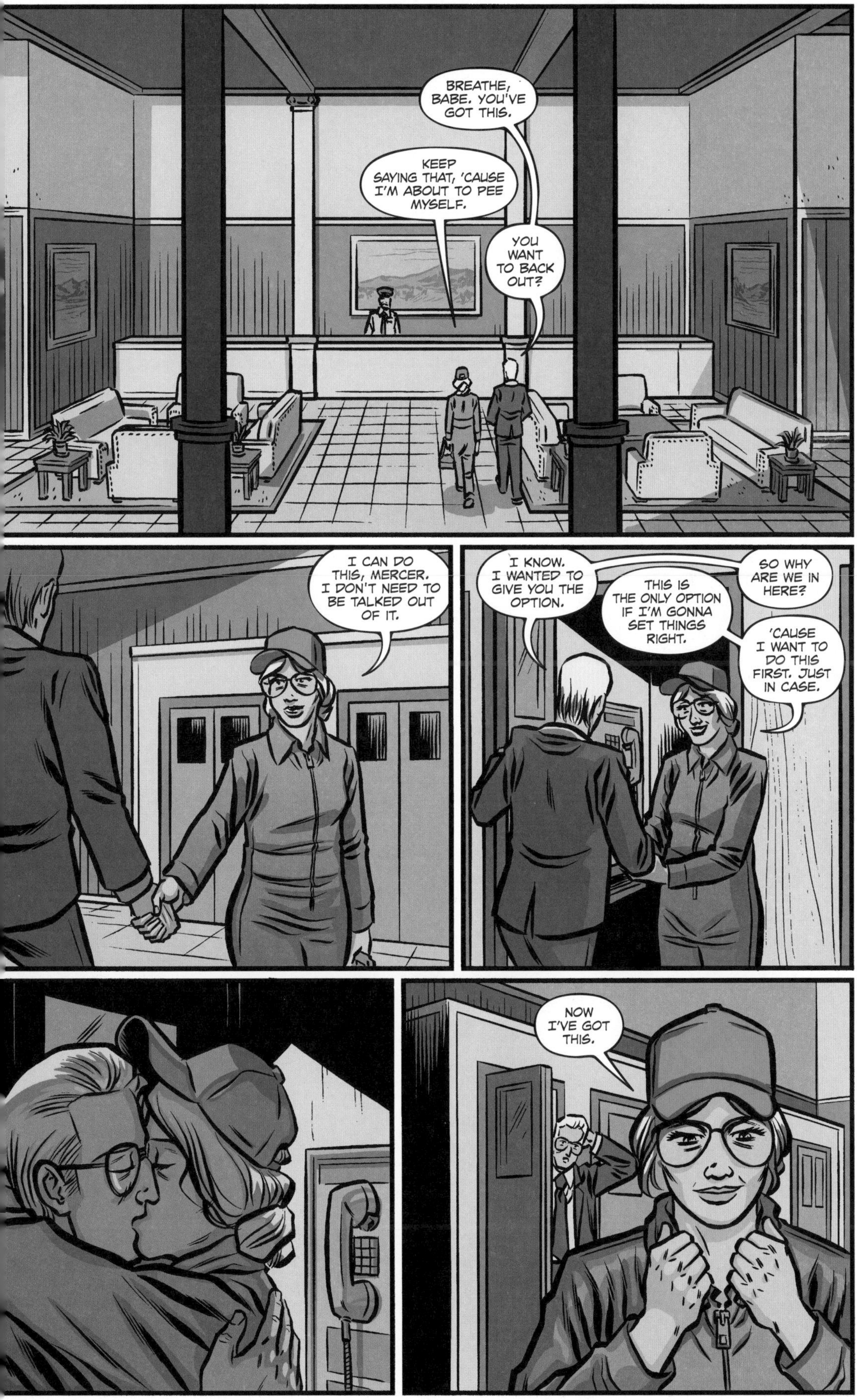

BREATHE, BABE. YOU'VE GOT THIS.
KEEP SAYING THAT, 'CAUSE I'M ABOUT TO PEE MYSELF.
YOU WANT TO BACK OUT?
I CAN DO THIS, MERCER. I DON'T NEED TO BE TALKED OUT OF IT.
I KNOW. I WANTED TO GIVE YOU THE OPTION.
SO WHY ARE WE IN HERE?
THIS IS THE ONLY OPTION IF I'M GONNA SET THINGS RIGHT.
'CAUSE I WANT TO DO THIS FIRST. JUST IN CASE.
NOW I'VE GOT THIS.

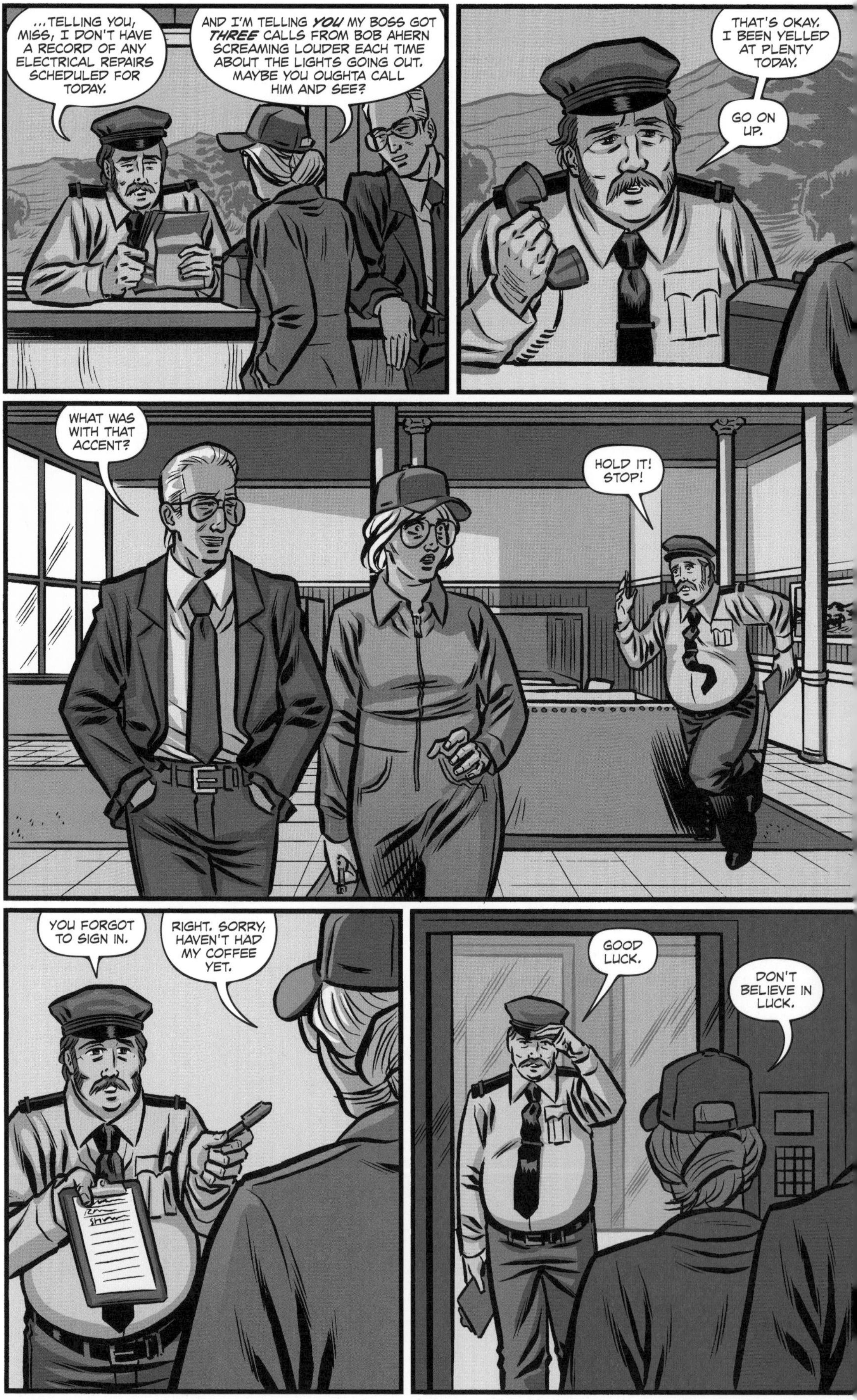
...TELLING YOU, MISS, I DON'T HAVE A RECORD OF ANY ELECTRICAL REPAIRS SCHEDULED FOR TODAY.
AND I'M TELLING *YOU* MY BOSS GOT *THREE* CALLS FROM BOB AHERN SCREAMING LOUDER EACH TIME ABOUT THE LIGHTS GOING OUT. MAYBE YOU OUGHTA CALL HIM AND SEE?
THAT'S OKAY. I BEEN YELLED AT PLENTY TODAY.
GO ON UP.
WHAT WAS WITH THAT ACCENT?
HOLD IT! STOP!
YOU FORGOT TO SIGN IN.
RIGHT. SORRY, HAVEN'T HAD MY COFFEE YET.
GOOD LUCK.
DON'T BELIEVE IN LUCK.

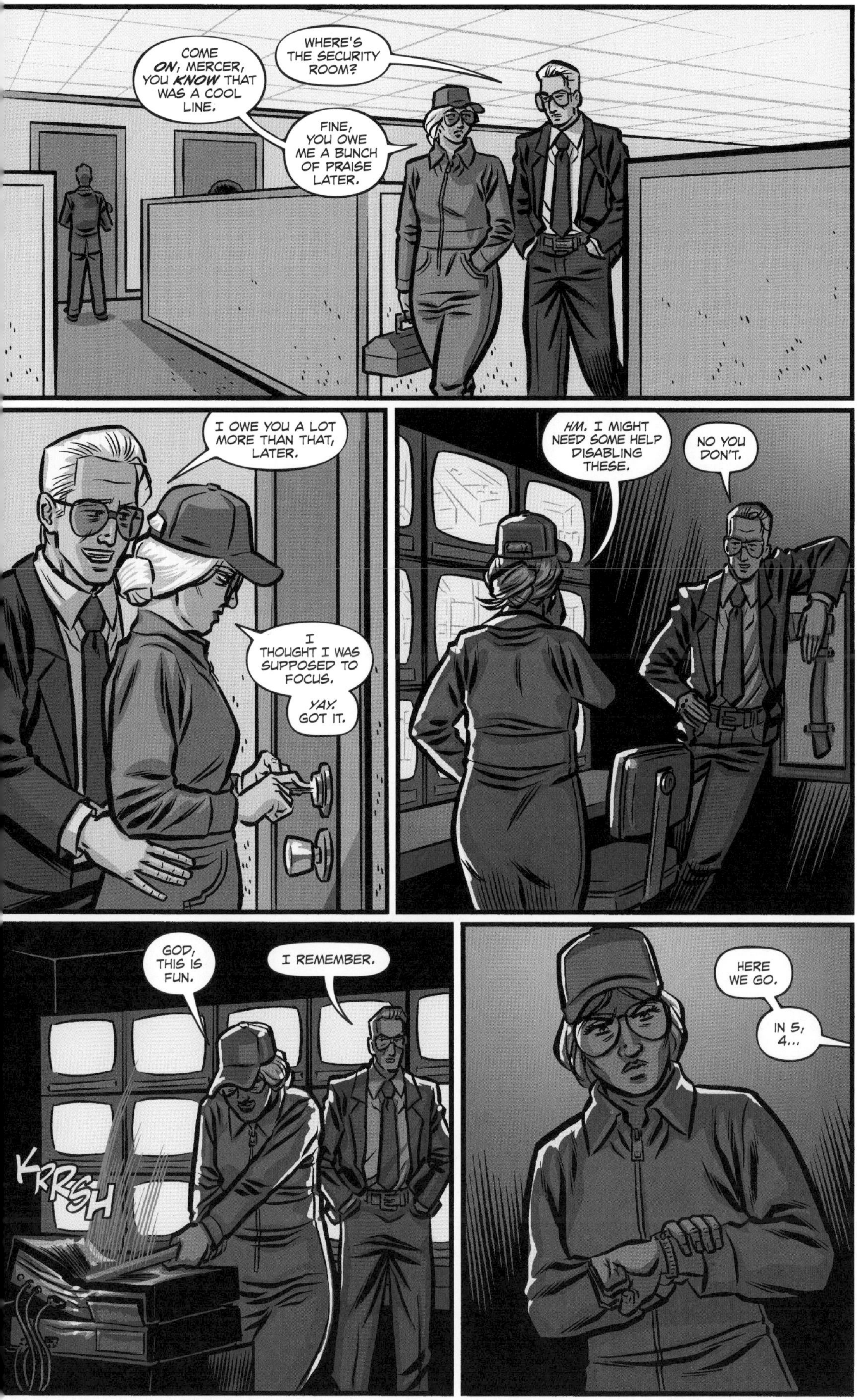
WHERE'S THE SECURITY ROOM?
COME *ON*, MERCER, YOU *KNOW* THAT WAS A COOL LINE.
FINE, YOU OWE ME A BUNCH OF PRAISE LATER.
I OWE YOU A LOT MORE THAN THAT, LATER.
I THOUGHT I WAS SUPPOSED TO FOCUS.
*YAY.* GOT IT.
*HM.* I MIGHT NEED SOME HELP DISABLING THESE.
NO YOU DON'T.
GOD, THIS IS FUN.
I REMEMBER.
KRR-SH
HERE WE GO.
IN 5, 4...

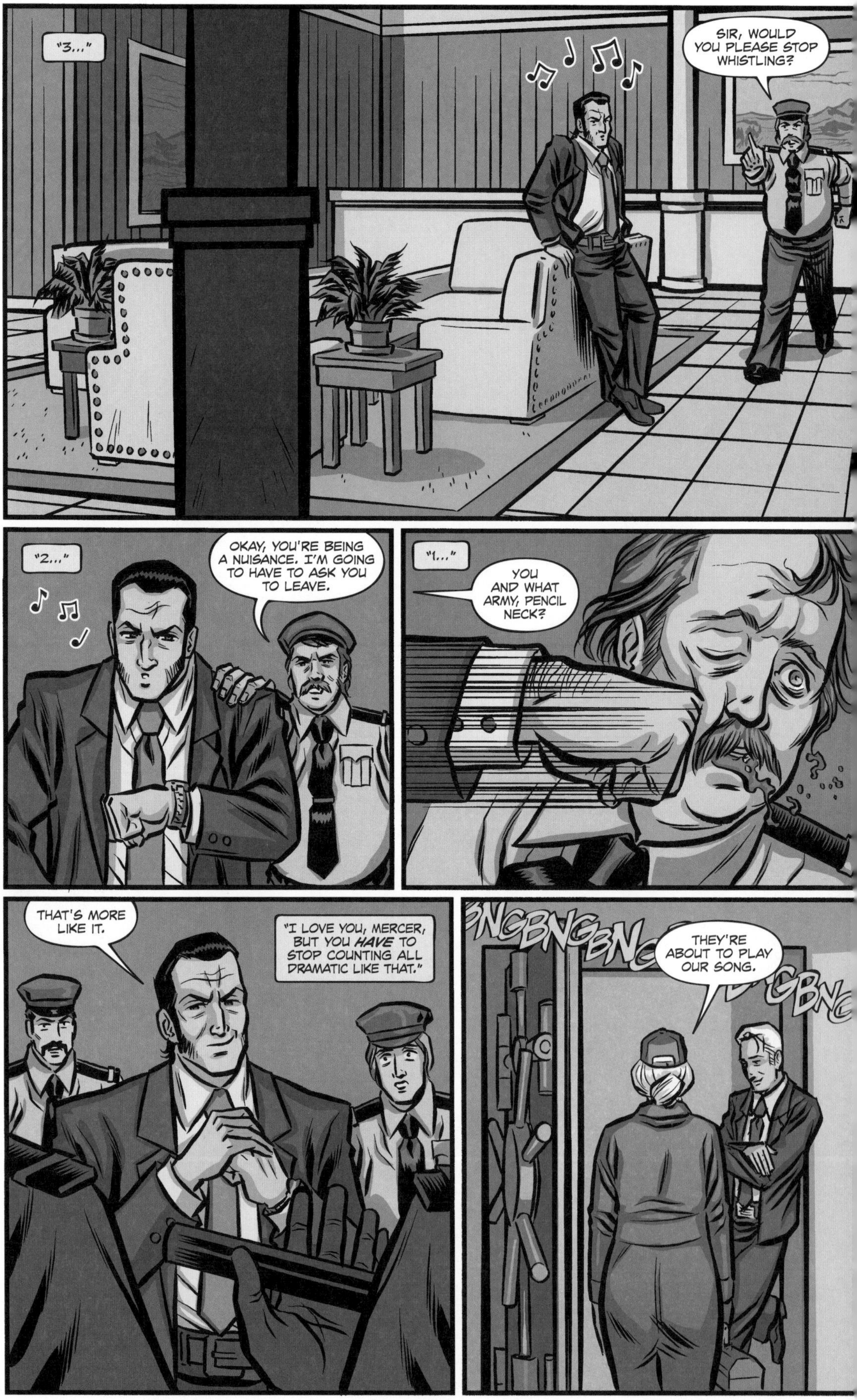
"3..."
SIR, WOULD YOU PLEASE STOP WHISTLING?
"2..."
OKAY, YOU'RE BEING A NUISANCE. I'M GOING TO HAVE TO ASK YOU TO LEAVE.
"1..."
YOU AND WHAT ARMY, PENCIL NECK?
THAT'S MORE LIKE IT.
"I LOVE YOU, MERCER, BUT YOU *HAVE* TO STOP COUNTING ALL DRAMATIC LIKE THAT."
THEY'RE ABOUT TO PLAY OUR SONG.

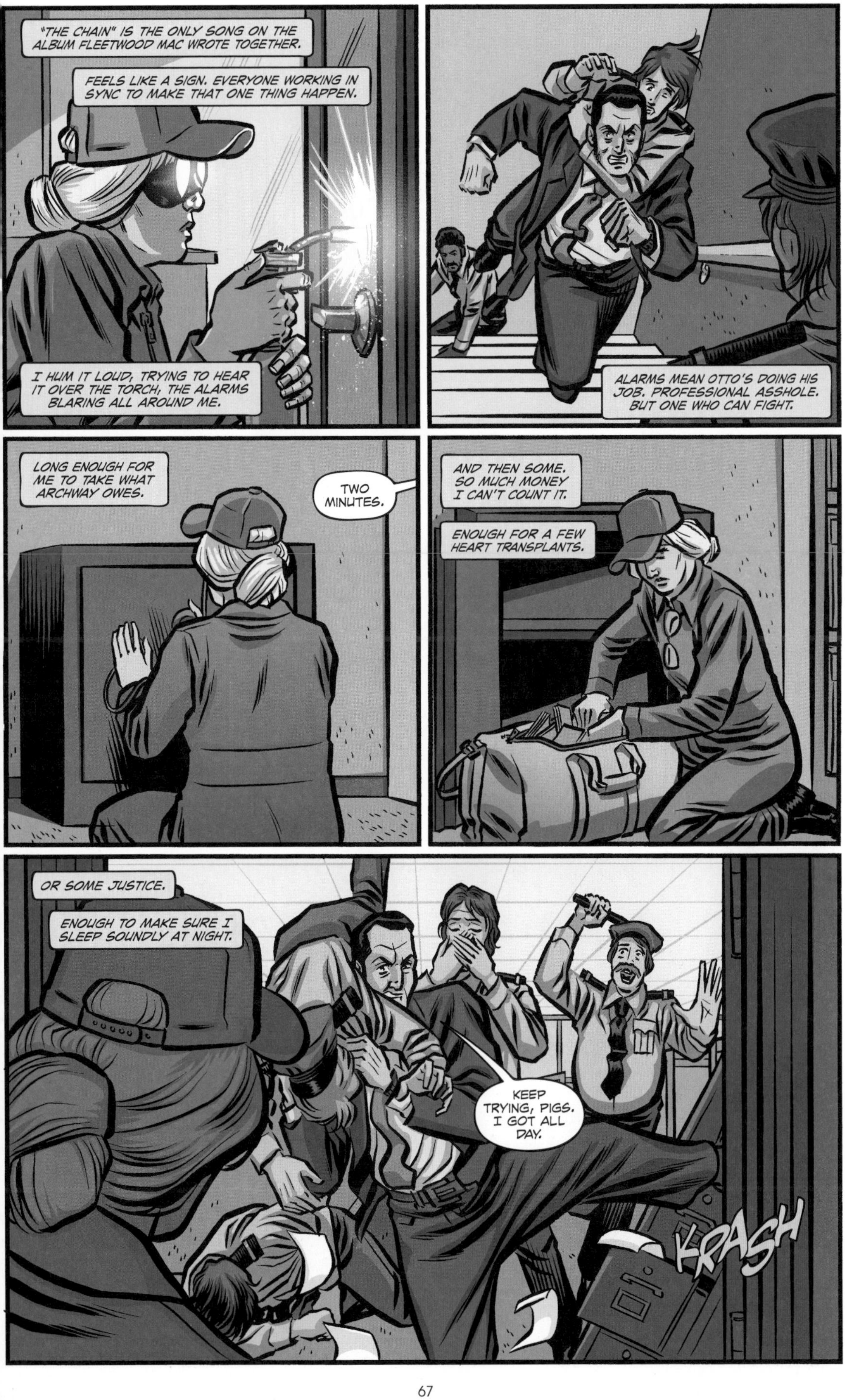
"THE CHAIN" IS THE ONLY SONG ON THE ALBUM FLEETWOOD MAC WROTE TOGETHER.
FEELS LIKE A SIGN. EVERYONE WORKING IN SYNC TO MAKE THAT ONE THING HAPPEN.
I HUM IT LOUD, TRYING TO HEAR IT OVER THE TORCH, THE ALARMS BLARING ALL AROUND ME.
ALARMS MEAN OTTO'S DOING HIS JOB. PROFESSIONAL ASSHOLE. BUT ONE WHO CAN FIGHT.
LONG ENOUGH FOR ME TO TAKE WHAT ARCHWAY OWES.
TWO MINUTES.
AND THEN SOME. SO MUCH MONEY I CAN'T COUNT IT.
ENOUGH FOR A FEW HEART TRANSPLANTS.
OR SOME JUSTICE.
ENOUGH TO MAKE SURE I SLEEP SOUNDLY AT NIGHT.
KEEP TRYING, PIGS. I GOT ALL DAY.
KRASH

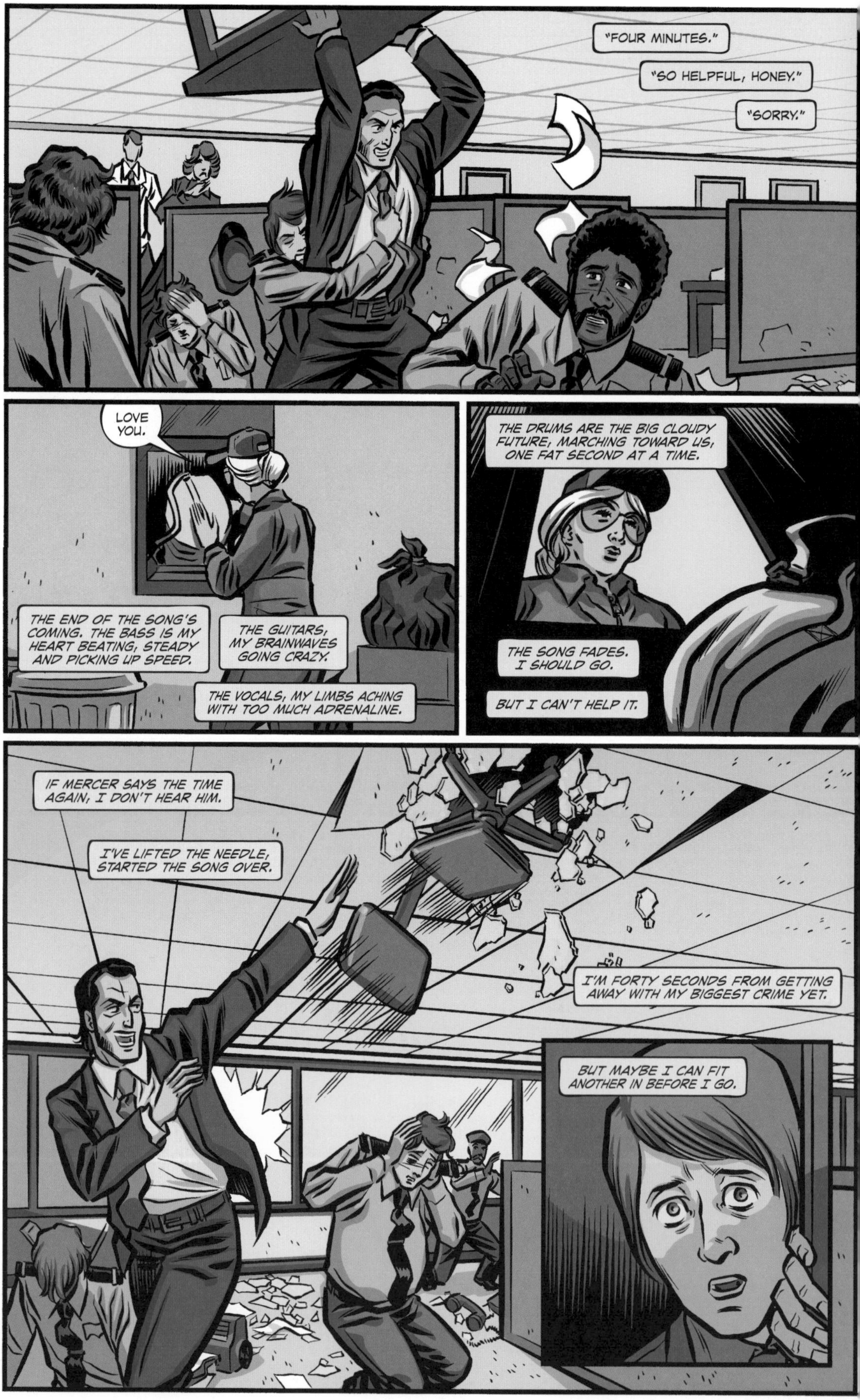
"FOUR MINUTES."
"SO HELPFUL, HONEY."
"SORRY."
LOVE YOU.
THE END OF THE SONG'S COMING. THE BASS IS MY HEART BEATING, STEADY AND PICKING UP SPEED.
THE GUITARS, MY BRAINWAVES GOING CRAZY.
THE VOCALS, MY LIMBS ACHING WITH TOO MUCH ADRENALINE.
THE DRUMS ARE THE BIG CLOUDY FUTURE, MARCHING TOWARD US, ONE FAT SECOND AT A TIME.
THE SONG FADES. I SHOULD GO.
BUT I CAN'T HELP IT.
IF MERCER SAYS THE TIME AGAIN, I DON'T HEAR HIM.
I'VE LIFTED THE NEEDLE, STARTED THE SONG OVER.
I'M FORTY SECONDS FROM GETTING AWAY WITH MY BIGGEST CRIME YET.
BUT MAYBE I CAN FIT ANOTHER IN BEFORE I GO.

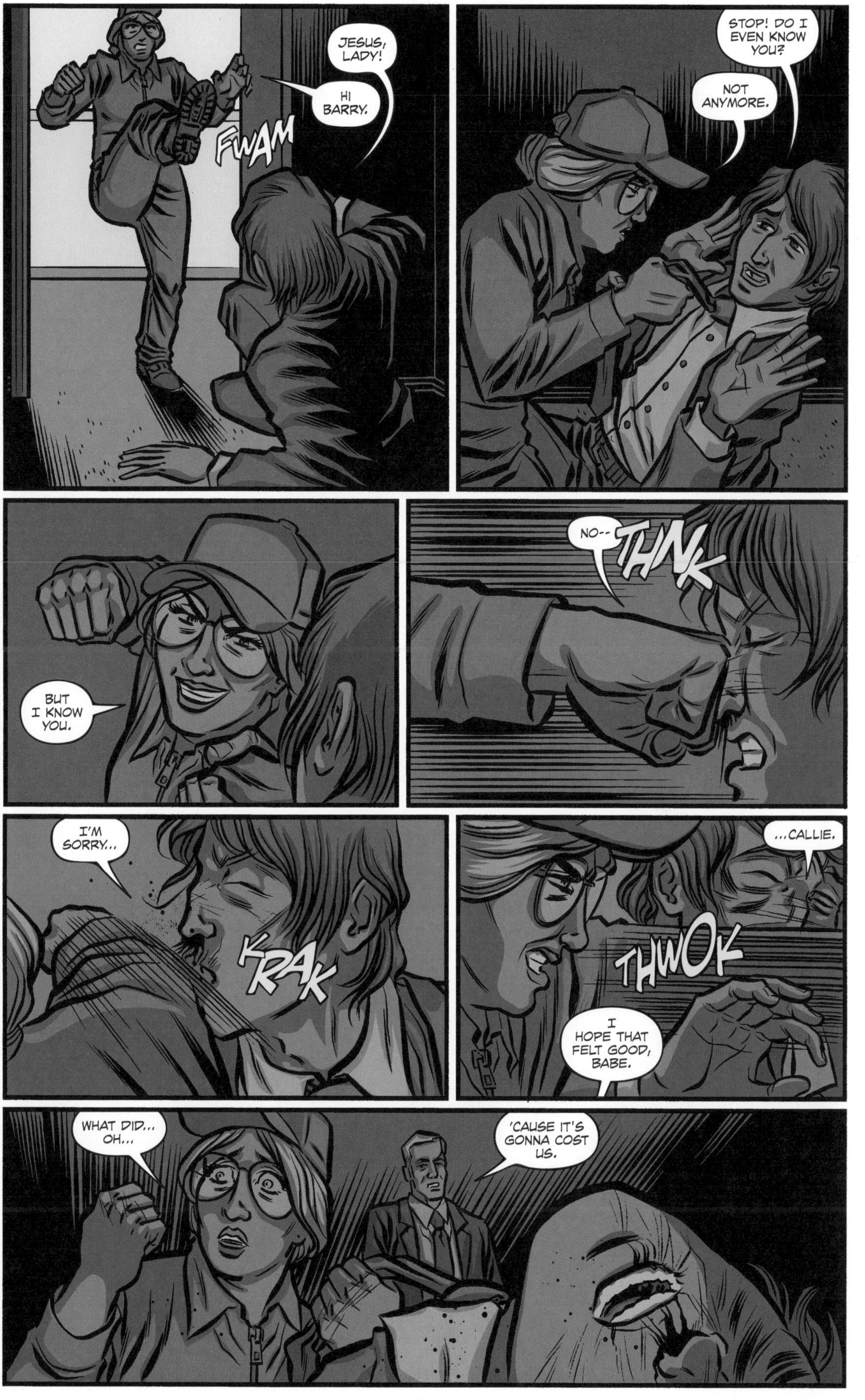

JESUS, LADY!
HI BARRY.
FWAM
STOP! DO I EVEN KNOW YOU?
NOT ANYMORE.
BUT I KNOW YOU.
NO--
THNK
I'M SORRY...
KRAK
...CALLIE.
THWOK
I HOPE THAT FELT GOOD, BABE.
WHAT DID... OH...
'CAUSE IT'S GONNA COST US.

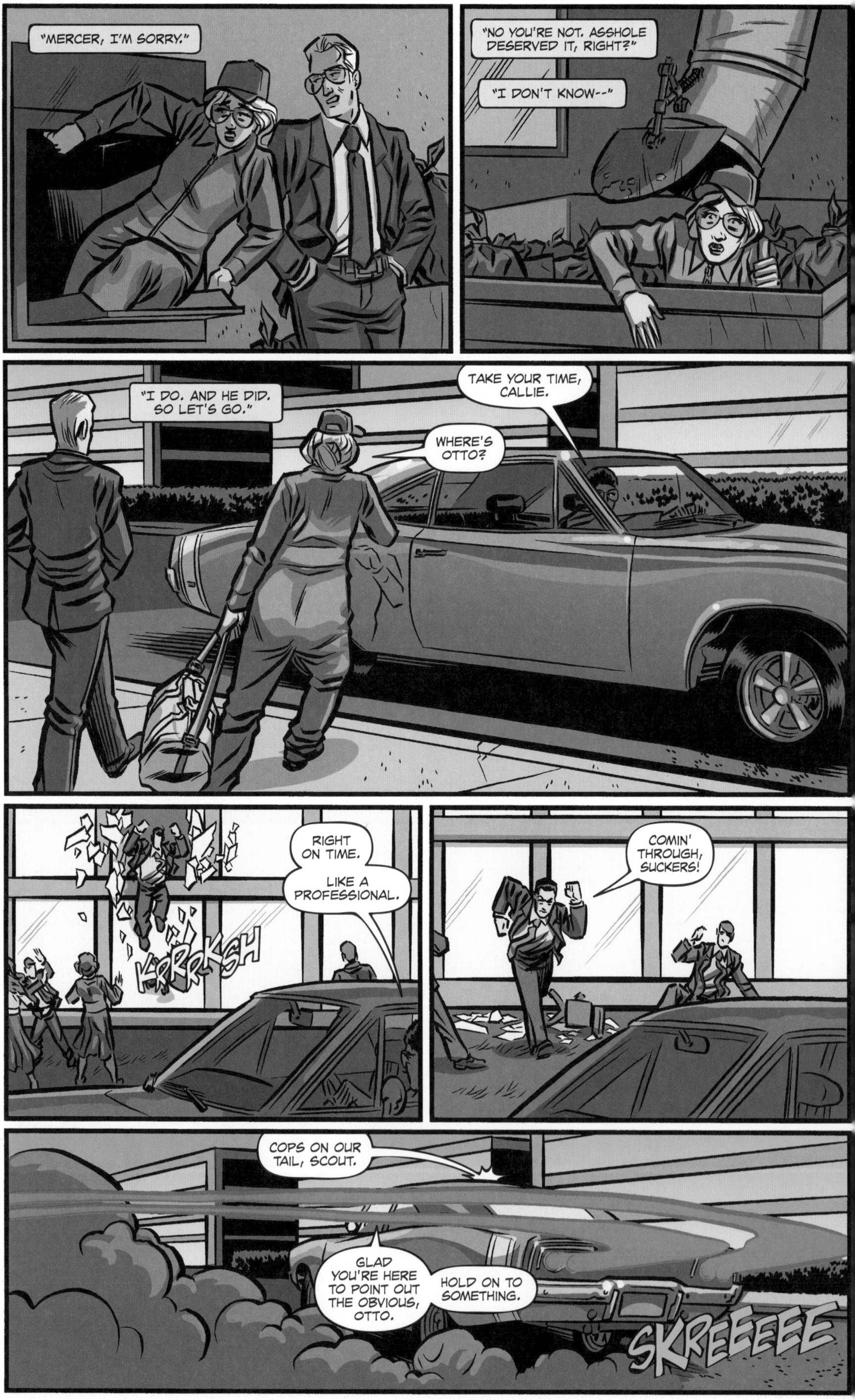
"MERCER, I'M SORRY."
"NO YOU'RE NOT. ASSHOLE DESERVED IT, RIGHT?"
"I DON'T KNOW--"
"I DO. AND HE DID. SO LET'S GO."
TAKE YOUR TIME, CALLIE.
WHERE'S OTTO?
KRRRKSH
RIGHT ON TIME.
LIKE A PROFESSIONAL.
COMIN' THROUGH, SUCKERS!
COPS ON OUR TAIL, SCOUT.
GLAD YOU'RE HERE TO POINT OUT THE OBVIOUS, OTTO.
HOLD ON TO SOMETHING.
SKREEEEEE

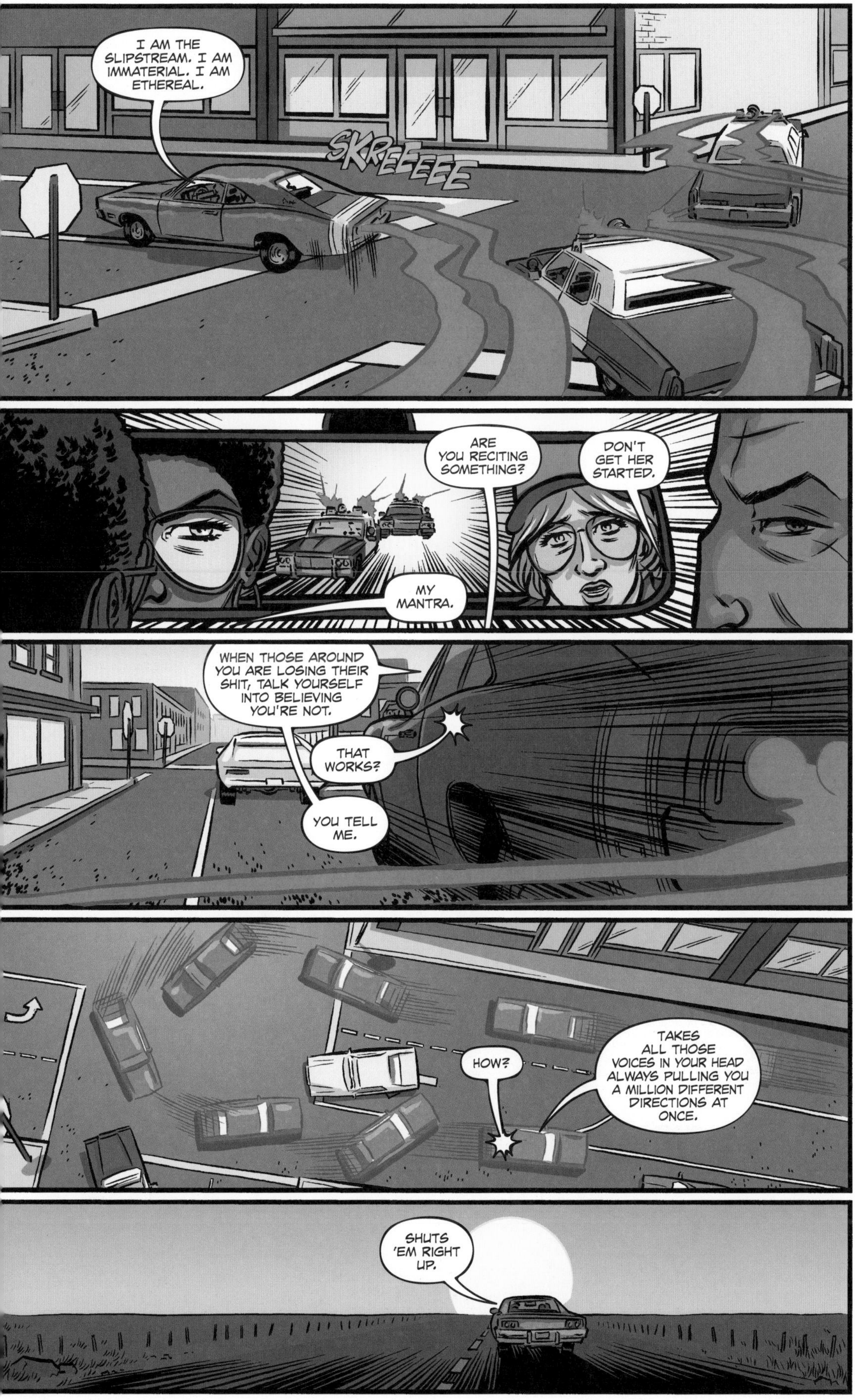
I AM THE SLIPSTREAM. I AM IMMATERIAL. I AM ETHEREAL.
SKREEEEEE
ARE YOU RECITING SOMETHING?
DON'T GET HER STARTED.
MY MANTRA.
WHEN THOSE AROUND YOU ARE LOSING THEIR SHIT, TALK YOURSELF INTO BELIEVING YOU'RE NOT.
THAT WORKS?
YOU TELL ME.
HOW?
TAKES ALL THOSE VOICES IN YOUR HEAD ALWAYS PULLING YOU A MILLION DIFFERENT DIRECTIONS AT ONCE.
SHUTS 'EM RIGHT UP.

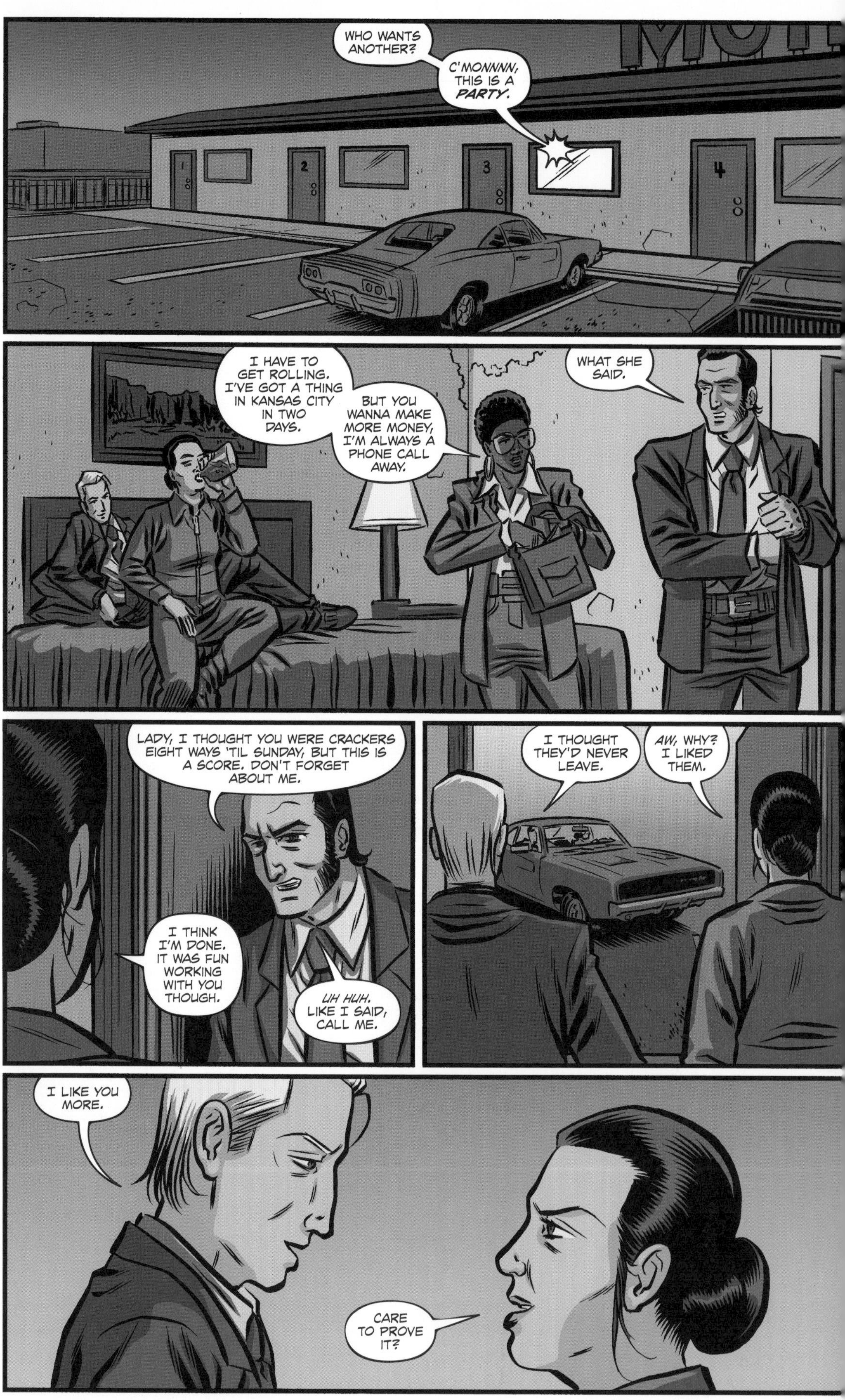
WHO WANTS ANOTHER?
C'MONNNN, THIS IS A *PARTY*.
I HAVE TO GET ROLLING. I'VE GOT A THING IN KANSAS CITY IN TWO DAYS.
BUT YOU WANNA MAKE MORE MONEY, I'M ALWAYS A PHONE CALL AWAY.
WHAT SHE SAID.
LADY, I THOUGHT YOU WERE CRACKERS EIGHT WAYS 'TIL SUNDAY, BUT THIS IS A SCORE. DON'T FORGET ABOUT ME.
I THINK I'M DONE. IT WAS FUN WORKING WITH YOU THOUGH.
*UH HUH.* LIKE I SAID, CALL ME.
I THOUGHT THEY'D NEVER LEAVE.
*AW,* WHY? I LIKED THEM.
I LIKE YOU MORE.
CARE TO PROVE IT?

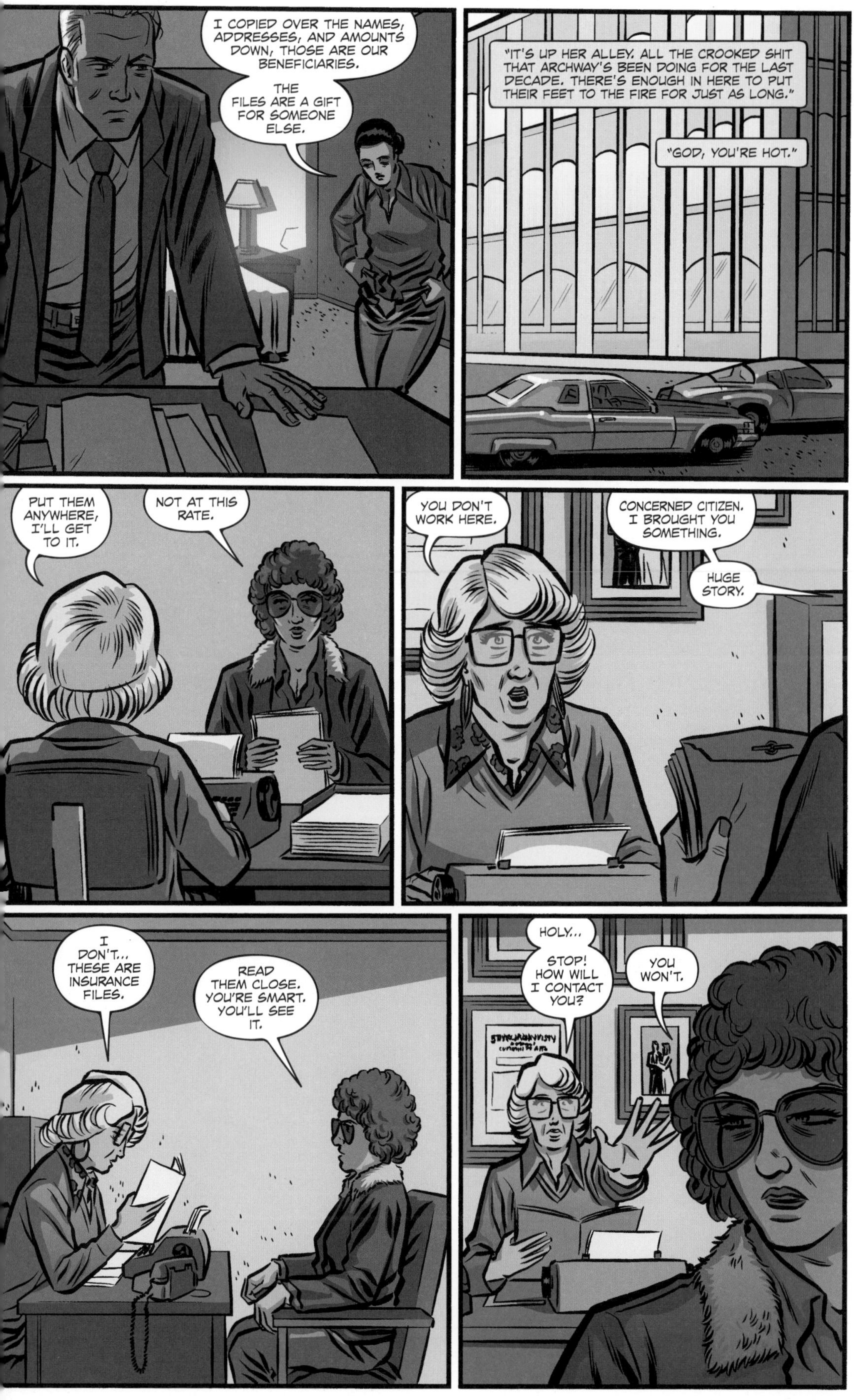
I COPIED OVER THE NAMES, ADDRESSES, AND AMOUNTS DOWN, THOSE ARE OUR BENEFICIARIES.
THE FILES ARE A GIFT FOR SOMEONE ELSE.
"IT'S UP HER ALLEY. ALL THE CROOKED SHIT THAT ARCHWAY'S BEEN DOING FOR THE LAST DECADE. THERE'S ENOUGH IN HERE TO PUT THEIR FEET TO THE FIRE FOR JUST AS LONG."
"GOD, YOU'RE HOT."
PUT THEM ANYWHERE, I'LL GET TO IT.
NOT AT THIS RATE.
YOU DON'T WORK HERE.
CONCERNED CITIZEN. I BROUGHT YOU SOMETHING.
HUGE STORY.
I DON'T... THESE ARE INSURANCE FILES.
READ THEM CLOSE. YOU'RE SMART. YOU'LL SEE IT.
HOLY...
STOP! HOW WILL I CONTACT YOU?
YOU WON'T.

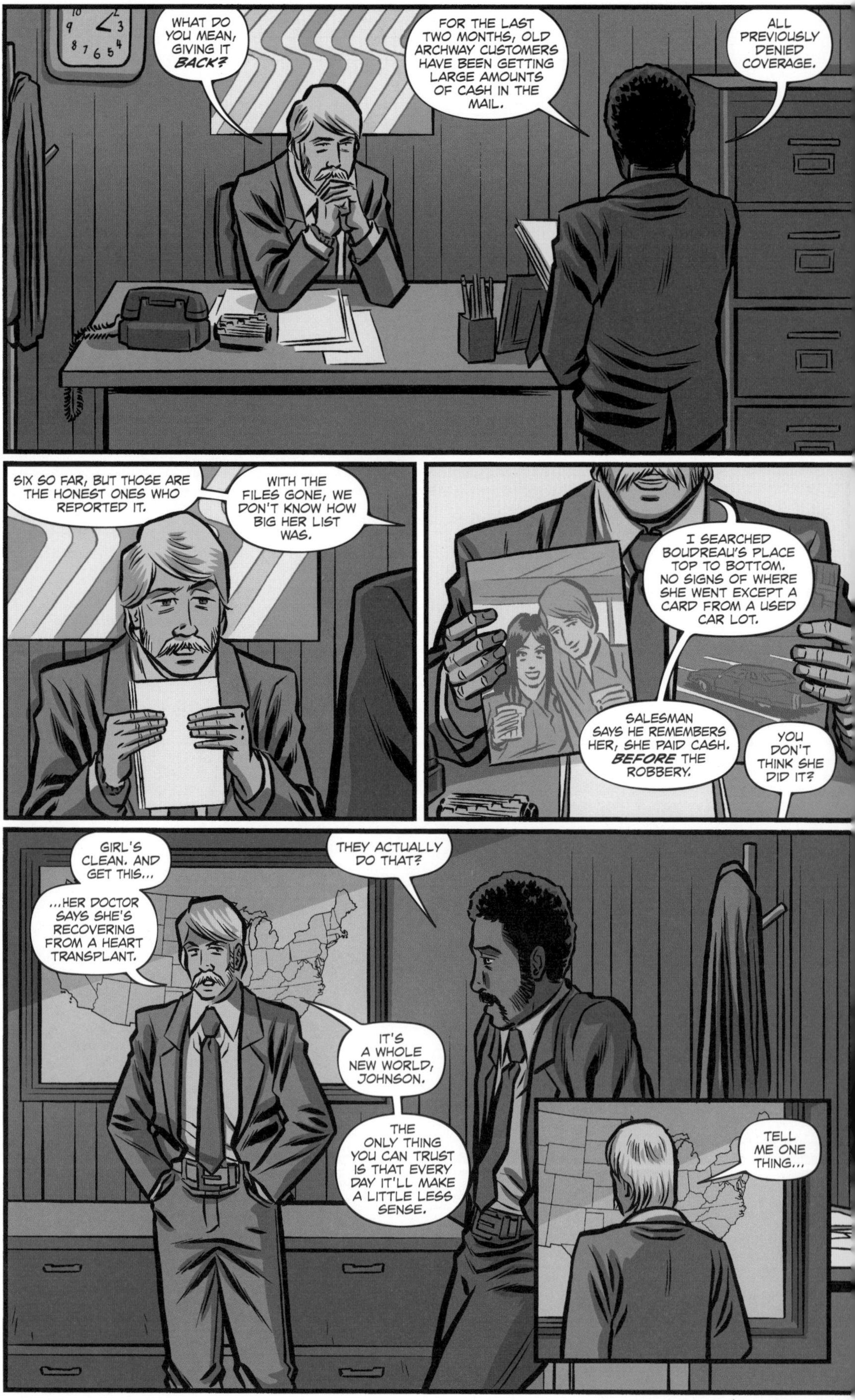
WHAT DO YOU MEAN, GIVING IT BACK?
FOR THE LAST TWO MONTHS, OLD ARCHWAY CUSTOMERS HAVE BEEN GETTING LARGE AMOUNTS OF CASH IN THE MAIL.
ALL PREVIOUSLY DENIED COVERAGE.
SIX SO FAR, BUT THOSE ARE THE HONEST ONES WHO REPORTED IT.
WITH THE FILES GONE, WE DON'T KNOW HOW BIG HER LIST WAS.
I SEARCHED BOUDREAU'S PLACE TOP TO BOTTOM. NO SIGNS OF WHERE SHE WENT EXCEPT A CARD FROM A USED CAR LOT.
SALESMAN SAYS HE REMEMBERS HER, SHE PAID CASH. BEFORE THE ROBBERY.
YOU DON'T THINK SHE DID IT?
GIRL'S CLEAN. AND GET THIS...
...HER DOCTOR SAYS SHE'S RECOVERING FROM A HEART TRANSPLANT.
THEY ACTUALLY DO THAT?
IT'S A WHOLE NEW WORLD, JOHNSON.
THE ONLY THING YOU CAN TRUST IS THAT EVERY DAY IT'LL MAKE A LITTLE LESS SENSE.
TELL ME ONE THING...

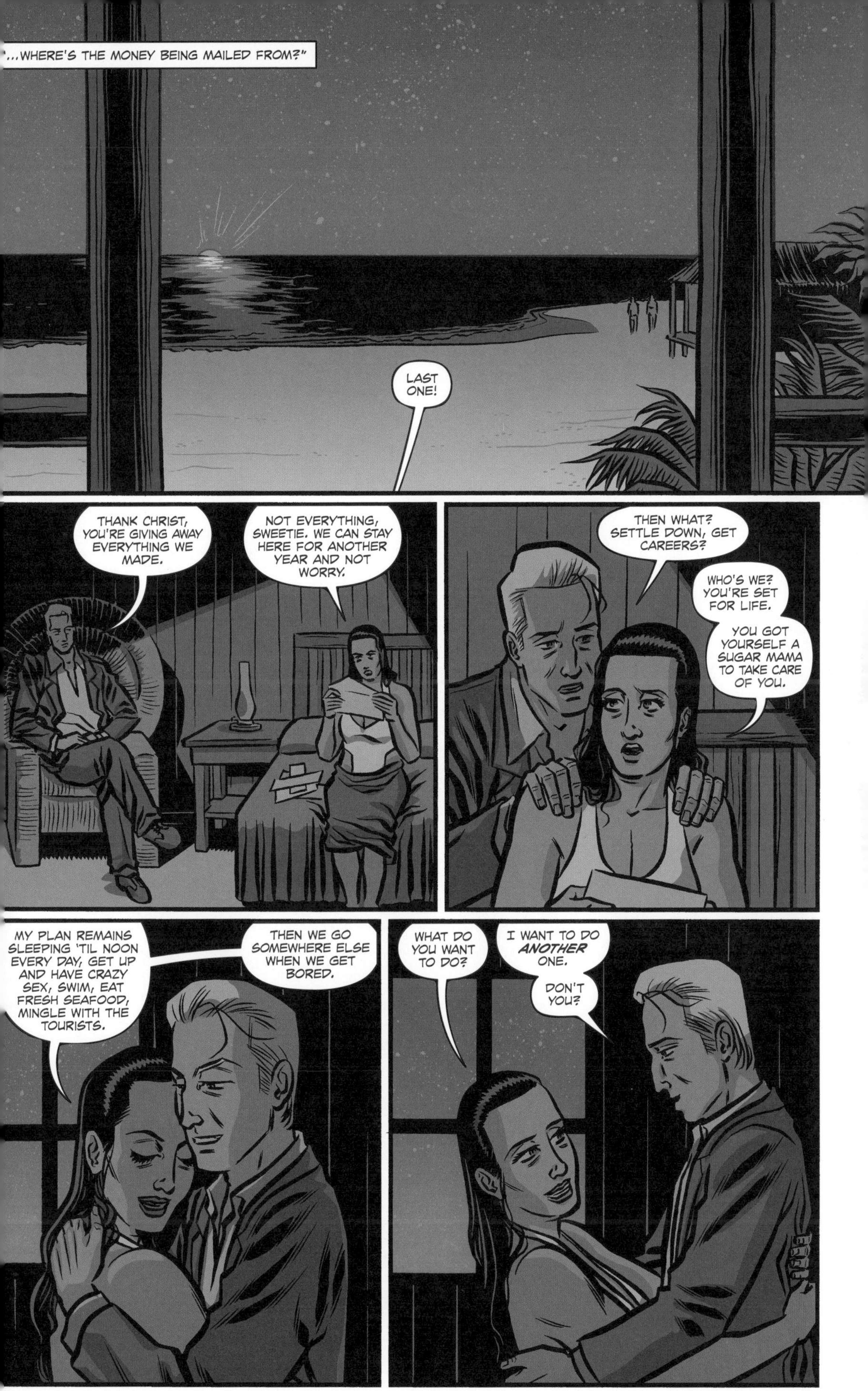
"...WHERE'S THE MONEY BEING MAILED FROM?"
LAST ONE!
THANK CHRIST, YOU'RE GIVING AWAY EVERYTHING WE MADE.
NOT EVERYTHING, SWEETIE. WE CAN STAY HERE FOR ANOTHER YEAR AND NOT WORRY.
THEN WHAT? SETTLE DOWN, GET CAREERS?
WHO'S WE? YOU'RE SET FOR LIFE.
YOU GOT YOURSELF A SUGAR MAMA TO TAKE CARE OF YOU.
MY PLAN REMAINS SLEEPING 'TIL NOON EVERY DAY; GET UP AND HAVE CRAZY SEX, SWIM, EAT FRESH SEAFOOD, MINGLE WITH THE TOURISTS.
THEN WE GO SOMEWHERE ELSE WHEN WE GET BORED.
WHAT DO YOU WANT TO DO?
I WANT TO DO ***ANOTHER*** ONE.
DON'T YOU?

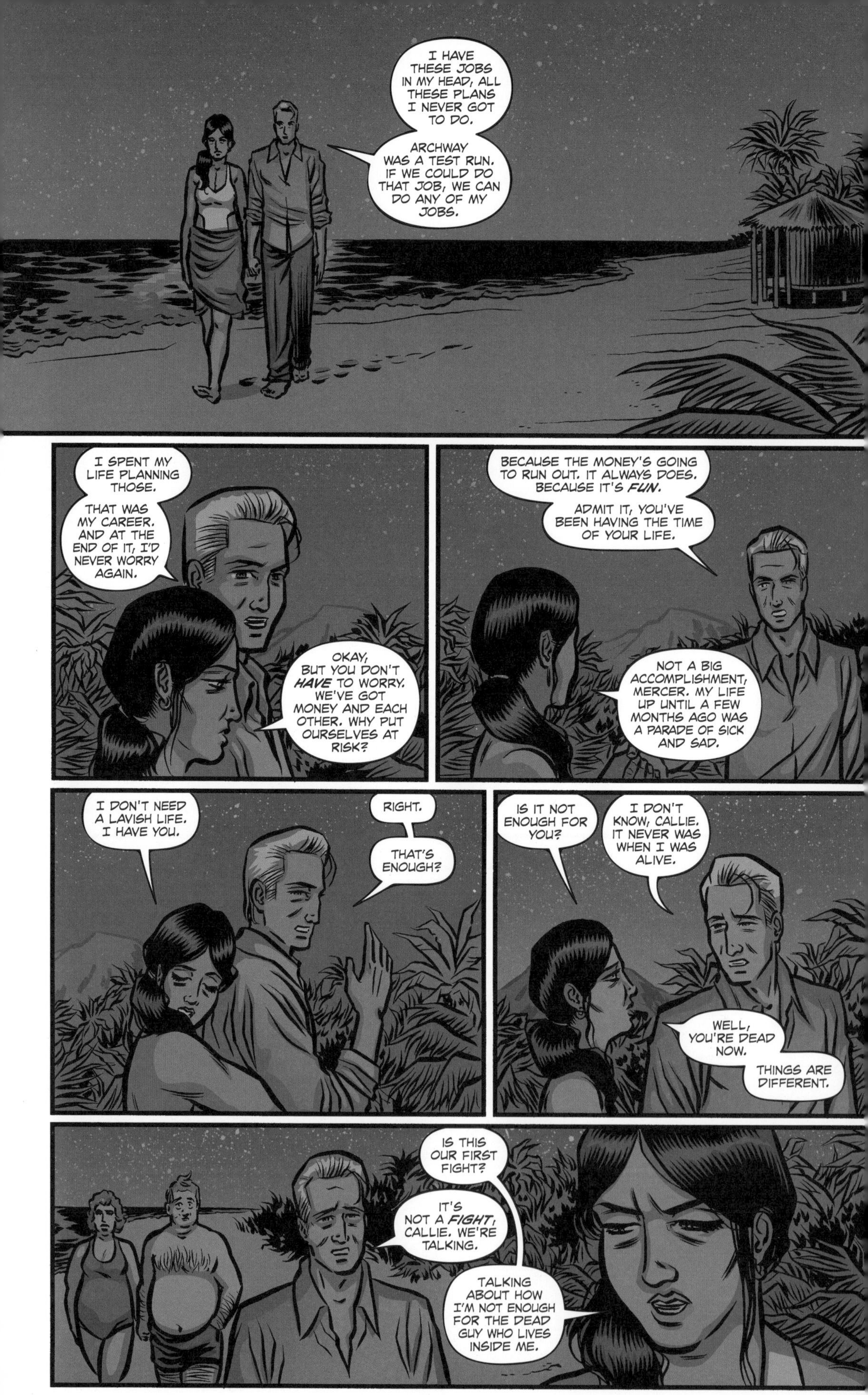
I HAVE THESE JOBS IN MY HEAD, ALL THESE PLANS I NEVER GOT TO DO.
ARCHWAY WAS A TEST RUN. IF WE COULD DO THAT JOB, WE CAN DO ANY OF MY JOBS.
I SPENT MY LIFE PLANNING THOSE.
THAT WAS MY CAREER. AND AT THE END OF IT, I'D NEVER WORRY AGAIN.
OKAY, BUT YOU DON'T *HAVE* TO WORRY. WE'VE GOT MONEY AND EACH OTHER. WHY PUT OURSELVES AT RISK?
BECAUSE THE MONEY'S GOING TO RUN OUT. IT ALWAYS DOES. BECAUSE IT'S *FUN*.
ADMIT IT, YOU'VE BEEN HAVING THE TIME OF YOUR LIFE.
NOT A BIG ACCOMPLISHMENT, MERCER. MY LIFE UP UNTIL A FEW MONTHS AGO WAS A PARADE OF SICK AND SAD.
I DON'T NEED A LAVISH LIFE. I HAVE YOU.
RIGHT.
THAT'S ENOUGH?
IS IT NOT ENOUGH FOR YOU?
I DON'T KNOW, CALLIE. IT NEVER WAS WHEN I WAS ALIVE.
WELL, YOU'RE DEAD NOW.
THINGS ARE DIFFERENT.
IS THIS OUR FIRST FIGHT?
IT'S NOT A *FIGHT*, CALLIE. WE'RE TALKING.
TALKING ABOUT HOW I'M NOT ENOUGH FOR THE DEAD GUY WHO LIVES INSIDE ME.

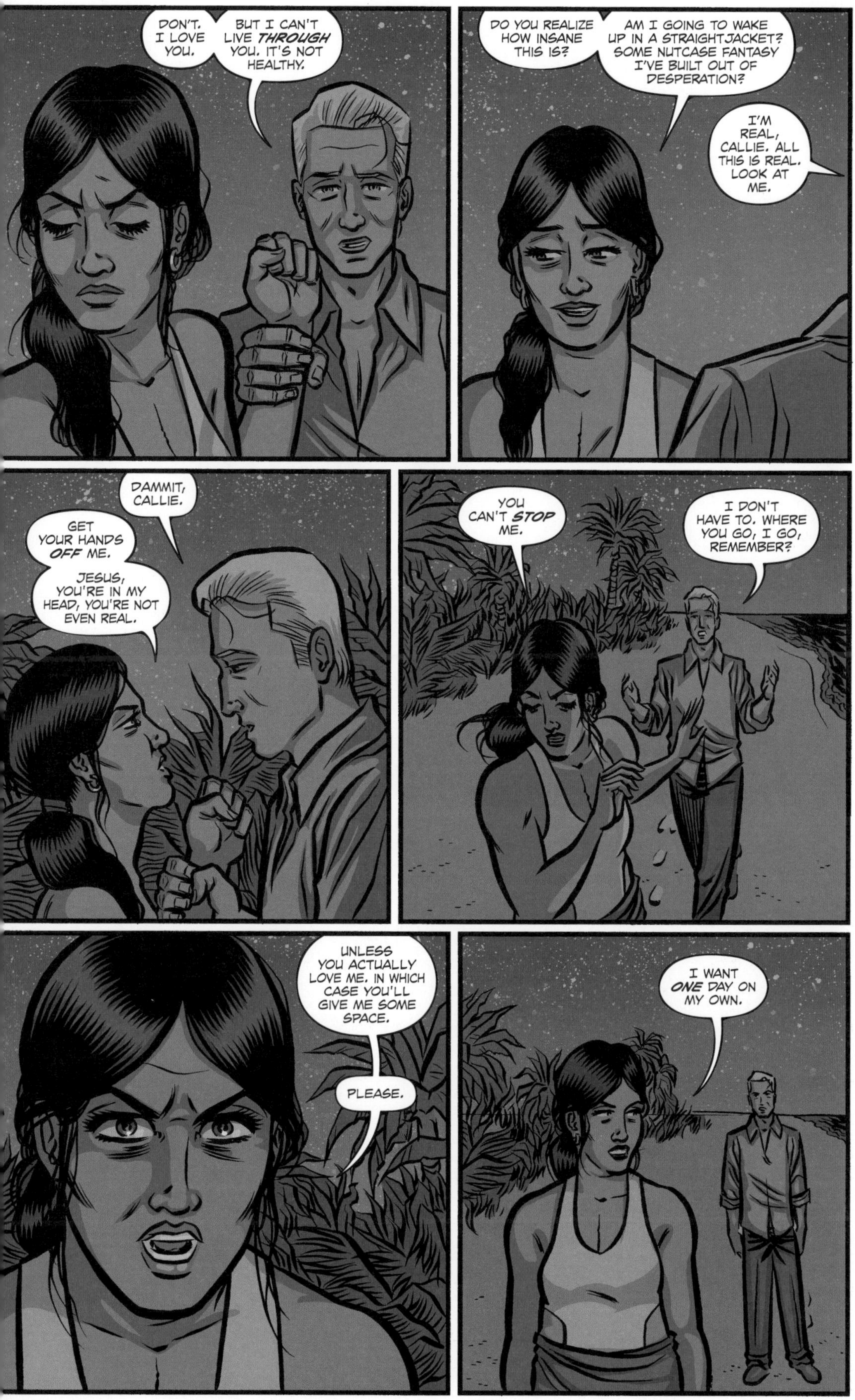
DON'T. I LOVE YOU.
BUT I CAN'T LIVE THROUGH YOU. IT'S NOT HEALTHY.
DO YOU REALIZE HOW INSANE THIS IS?
AM I GOING TO WAKE UP IN A STRAIGHTJACKET? SOME NUTCASE FANTASY I'VE BUILT OUT OF DESPERATION?
I'M REAL, CALLIE. ALL THIS IS REAL. LOOK AT ME.
DAMMIT, CALLIE.
GET YOUR HANDS OFF ME.
JESUS, YOU'RE IN MY HEAD, YOU'RE NOT EVEN REAL.
YOU CAN'T STOP ME.
I DON'T HAVE TO. WHERE YOU GO, I GO, REMEMBER?
UNLESS YOU ACTUALLY LOVE ME. IN WHICH CASE YOU'LL GIVE ME SOME SPACE.
PLEASE.
I WANT ONE DAY ON MY OWN.

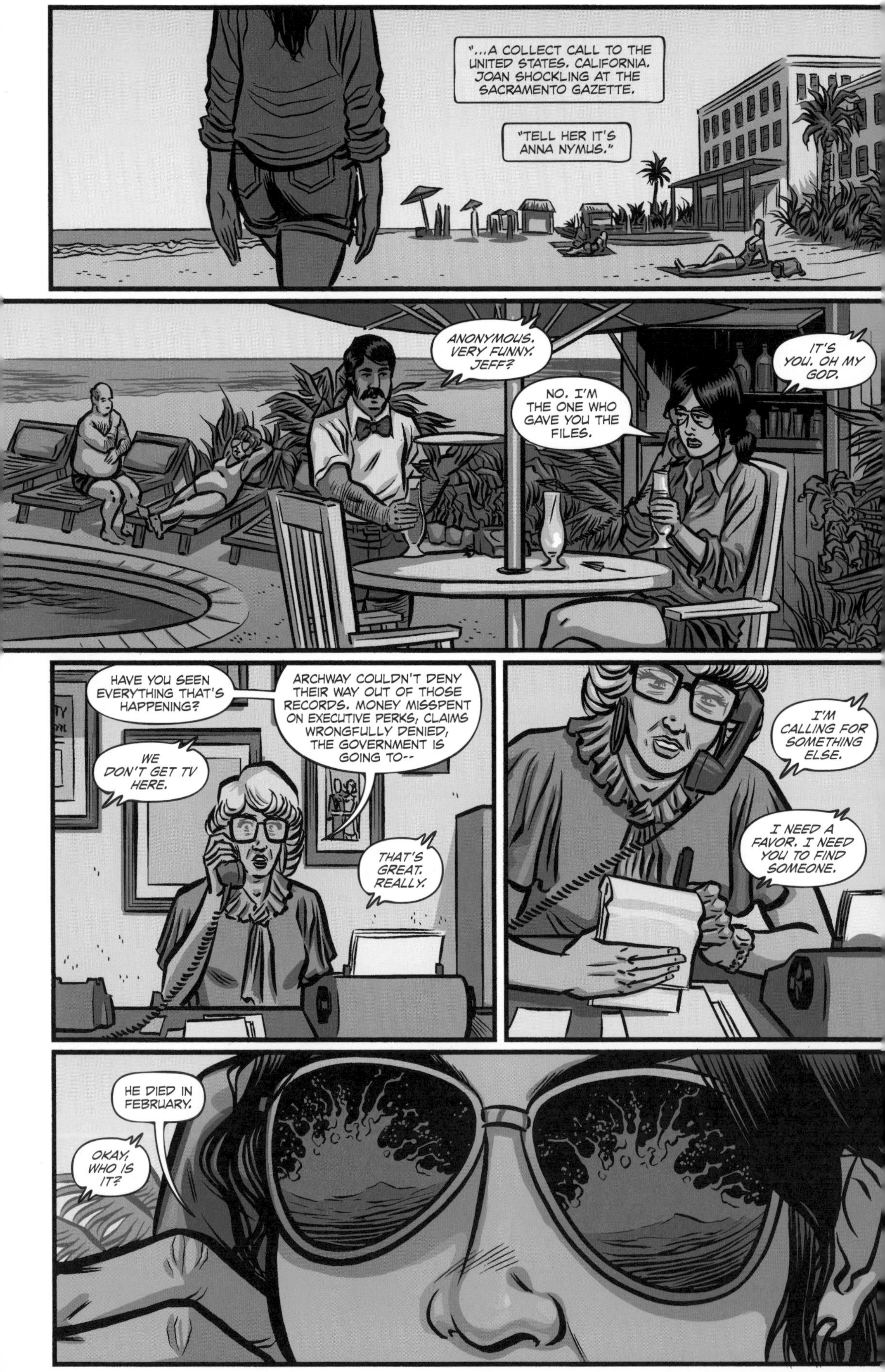
"...A COLLECT CALL TO THE UNITED STATES. CALIFORNIA. JOAN SHOCKLING AT THE SACRAMENTO GAZETTE.
"TELL HER IT'S ANNA NYMUS."
ANONYMOUS. VERY FUNNY. JEFF?
NO. I'M THE ONE WHO GAVE YOU THE FILES.
IT'S YOU. OH MY GOD.
HAVE YOU SEEN EVERYTHING THAT'S HAPPENING?
ARCHWAY COULDN'T DENY THEIR WAY OUT OF THOSE RECORDS. MONEY MISSPENT ON EXECUTIVE PERKS, CLAIMS WRONGFULLY DENIED, THE GOVERNMENT IS GOING TO--
WE DON'T GET TV HERE.
THAT'S GREAT. REALLY.
I'M CALLING FOR SOMETHING ELSE.
I NEED A FAVOR. I NEED YOU TO FIND SOMEONE.
OKAY, WHO IS IT?
HE DIED IN FEBRUARY.

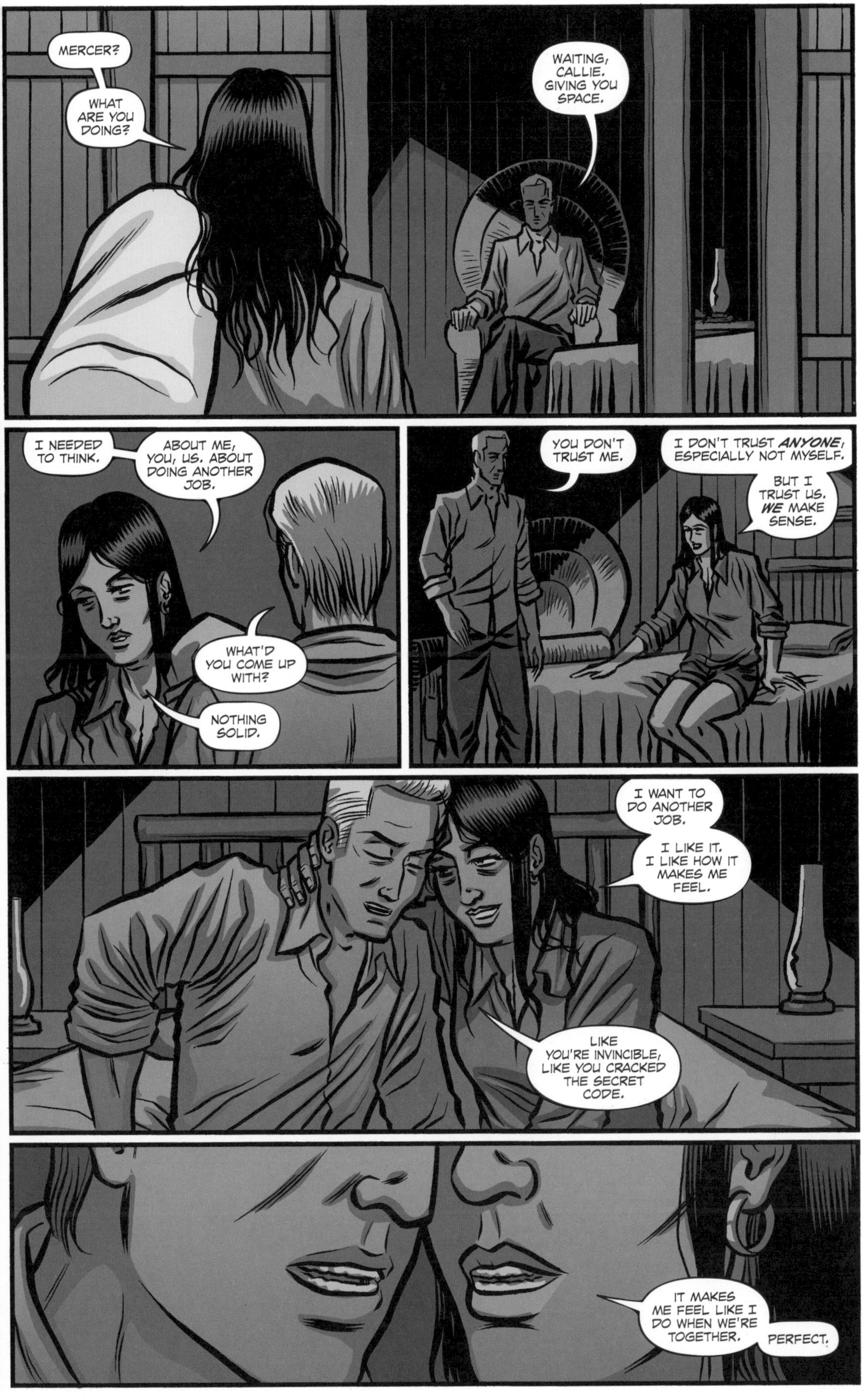
MERCER?
WHAT ARE YOU DOING?
WAITING, CALLIE. GIVING YOU SPACE.
I NEEDED TO THINK.
ABOUT ME, YOU, US. ABOUT DOING ANOTHER JOB.
WHAT'D YOU COME UP WITH?
NOTHING SOLID.
YOU DON'T TRUST ME.
I DON'T TRUST ANYONE, ESPECIALLY NOT MYSELF.
BUT I TRUST US. WE MAKE SENSE.
I WANT TO DO ANOTHER JOB.
I LIKE IT. I LIKE HOW IT MAKES ME FEEL.
LIKE YOU'RE INVINCIBLE, LIKE YOU CRACKED THE SECRET CODE.
IT MAKES ME FEEL LIKE I DO WHEN WE'RE TOGETHER.
PERFECT.

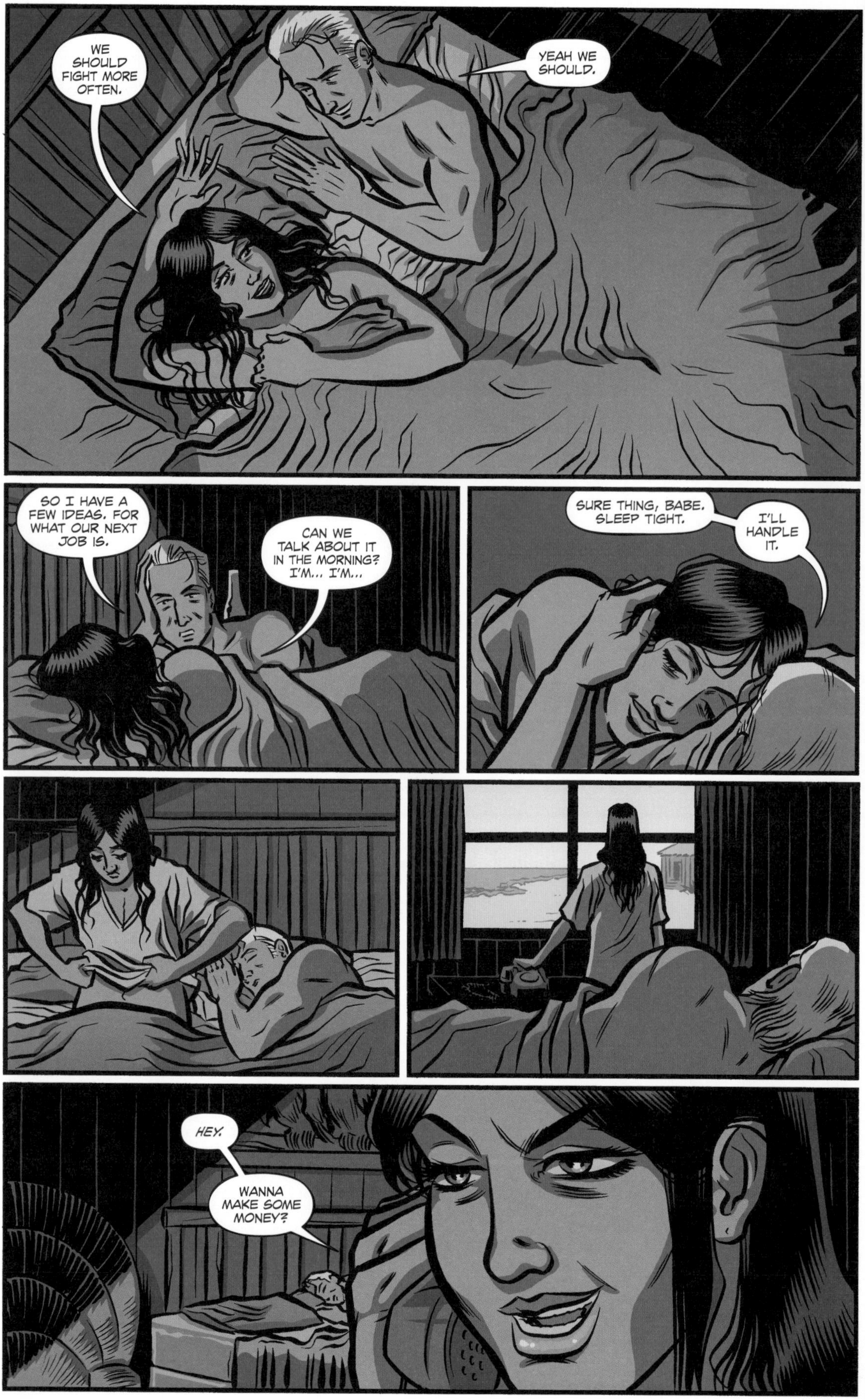
WE SHOULD FIGHT MORE OFTEN.
YEAH WE SHOULD.
SO I HAVE A FEW IDEAS. FOR WHAT OUR NEXT JOB IS.
CAN WE TALK ABOUT IT IN THE MORNING? I'M... I'M...
SURE THING, BABE. SLEEP TIGHT.
I'LL HANDLE IT.
HEY.
WANNA MAKE SOME MONEY?

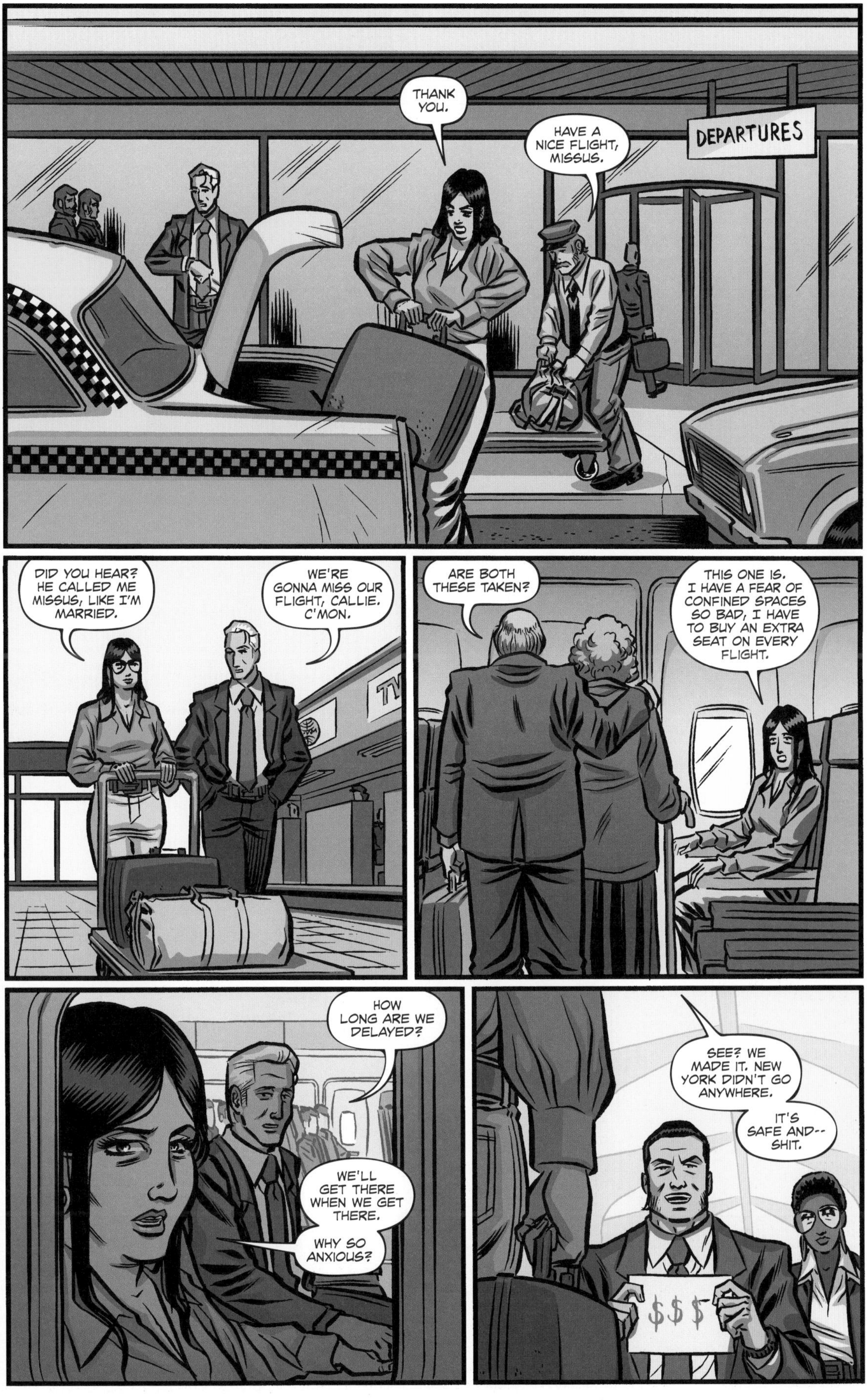
THANK YOU.
HAVE A NICE FLIGHT, MISSUS.
DEPARTURES
DID YOU HEAR? HE CALLED ME MISSUS, LIKE I'M MARRIED.
WE'RE GONNA MISS OUR FLIGHT, CALLIE. C'MON.
ARE BOTH THESE TAKEN?
THIS ONE IS. I HAVE A FEAR OF CONFINED SPACES SO BAD, I HAVE TO BUY AN EXTRA SEAT ON EVERY FLIGHT.
HOW LONG ARE WE DELAYED?
WE'LL GET THERE WHEN WE GET THERE.
WHY SO ANXIOUS?
SEE? WE MADE IT. NEW YORK DIDN'T GO ANYWHERE.
IT'S SAFE AND-- SHIT.
$$$

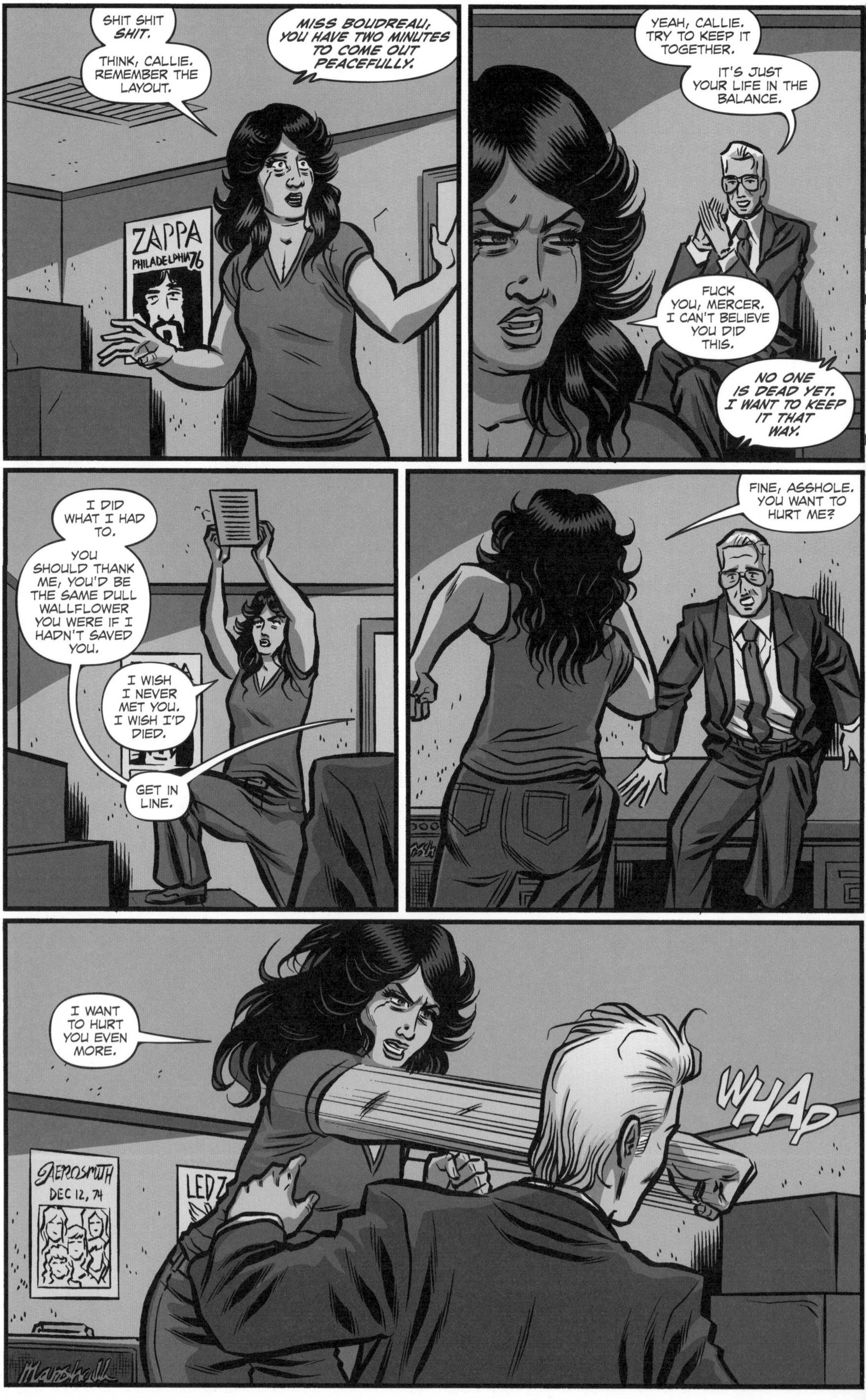
SHIT SHIT SHIT.
THINK, CALLIE. REMEMBER THE LAYOUT.
MISS BOUDREAU, YOU HAVE TWO MINUTES TO COME OUT PEACEFULLY.
ZAPPA PHILADELPHIA 76
YEAH, CALLIE. TRY TO KEEP IT TOGETHER.
IT'S JUST YOUR LIFE IN THE BALANCE.
FUCK YOU, MERCER. I CAN'T BELIEVE YOU DID THIS.
NO ONE IS DEAD YET. I WANT TO KEEP IT THAT WAY.
I DID WHAT I HAD TO.
YOU SHOULD THANK ME; YOU'D BE THE SAME DULL WALLFLOWER YOU WERE IF I HADN'T SAVED YOU.
I WISH I NEVER MET YOU. I WISH I'D DIED.
GET IN LINE.
FINE, ASSHOLE. YOU WANT TO HURT ME?
I WANT TO HURT YOU EVEN MORE.
WHAP
AEROSMITH DEC 12, 74
Marshall

# CHAPTER 4

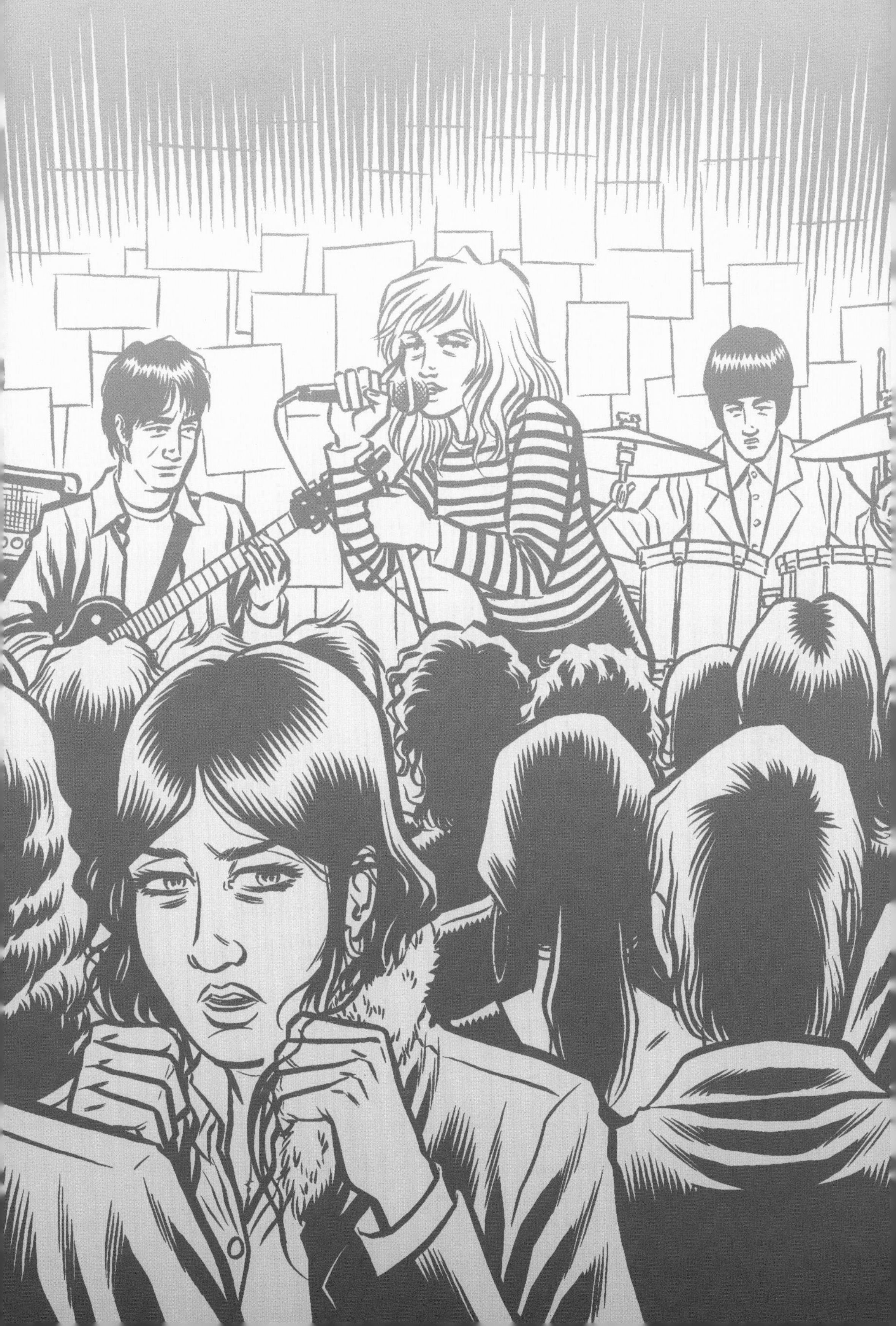

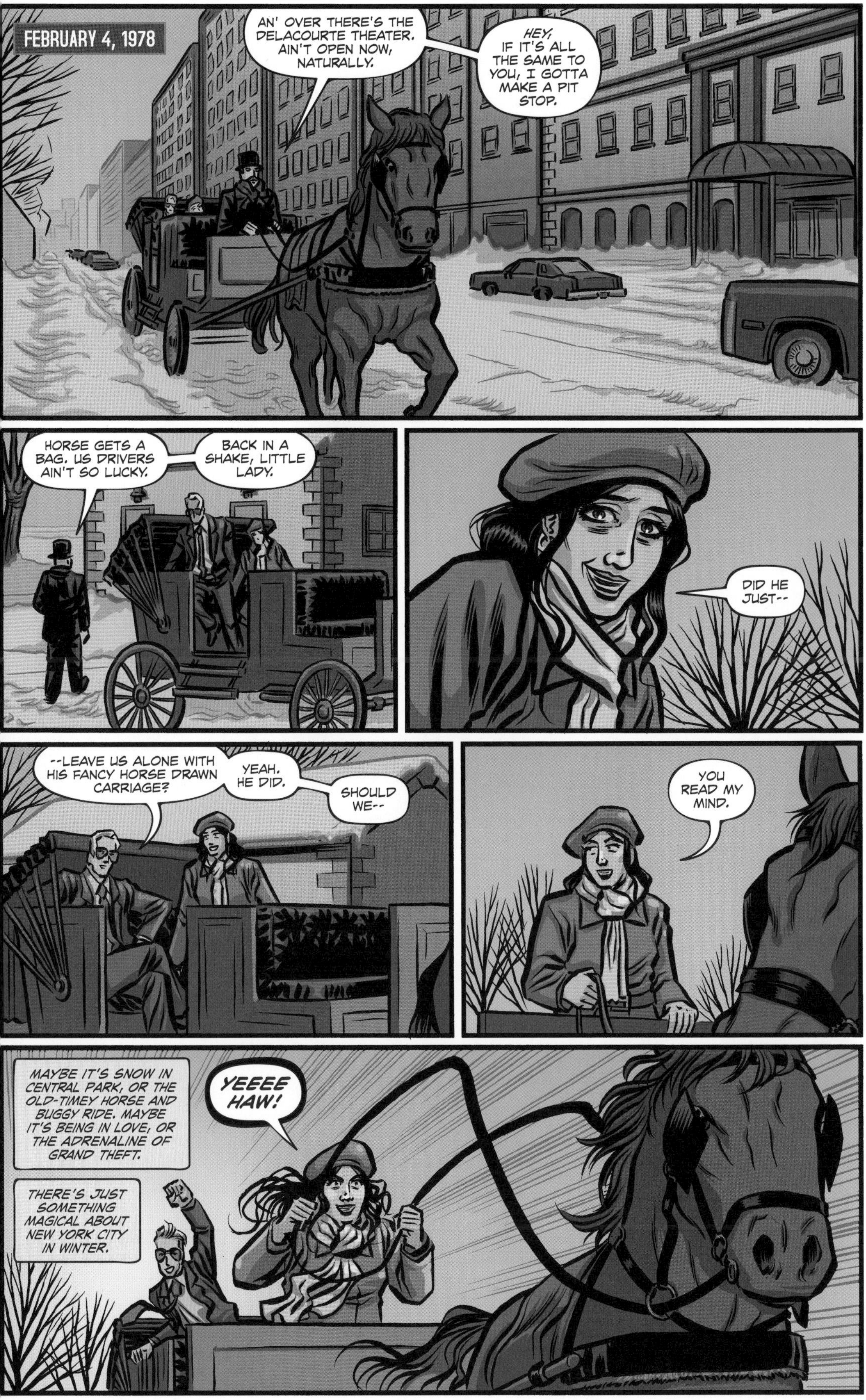
FEBRUARY 4, 1978
AN' OVER THERE'S THE DELACOURTE THEATER. AIN'T OPEN NOW, NATURALLY.
HEY, IF IT'S ALL THE SAME TO YOU, I GOTTA MAKE A PIT STOP.
HORSE GETS A BAG. US DRIVERS AIN'T SO LUCKY.
BACK IN A SHAKE, LITTLE LADY.
DID HE JUST--
--LEAVE US ALONE WITH HIS FANCY HORSE DRAWN CARRIAGE?
YEAH. HE DID.
SHOULD WE--
YOU READ MY MIND.
MAYBE IT'S SNOW IN CENTRAL PARK, OR THE OLD-TIMEY HORSE AND BUGGY RIDE. MAYBE IT'S BEING IN LOVE, OR THE ADRENALINE OF GRAND THEFT.
YEEEE HAW!
THERE'S JUST SOMETHING MAGICAL ABOUT NEW YORK CITY IN WINTER.

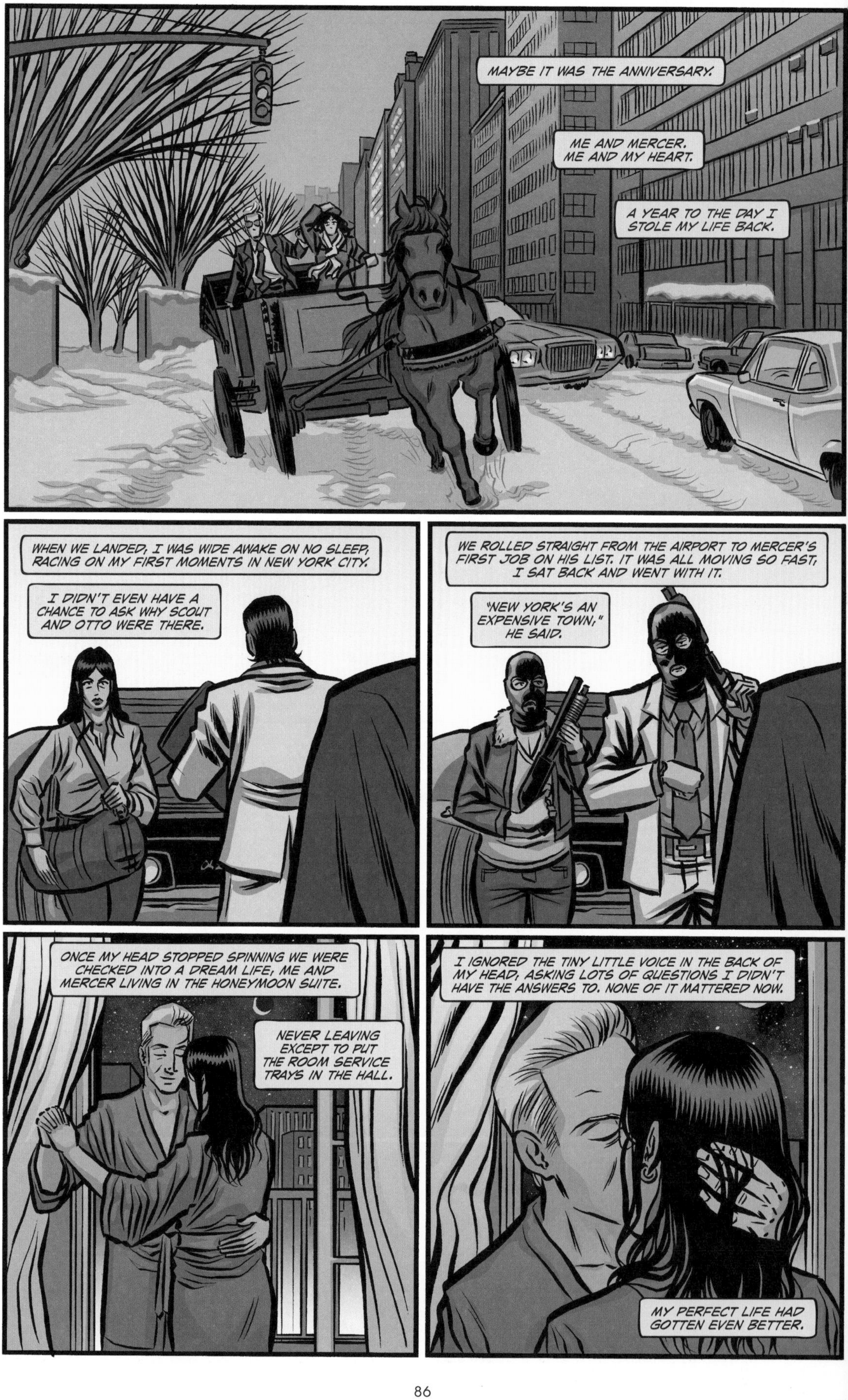
MAYBE IT WAS THE ANNIVERSARY.
ME AND MERCER. ME AND MY HEART.
A YEAR TO THE DAY I STOLE MY LIFE BACK.
WHEN WE LANDED, I WAS WIDE AWAKE ON NO SLEEP, RACING ON MY FIRST MOMENTS IN NEW YORK CITY.
I DIDN'T EVEN HAVE A CHANCE TO ASK WHY SCOUT AND OTTO WERE THERE.
WE ROLLED STRAIGHT FROM THE AIRPORT TO MERCER'S FIRST JOB ON HIS LIST. IT WAS ALL MOVING SO FAST, I SAT BACK AND WENT WITH IT.
"NEW YORK'S AN EXPENSIVE TOWN," HE SAID.
ONCE MY HEAD STOPPED SPINNING WE WERE CHECKED INTO A DREAM LIFE, ME AND MERCER LIVING IN THE HONEYMOON SUITE.
NEVER LEAVING EXCEPT TO PUT THE ROOM SERVICE TRAYS IN THE HALL.
I IGNORED THE TINY LITTLE VOICE IN THE BACK OF MY HEAD, ASKING LOTS OF QUESTIONS I DIDN'T HAVE THE ANSWERS TO. NONE OF IT MATTERED NOW.
MY PERFECT LIFE HAD GOTTEN EVEN BETTER.

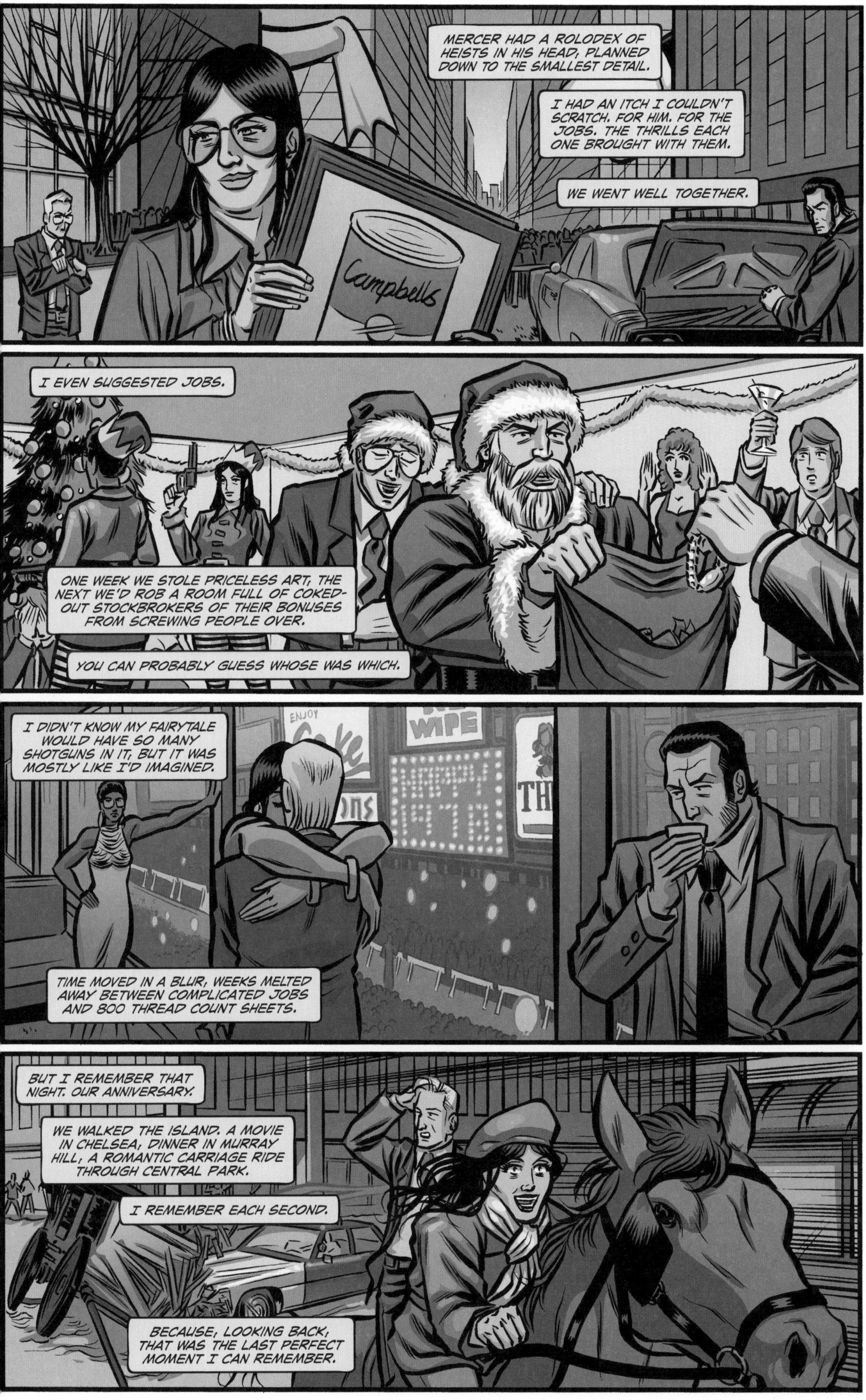
MERCER HAD A ROLODEX OF HEISTS IN HIS HEAD, PLANNED DOWN TO THE SMALLEST DETAIL.
I HAD AN ITCH I COULDN'T SCRATCH. FOR HIM. FOR THE JOBS. THE THRILLS EACH ONE BROUGHT WITH THEM.
WE WENT WELL TOGETHER.
Campbells
I EVEN SUGGESTED JOBS.
ONE WEEK WE STOLE PRICELESS ART, THE NEXT WE'D ROB A ROOM FULL OF COKED-OUT STOCKBROKERS OF THEIR BONUSES FROM SCREWING PEOPLE OVER.
YOU CAN PROBABLY GUESS WHOSE WAS WHICH.
I DIDN'T KNOW MY FAIRYTALE WOULD HAVE SO MANY SHOTGUNS IN IT, BUT IT WAS MOSTLY LIKE I'D IMAGINED.
ENJOY
WIPE
TIME MOVED IN A BLUR, WEEKS MELTED AWAY BETWEEN COMPLICATED JOBS AND 800 THREAD COUNT SHEETS.
BUT I REMEMBER THAT NIGHT. OUR ANNIVERSARY.
WE WALKED THE ISLAND. A MOVIE IN CHELSEA, DINNER IN MURRAY HILL, A ROMANTIC CARRIAGE RIDE THROUGH CENTRAL PARK.
I REMEMBER EACH SECOND.
BECAUSE, LOOKING BACK, THAT WAS THE LAST PERFECT MOMENT I CAN REMEMBER.

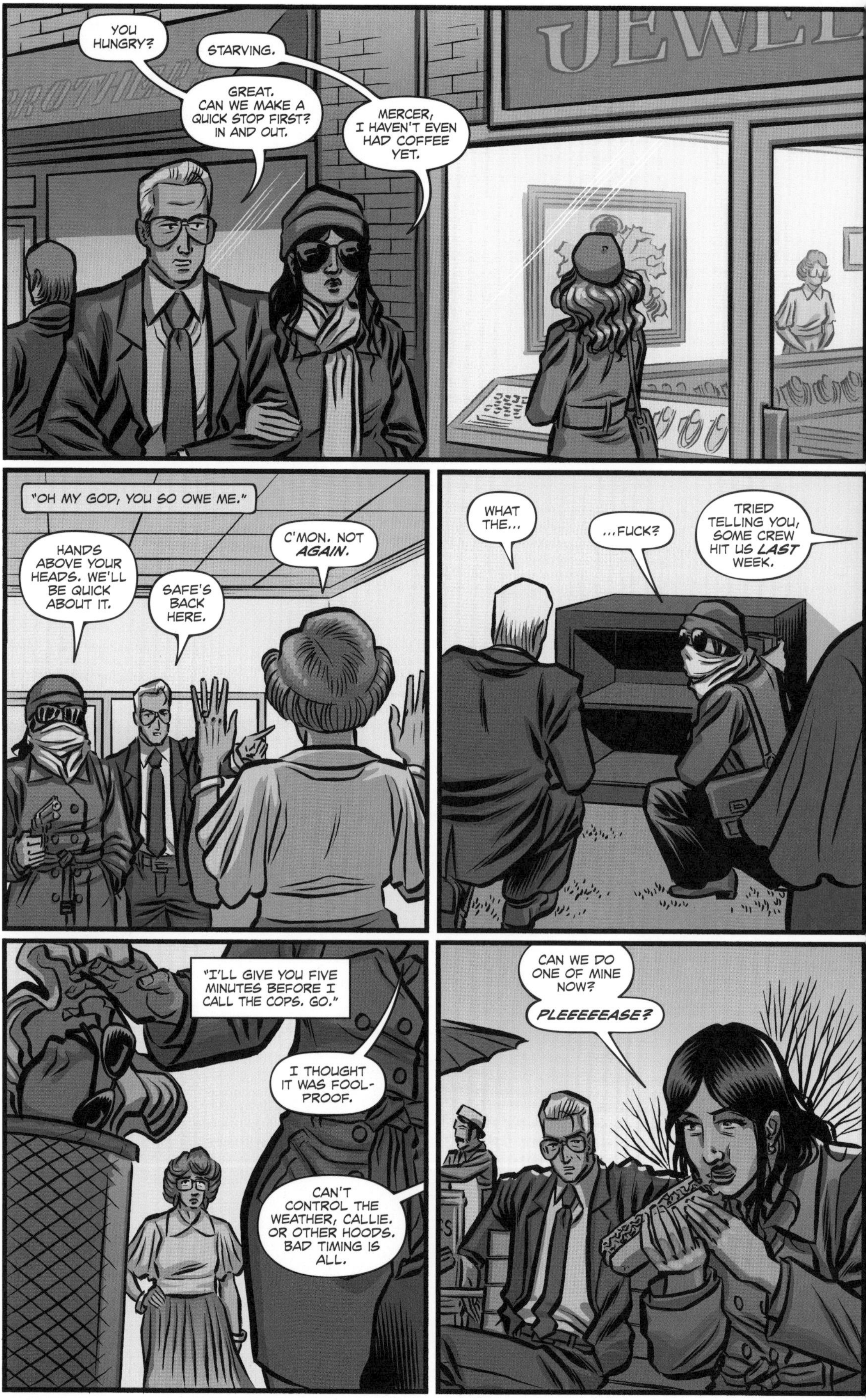
YOU HUNGRY?
STARVING.
GREAT. CAN WE MAKE A QUICK STOP FIRST? IN AND OUT.
MERCER, I HAVEN'T EVEN HAD COFFEE YET.
JEWEL
BROTHERS
"OH MY GOD, YOU SO OWE ME."
HANDS ABOVE YOUR HEADS. WE'LL BE QUICK ABOUT IT.
SAFE'S BACK HERE.
C'MON. NOT *AGAIN*.
WHAT THE...
...FUCK?
TRIED TELLING YOU, SOME CREW HIT US *LAST* WEEK.
"I'LL GIVE YOU FIVE MINUTES BEFORE I CALL THE COPS. GO."
I THOUGHT IT WAS FOOL-PROOF.
CAN'T CONTROL THE WEATHER, CALLIE. OR OTHER HOODS. BAD TIMING IS ALL.
CAN WE DO ONE OF MINE NOW?
*PLEEEEEASE?*

ONE OF MINE.

YOU KNOW WHO YOU'RE RIPPING OFF, TOUGH GUY?

WHY DO YOU THINK WE'RE *HERE*, WISE GUY?

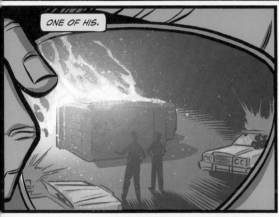

ONE OF HIS.

AW, CHRIST. I THOUGHT YOU SAID THIS WAS ALL SET!

CUT HER A BREAK, OTTO.

THEN ALL MINE STARTED GOING PERFECT.

BOSS, I GOTTA SAY, I HAD MY DOUBTS, BUT YOU'RE A GENIUS.

WHILE ALL HIS...

IT'S OKAY. I DON'T MIND. WE CAN TRY AGAIN.

IT HAPPENS TO EVERYONE.

555-3721

MERCER? WHERE'D YOU GO?

OH GOD, HOW LATE IS IT?

2:24 PM

YOU AWAKE IN THERE?

'CAUSE I'M GONNA GET BREAKFA--LUNCH. FOOD.

MISS PARKER, HOW ARE YOU TODAY?

CAN'T TALK. NEED COFFEE.

YOU COMING OUT?

OR ARE YOU GONNA SULK ALL DAY?

WHAT DID I DO?

IT'S JUST A ROUGH PATCH, I TOLD MYSELF.

HE'LL GET OVER IT, I THOUGHT.

AND THAT LITTLE VOICE GOT LOUDER, PANICKING. WHAT IF HE DIDN'T?

NEW YORK TIMES

UPPER CRUST CRIME SPR
SHOCKS NEWYOR

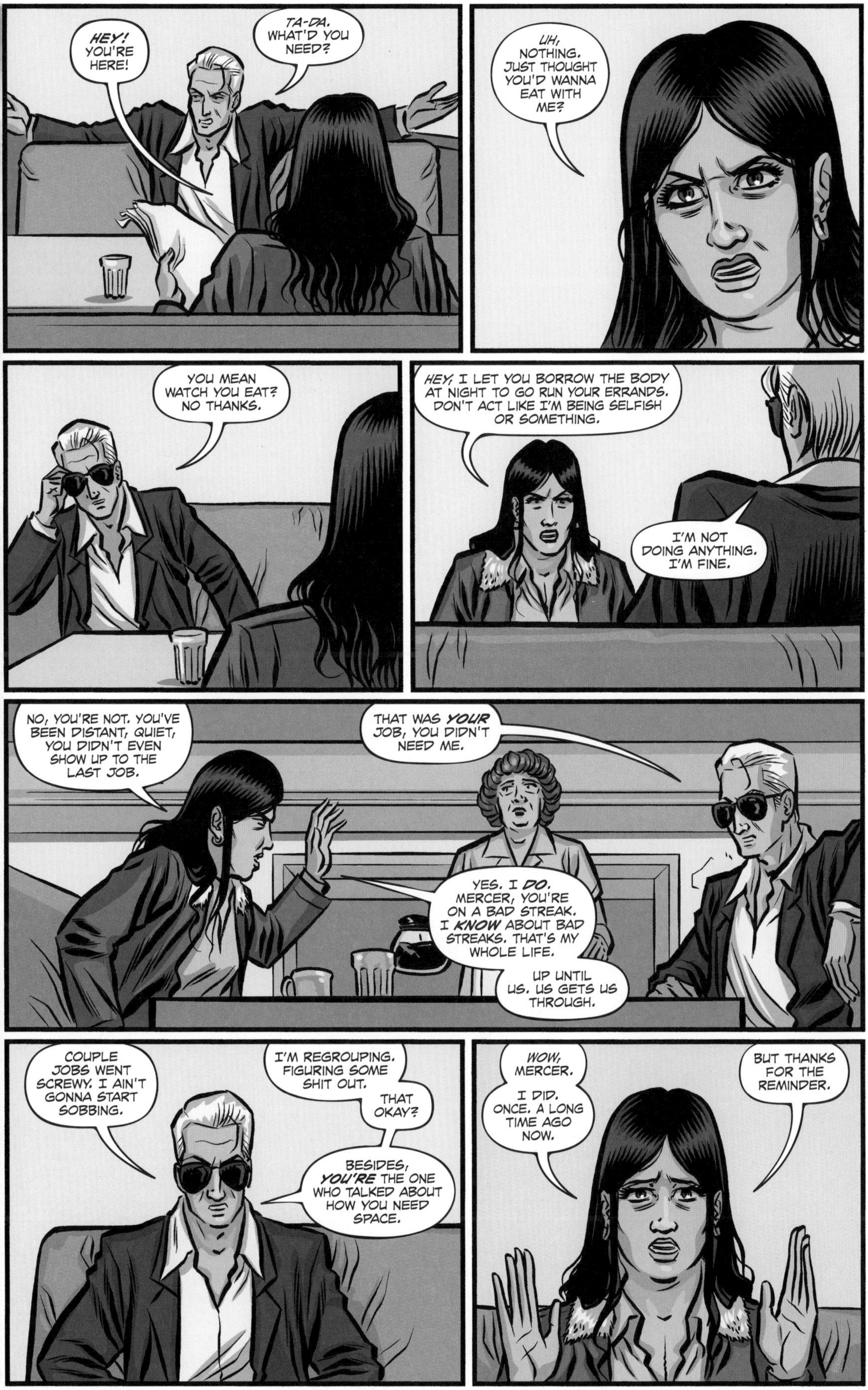
HEY! YOU'RE HERE!
TA-DA. WHAT'D YOU NEED?
UH, NOTHING. JUST THOUGHT YOU'D WANNA EAT WITH ME?
YOU MEAN WATCH YOU EAT? NO THANKS.
HEY, I LET YOU BORROW THE BODY AT NIGHT TO GO RUN YOUR ERRANDS. DON'T ACT LIKE I'M BEING SELFISH OR SOMETHING.
I'M NOT DOING ANYTHING. I'M FINE.
NO, YOU'RE NOT. YOU'VE BEEN DISTANT, QUIET, YOU DIDN'T EVEN SHOW UP TO THE LAST JOB.
THAT WAS YOUR JOB, YOU DIDN'T NEED ME.
YES. I DO. MERCER, YOU'RE ON A BAD STREAK. I KNOW ABOUT BAD STREAKS. THAT'S MY WHOLE LIFE.
UP UNTIL US. US GETS US THROUGH.
COUPLE JOBS WENT SCREWY. I AIN'T GONNA START SOBBING.
I'M REGROUPING. FIGURING SOME SHIT OUT.
THAT OKAY?
BESIDES, YOU'RE THE ONE WHO TALKED ABOUT HOW YOU NEED SPACE.
WOW, MERCER.
I DID. ONCE. A LONG TIME AGO NOW.
BUT THANKS FOR THE REMINDER.

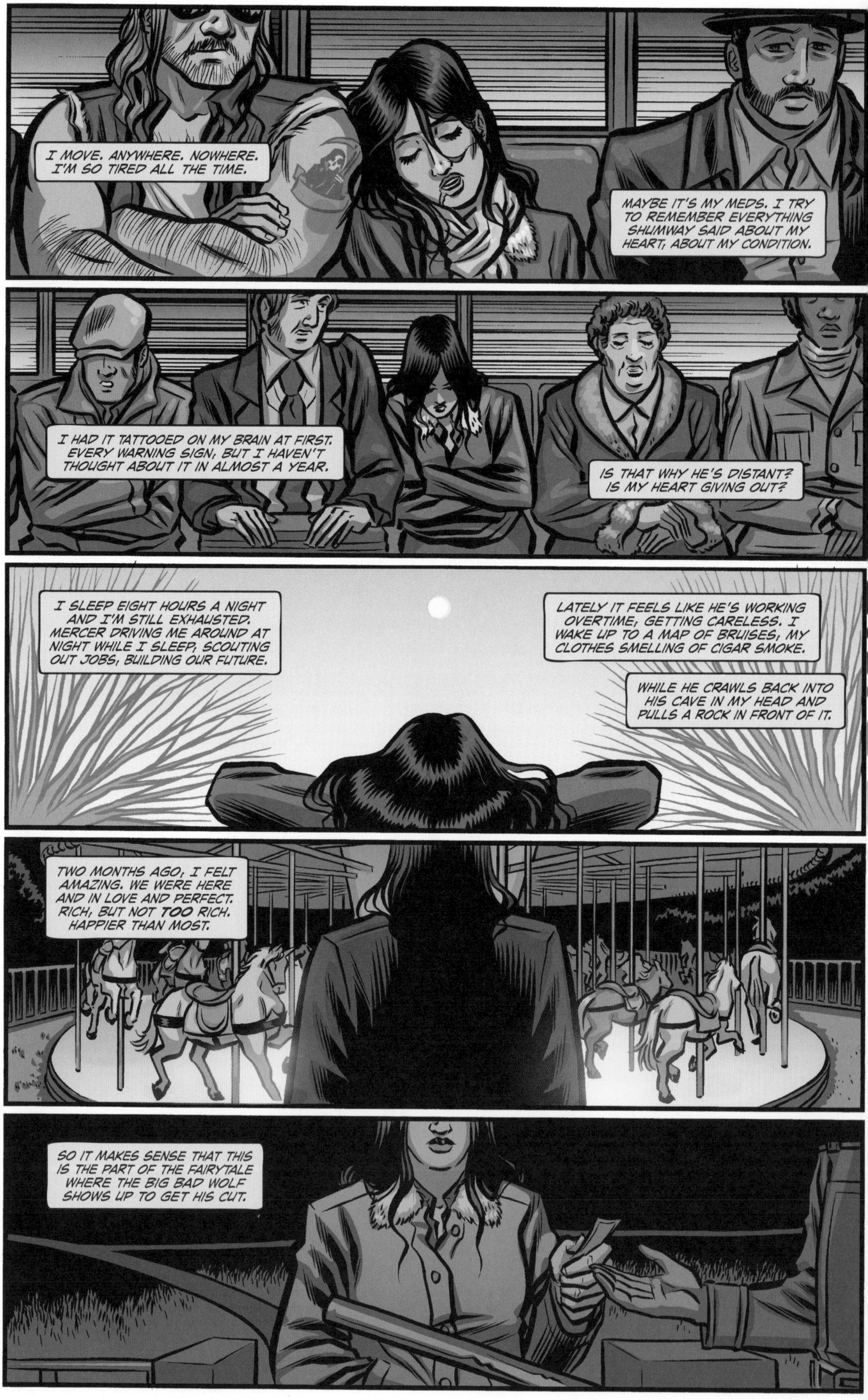
I MOVE. ANYWHERE. NOWHERE. I'M SO TIRED ALL THE TIME.
MAYBE IT'S MY MEDS. I TRY TO REMEMBER EVERYTHING SHUMWAY SAID ABOUT MY HEART, ABOUT MY CONDITION.
I HAD IT TATTOOED ON MY BRAIN AT FIRST. EVERY WARNING SIGN, BUT I HAVEN'T THOUGHT ABOUT IT IN ALMOST A YEAR.
IS THAT WHY HE'S DISTANT? IS MY HEART GIVING OUT?
I SLEEP EIGHT HOURS A NIGHT AND I'M STILL EXHAUSTED. MERCER DRIVING ME AROUND AT NIGHT WHILE I SLEEP, SCOUTING OUT JOBS, BUILDING OUR FUTURE.
LATELY IT FEELS LIKE HE'S WORKING OVERTIME, GETTING CARELESS. I WAKE UP TO A MAP OF BRUISES, MY CLOTHES SMELLING OF CIGAR SMOKE.
WHILE HE CRAWLS BACK INTO HIS CAVE IN MY HEAD AND PULLS A ROCK IN FRONT OF IT.
TWO MONTHS AGO, I FELT AMAZING. WE WERE HERE AND IN LOVE AND PERFECT. RICH, BUT NOT TOO RICH. HAPPIER THAN MOST.
SO IT MAKES SENSE THAT THIS IS THE PART OF THE FAIRYTALE WHERE THE BIG BAD WOLF SHOWS UP TO GET HIS CUT.

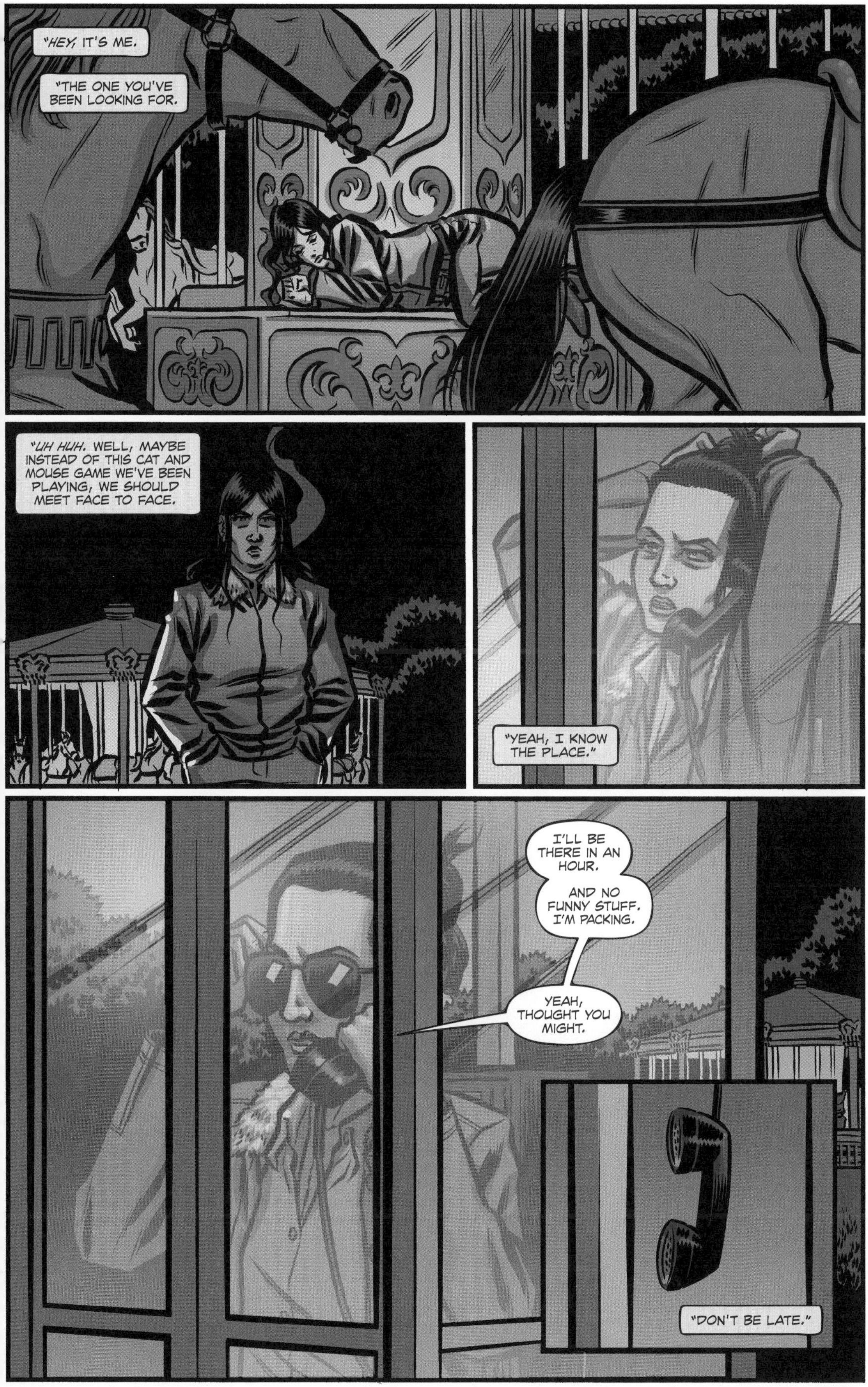
"HEY, IT'S ME.
"THE ONE YOU'VE BEEN LOOKING FOR.
"UH HUH. WELL, MAYBE INSTEAD OF THIS CAT AND MOUSE GAME WE'VE BEEN PLAYING, WE SHOULD MEET FACE TO FACE.
"YEAH, I KNOW THE PLACE."
I'LL BE THERE IN AN HOUR.
AND NO FUNNY STUFF. I'M PACKING.
YEAH, THOUGHT YOU MIGHT.
"DON'T BE LATE."

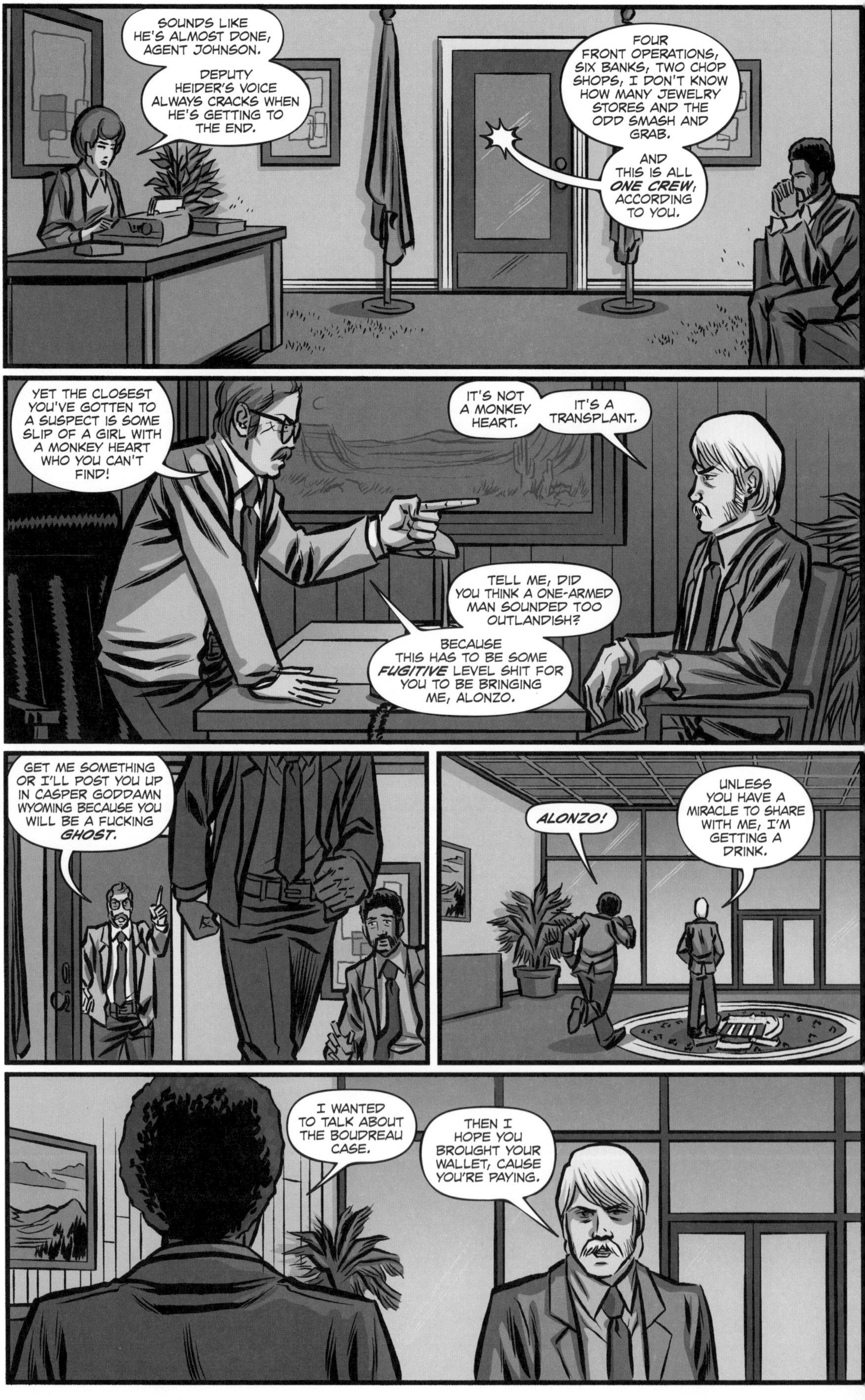
SOUNDS LIKE HE'S ALMOST DONE, AGENT JOHNSON.
DEPUTY HEIDER'S VOICE ALWAYS CRACKS WHEN HE'S GETTING TO THE END.
FOUR FRONT OPERATIONS, SIX BANKS, TWO CHOP SHOPS, I DON'T KNOW HOW MANY JEWELRY STORES AND THE ODD SMASH AND GRAB.
AND THIS IS ALL ONE CREW, ACCORDING TO YOU.
YET THE CLOSEST YOU'VE GOTTEN TO A SUSPECT IS SOME SLIP OF A GIRL WITH A MONKEY HEART WHO YOU CAN'T FIND!
IT'S NOT A MONKEY HEART.
IT'S A TRANSPLANT.
TELL ME, DID YOU THINK A ONE-ARMED MAN SOUNDED TOO OUTLANDISH?
BECAUSE THIS HAS TO BE SOME FUGITIVE LEVEL SHIT FOR YOU TO BE BRINGING ME, ALONZO.
GET ME SOMETHING OR I'LL POST YOU UP IN CASPER GODDAMN WYOMING BECAUSE YOU WILL BE A FUCKING GHOST.
ALONZO!
UNLESS YOU HAVE A MIRACLE TO SHARE WITH ME, I'M GETTING A DRINK.
I WANTED TO TALK ABOUT THE BOUDREAU CASE.
THEN I HOPE YOU BROUGHT YOUR WALLET, CAUSE YOU'RE PAYING.

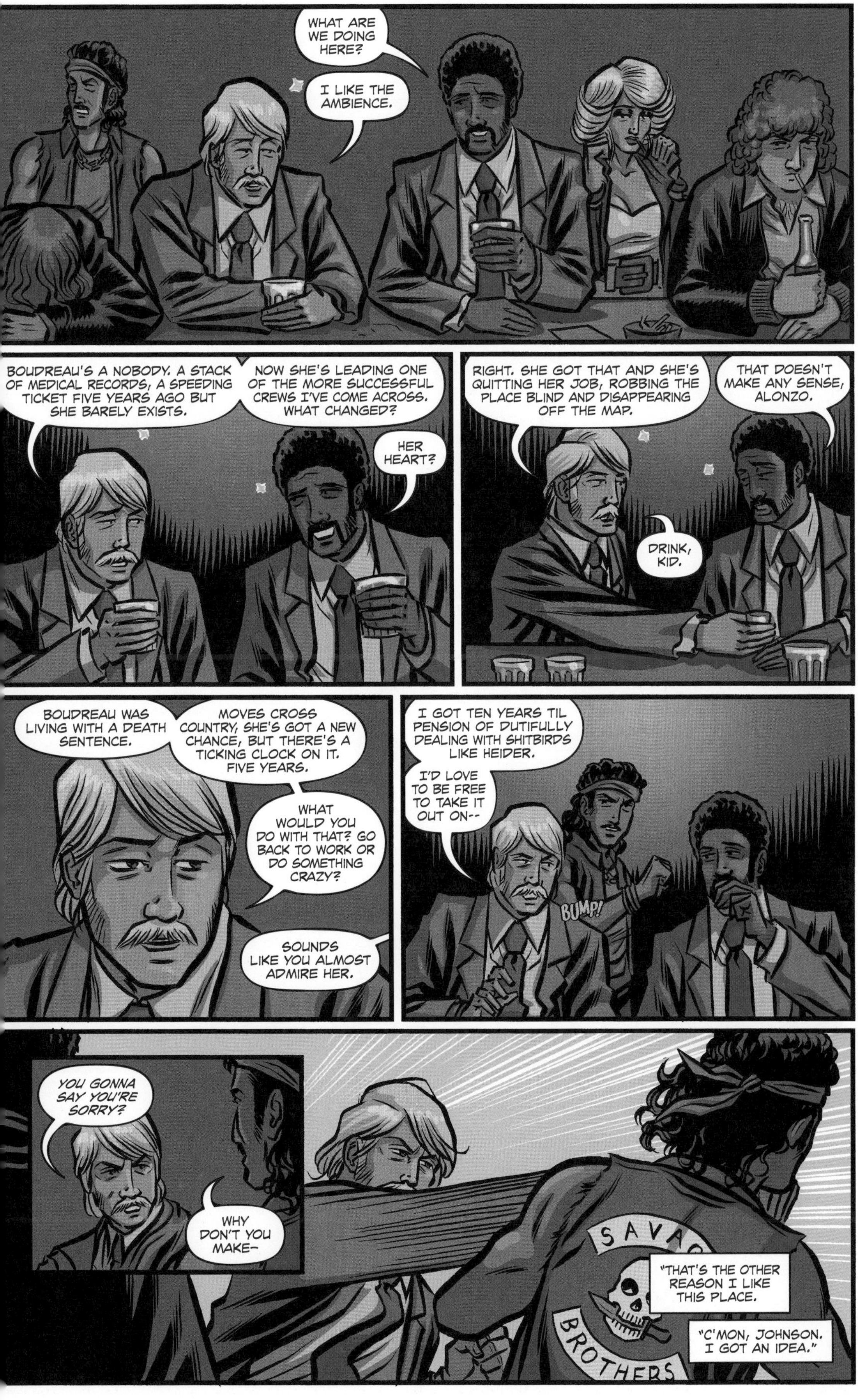
WHAT ARE WE DOING HERE?
I LIKE THE AMBIENCE.
BOUDREAU'S A NOBODY. A STACK OF MEDICAL RECORDS, A SPEEDING TICKET FIVE YEARS AGO BUT SHE BARELY EXISTS.
NOW SHE'S LEADING ONE OF THE MORE SUCCESSFUL CREWS I'VE COME ACROSS. WHAT CHANGED?
HER HEART?
RIGHT. SHE GOT THAT AND SHE'S QUITTING HER JOB, ROBBING THE PLACE BLIND AND DISAPPEARING OFF THE MAP.
THAT DOESN'T MAKE ANY SENSE, ALONZO.
DRINK, KID.
BOUDREAU WAS LIVING WITH A DEATH SENTENCE.
MOVES CROSS COUNTRY, SHE'S GOT A NEW CHANCE, BUT THERE'S A TICKING CLOCK ON IT. FIVE YEARS.
WHAT WOULD YOU DO WITH THAT? GO BACK TO WORK OR DO SOMETHING CRAZY?
SOUNDS LIKE YOU ALMOST ADMIRE HER.
I GOT TEN YEARS TIL PENSION OF DUTIFULLY DEALING WITH SHITBIRDS LIKE HEIDER.
I'D LOVE TO BE FREE TO TAKE IT OUT ON--
BUMP!
YOU GONNA SAY YOU'RE SORRY?
WHY DON'T YOU MAKE-
SAVAG
BROTHERS
"THAT'S THE OTHER REASON I LIKE THIS PLACE.
"C'MON, JOHNSON. I GOT AN IDEA."

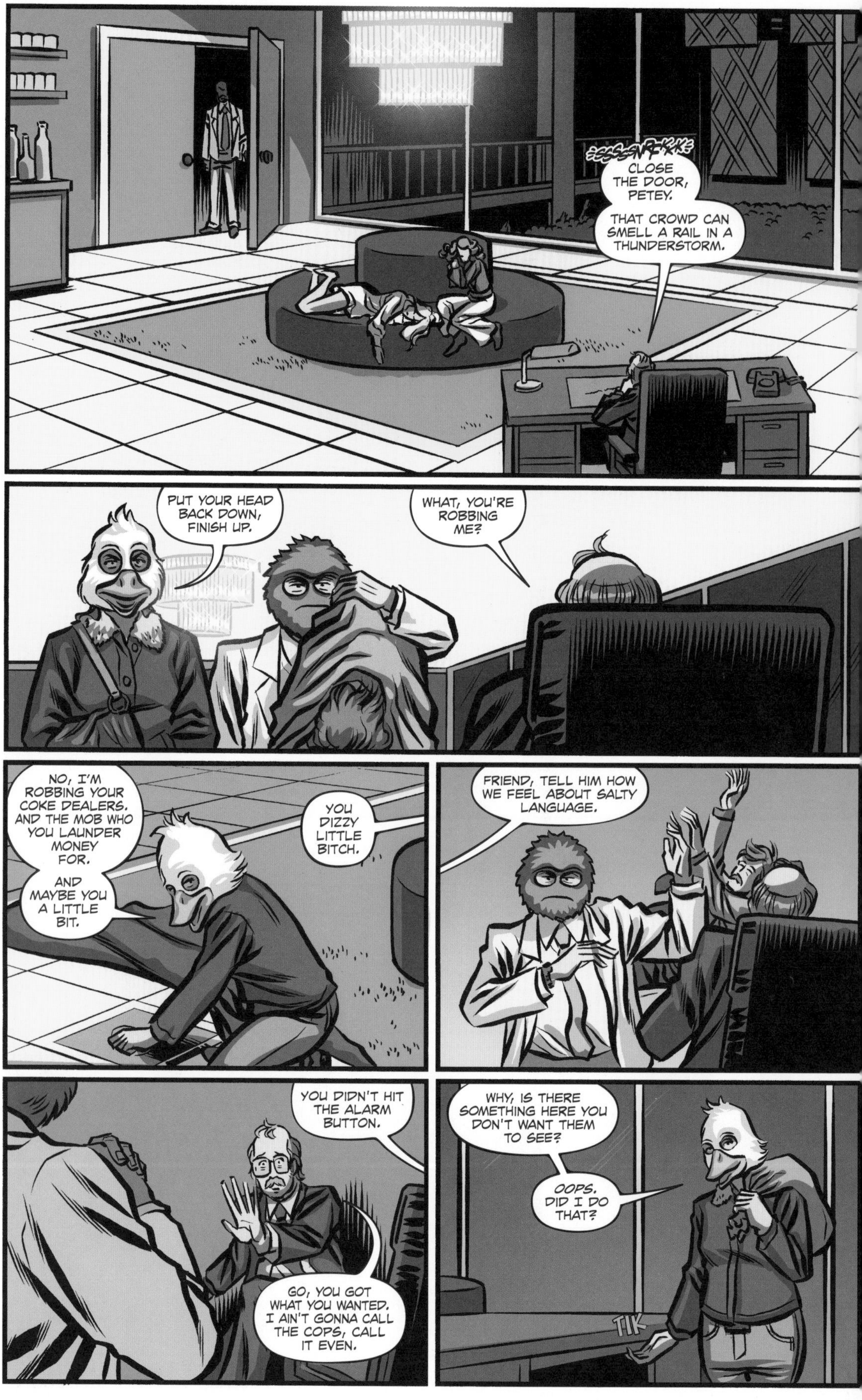
SSSSSNRFKK
CLOSE THE DOOR, PETEY.
THAT CROWD CAN SMELL A RAIL IN A THUNDERSTORM.
PUT YOUR HEAD BACK DOWN, FINISH UP.
WHAT, YOU'RE ROBBING ME?
NO, I'M ROBBING YOUR COKE DEALERS. AND THE MOB WHO YOU LAUNDER MONEY FOR.
AND MAYBE YOU A LITTLE BIT.
YOU DIZZY LITTLE BITCH.
FRIEND, TELL HIM HOW WE FEEL ABOUT SALTY LANGUAGE.
YOU DIDN'T HIT THE ALARM BUTTON.
GO, YOU GOT WHAT YOU WANTED. I AIN'T GONNA CALL THE COPS, CALL IT EVEN.
WHY, IS THERE SOMETHING HERE YOU DON'T WANT THEM TO SEE?
OOPS. DID I DO THAT?
TIK

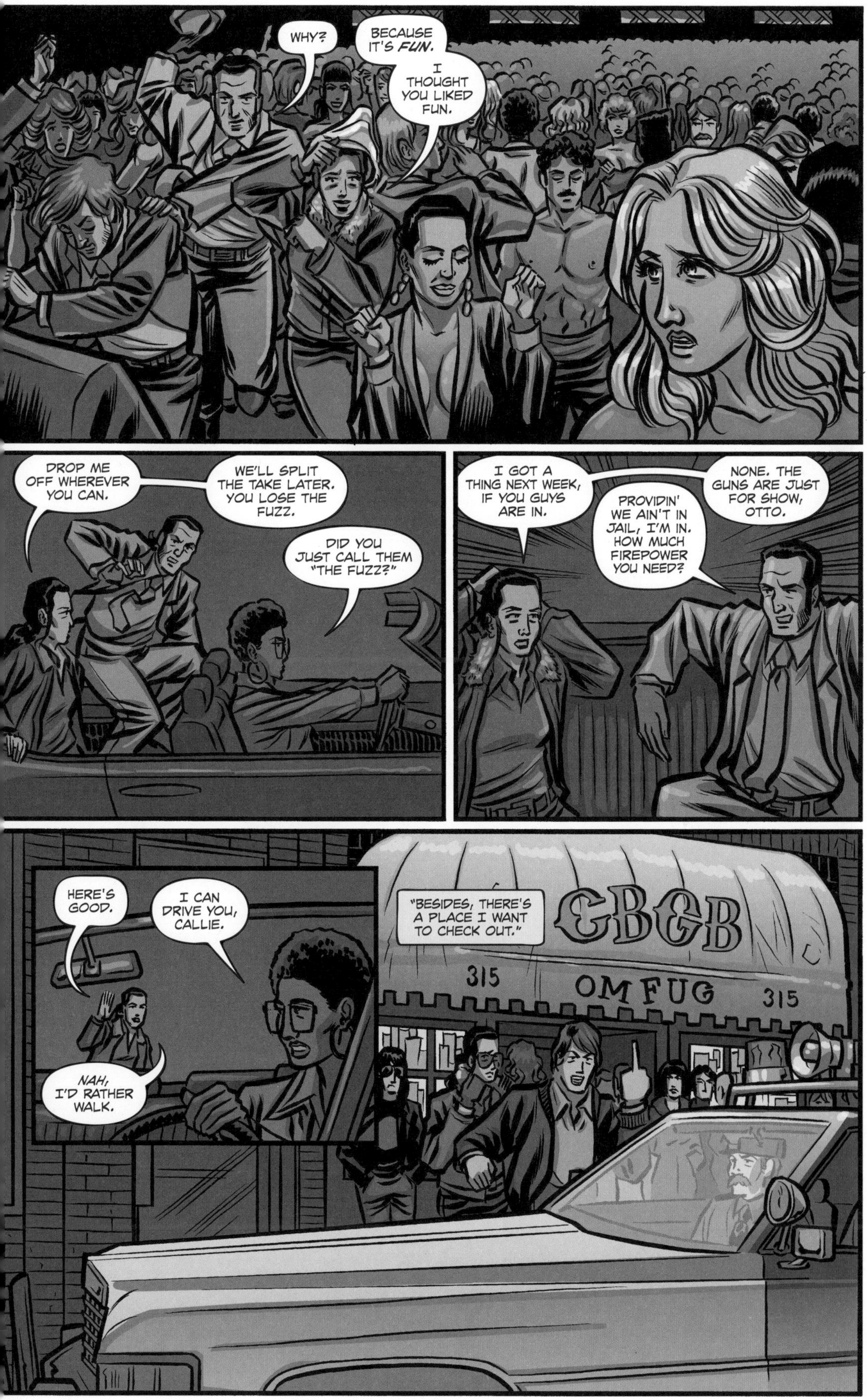
WHY?
BECAUSE IT'S *FUN*.
I THOUGHT YOU LIKED FUN.
DROP ME OFF WHEREVER YOU CAN.
WE'LL SPLIT THE TAKE LATER. YOU LOSE THE FUZZ.
DID YOU JUST CALL THEM "THE FUZZ?"
I GOT A THING NEXT WEEK, IF YOU GUYS ARE IN.
PROVIDIN' WE AIN'T IN JAIL, I'M IN. HOW MUCH FIREPOWER YOU NEED?
NONE. THE GUNS ARE JUST FOR SHOW, OTTO.
HERE'S GOOD.
I CAN DRIVE YOU, CALLIE.
*NAH*, I'D RATHER WALK.
"BESIDES, THERE'S A PLACE I WANT TO CHECK OUT."
CBGB
315
OMFUG
315

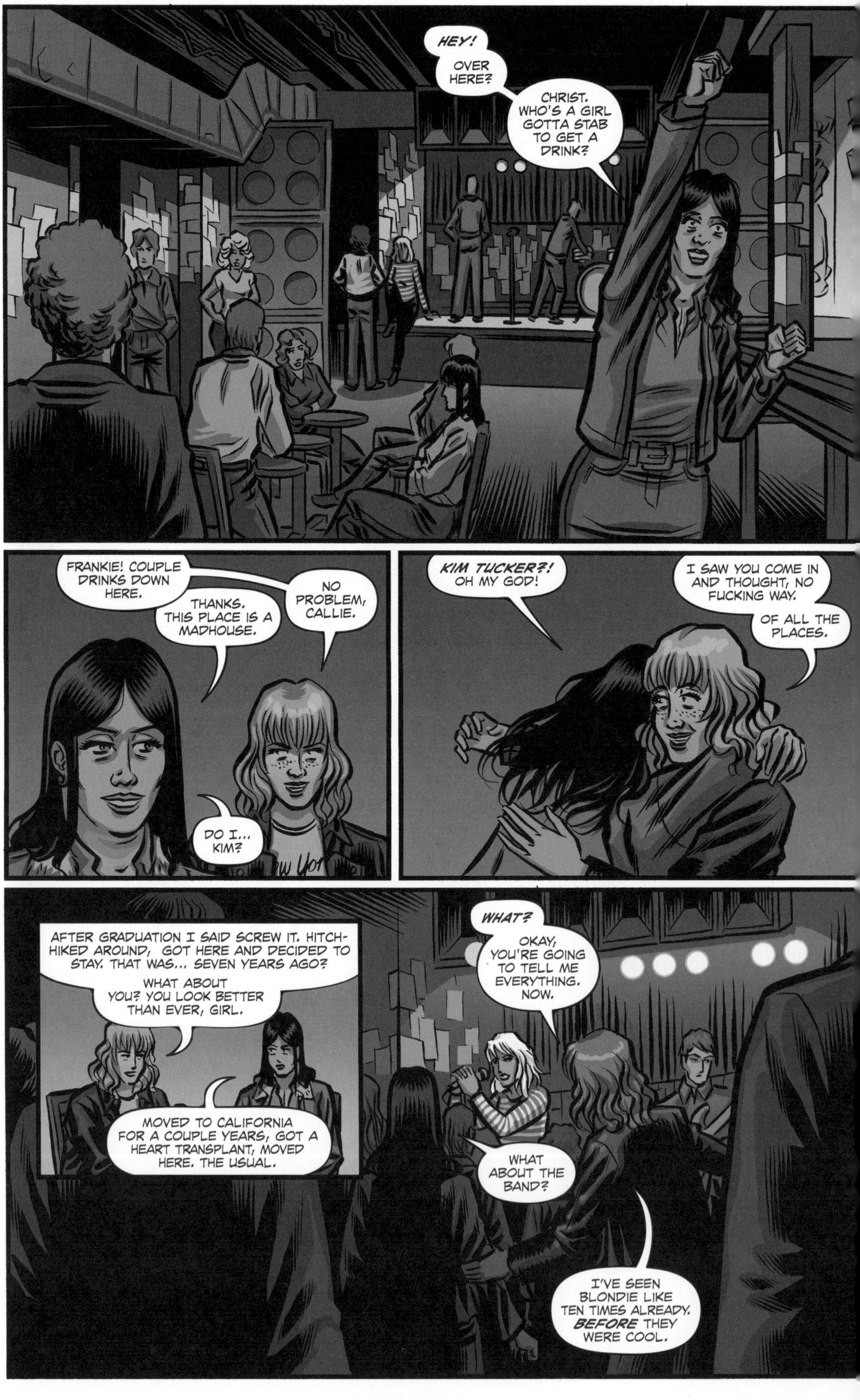

HEY!
OVER HERE?
CHRIST. WHO'S A GIRL GOTTA STAB TO GET A DRINK?
FRANKIE! COUPLE DRINKS DOWN HERE.
NO PROBLEM, CALLIE.
THANKS. THIS PLACE IS A MADHOUSE.
DO I... KIM?
KIM TUCKER?! OH MY GOD!
I SAW YOU COME IN AND THOUGHT, NO FUCKING WAY.
OF ALL THE PLACES.
AFTER GRADUATION I SAID SCREW IT. HITCH-HIKED AROUND, GOT HERE AND DECIDED TO STAY. THAT WAS... SEVEN YEARS AGO?
WHAT ABOUT YOU? YOU LOOK BETTER THAN EVER, GIRL.
MOVED TO CALIFORNIA FOR A COUPLE YEARS, GOT A HEART TRANSPLANT, MOVED HERE. THE USUAL.
WHAT?
OKAY, YOU'RE GOING TO TELL ME EVERYTHING. NOW.
WHAT ABOUT THE BAND?
I'VE SEEN BLONDIE LIKE TEN TIMES ALREADY. BEFORE THEY WERE COOL.

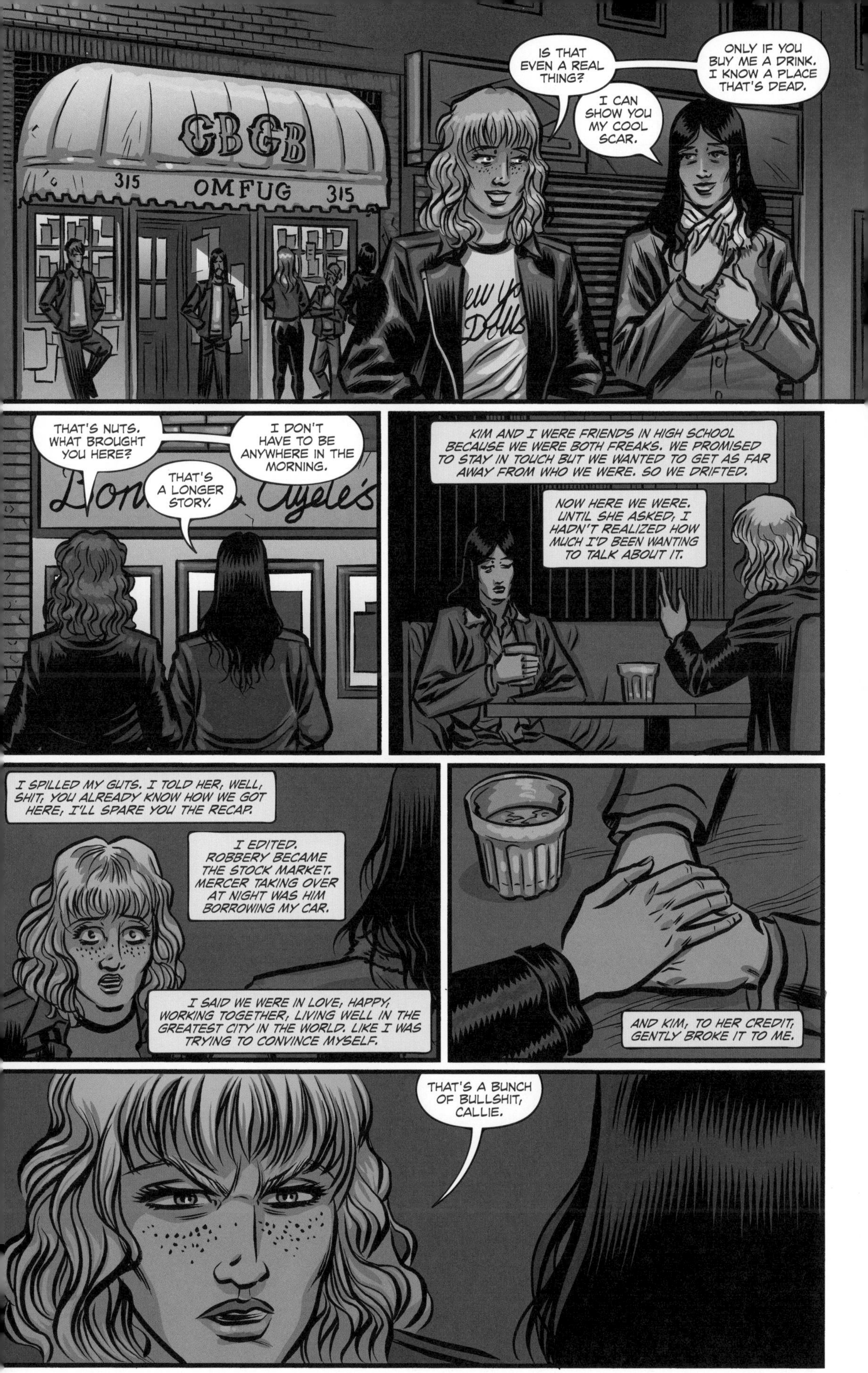
GBGB
315
OMFUG
315
IS THAT EVEN A REAL THING?
ONLY IF YOU BUY ME A DRINK. I KNOW A PLACE THAT'S DEAD.
I CAN SHOW YOU MY COOL SCAR.
THAT'S NUTS. WHAT BROUGHT YOU HERE?
I DON'T HAVE TO BE ANYWHERE IN THE MORNING.
THAT'S A LONGER STORY.
KIM AND I WERE FRIENDS IN HIGH SCHOOL BECAUSE WE WERE BOTH FREAKS. WE PROMISED TO STAY IN TOUCH BUT WE WANTED TO GET AS FAR AWAY FROM WHO WE WERE. SO WE DRIFTED.
NOW HERE WE WERE. UNTIL SHE ASKED, I HADN'T REALIZED HOW MUCH I'D BEEN WANTING TO TALK ABOUT IT.
I SPILLED MY GUTS. I TOLD HER, WELL, SHIT, YOU ALREADY KNOW HOW WE GOT HERE; I'LL SPARE YOU THE RECAP.
I EDITED. ROBBERY BECAME THE STOCK MARKET. MERCER TAKING OVER AT NIGHT WAS HIM BORROWING MY CAR.
I SAID WE WERE IN LOVE, HAPPY, WORKING TOGETHER, LIVING WELL IN THE GREATEST CITY IN THE WORLD. LIKE I WAS TRYING TO CONVINCE MYSELF.
AND KIM, TO HER CREDIT, GENTLY BROKE IT TO ME.
THAT'S A BUNCH OF BULLSHIT, CALLIE.

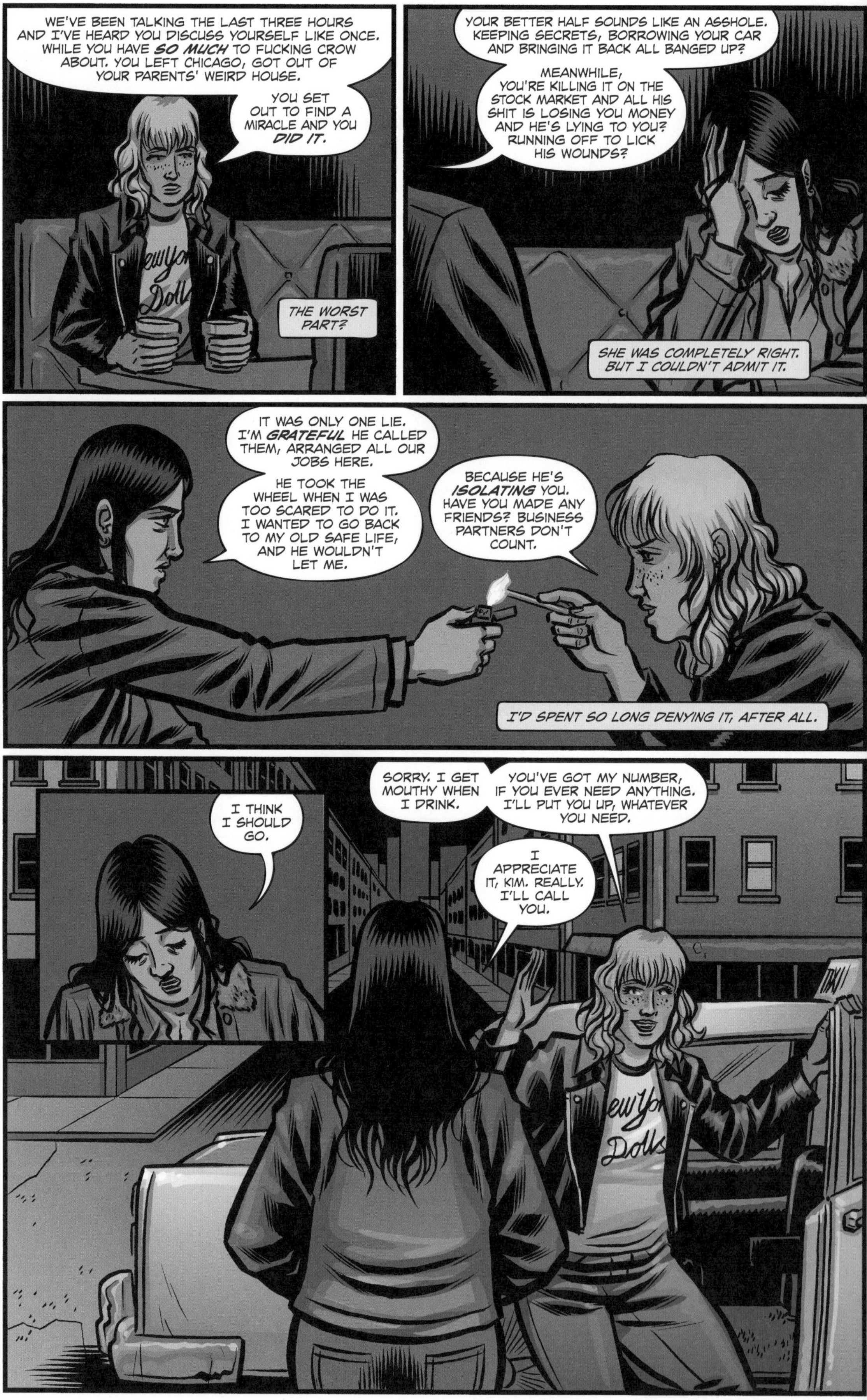
WE'VE BEEN TALKING THE LAST THREE HOURS AND I'VE HEARD YOU DISCUSS YOURSELF LIKE ONCE. WHILE YOU HAVE SO MUCH TO FUCKING CROW ABOUT. YOU LEFT CHICAGO, GOT OUT OF YOUR PARENTS' WEIRD HOUSE.
YOU SET OUT TO FIND A MIRACLE AND YOU DID IT.
THE WORST PART?
YOUR BETTER HALF SOUNDS LIKE AN ASSHOLE. KEEPING SECRETS, BORROWING YOUR CAR AND BRINGING IT BACK ALL BANGED UP?
MEANWHILE, YOU'RE KILLING IT ON THE STOCK MARKET AND ALL HIS SHIT IS LOSING YOU MONEY AND HE'S LYING TO YOU? RUNNING OFF TO LICK HIS WOUNDS?
SHE WAS COMPLETELY RIGHT. BUT I COULDN'T ADMIT IT.
IT WAS ONLY ONE LIE. I'M GRATEFUL HE CALLED THEM, ARRANGED ALL OUR JOBS HERE.
HE TOOK THE WHEEL WHEN I WAS TOO SCARED TO DO IT. I WANTED TO GO BACK TO MY OLD SAFE LIFE, AND HE WOULDN'T LET ME.
BECAUSE HE'S ISOLATING YOU. HAVE YOU MADE ANY FRIENDS? BUSINESS PARTNERS DON'T COUNT.
I'D SPENT SO LONG DENYING IT, AFTER ALL.
I THINK I SHOULD GO.
SORRY. I GET MOUTHY WHEN I DRINK.
YOU'VE GOT MY NUMBER, IF YOU EVER NEED ANYTHING. I'LL PUT YOU UP, WHATEVER YOU NEED.
I APPRECIATE IT, KIM. REALLY. I'LL CALL YOU.
TAXI

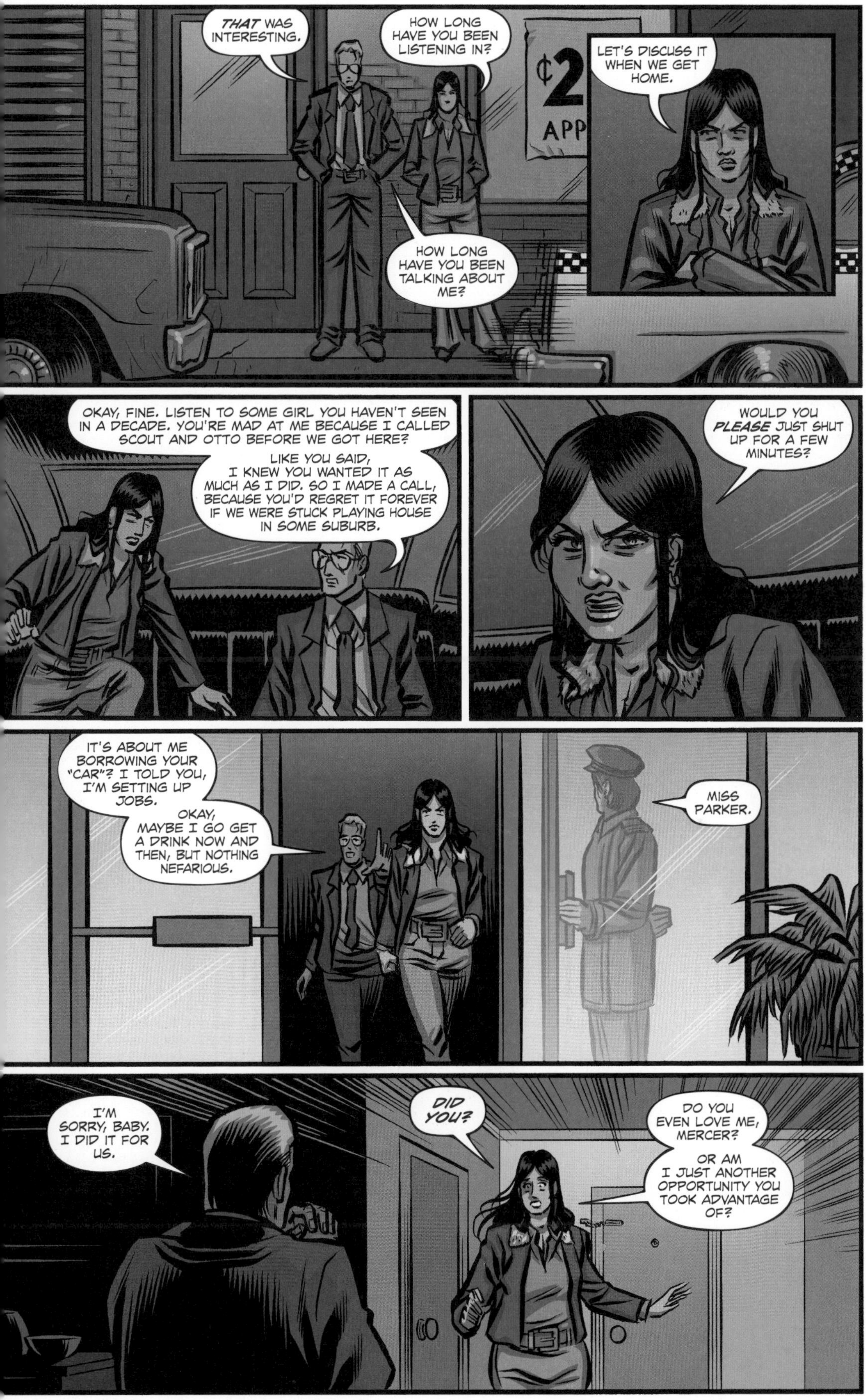
THAT WAS INTERESTING.
HOW LONG HAVE YOU BEEN LISTENING IN?
HOW LONG HAVE YOU BEEN TALKING ABOUT ME?
LET'S DISCUSS IT WHEN WE GET HOME.
OKAY, FINE. LISTEN TO SOME GIRL YOU HAVEN'T SEEN IN A DECADE. YOU'RE MAD AT ME BECAUSE I CALLED SCOUT AND OTTO BEFORE WE GOT HERE?
LIKE YOU SAID, I KNEW YOU WANTED IT AS MUCH AS I DID. SO I MADE A CALL, BECAUSE YOU'D REGRET IT FOREVER IF WE WERE STUCK PLAYING HOUSE IN SOME SUBURB.
WOULD YOU PLEASE JUST SHUT UP FOR A FEW MINUTES?
IT'S ABOUT ME BORROWING YOUR "CAR"? I TOLD YOU, I'M SETTING UP JOBS.
OKAY, MAYBE I GO GET A DRINK NOW AND THEN, BUT NOTHING NEFARIOUS.
MISS PARKER.
I'M SORRY, BABY. I DID IT FOR US.
DID YOU?
DO YOU EVEN LOVE ME, MERCER?
OR AM I JUST ANOTHER OPPORTUNITY YOU TOOK ADVANTAGE OF?

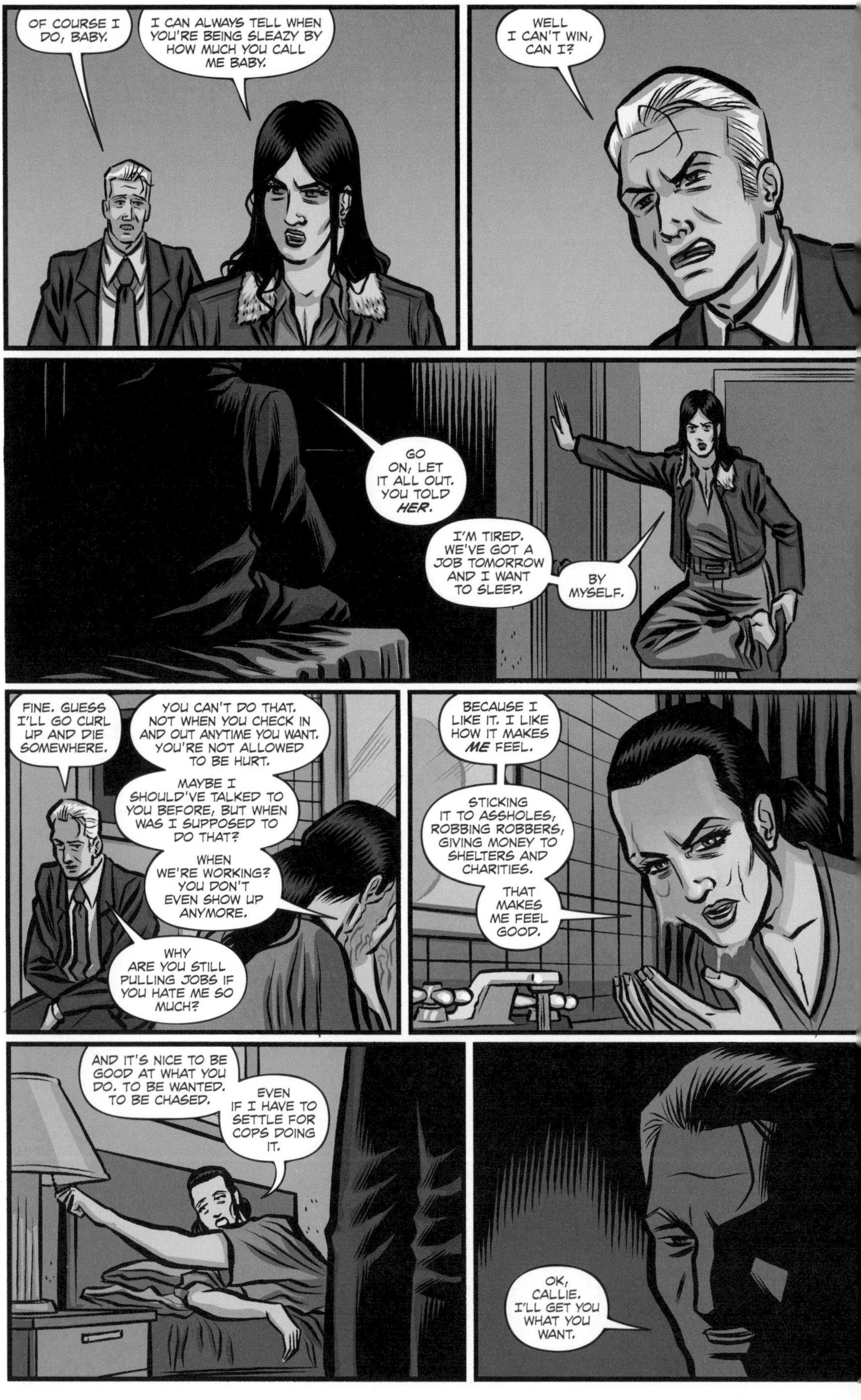
OF COURSE I DO, BABY.
I CAN ALWAYS TELL WHEN YOU'RE BEING SLEAZY BY HOW MUCH YOU CALL ME BABY.
WELL I CAN'T WIN, CAN I?
GO ON, LET IT ALL OUT. YOU TOLD *HER*.
I'M TIRED. WE'VE GOT A JOB TOMORROW AND I WANT TO SLEEP.
BY MYSELF.
FINE. GUESS I'LL GO CURL UP AND DIE SOMEWHERE.
YOU CAN'T DO THAT. NOT WHEN YOU CHECK IN AND OUT ANYTIME YOU WANT. YOU'RE NOT ALLOWED TO BE HURT.
MAYBE I SHOULD'VE TALKED TO YOU BEFORE, BUT WHEN WAS I SUPPOSED TO DO THAT?
WHEN WE'RE WORKING? YOU DON'T EVEN SHOW UP ANYMORE.
WHY ARE YOU STILL PULLING JOBS IF YOU HATE ME SO MUCH?
BECAUSE I LIKE IT. I LIKE HOW IT MAKES *ME* FEEL.
STICKING IT TO ASSHOLES, ROBBING ROBBERS, GIVING MONEY TO SHELTERS AND CHARITIES.
THAT MAKES ME FEEL GOOD.
AND IT'S NICE TO BE GOOD AT WHAT YOU DO. TO BE WANTED. TO BE CHASED.
EVEN IF I HAVE TO SETTLE FOR COPS DOING IT.
OK, CALLIE. I'LL GET YOU WHAT YOU WANT.

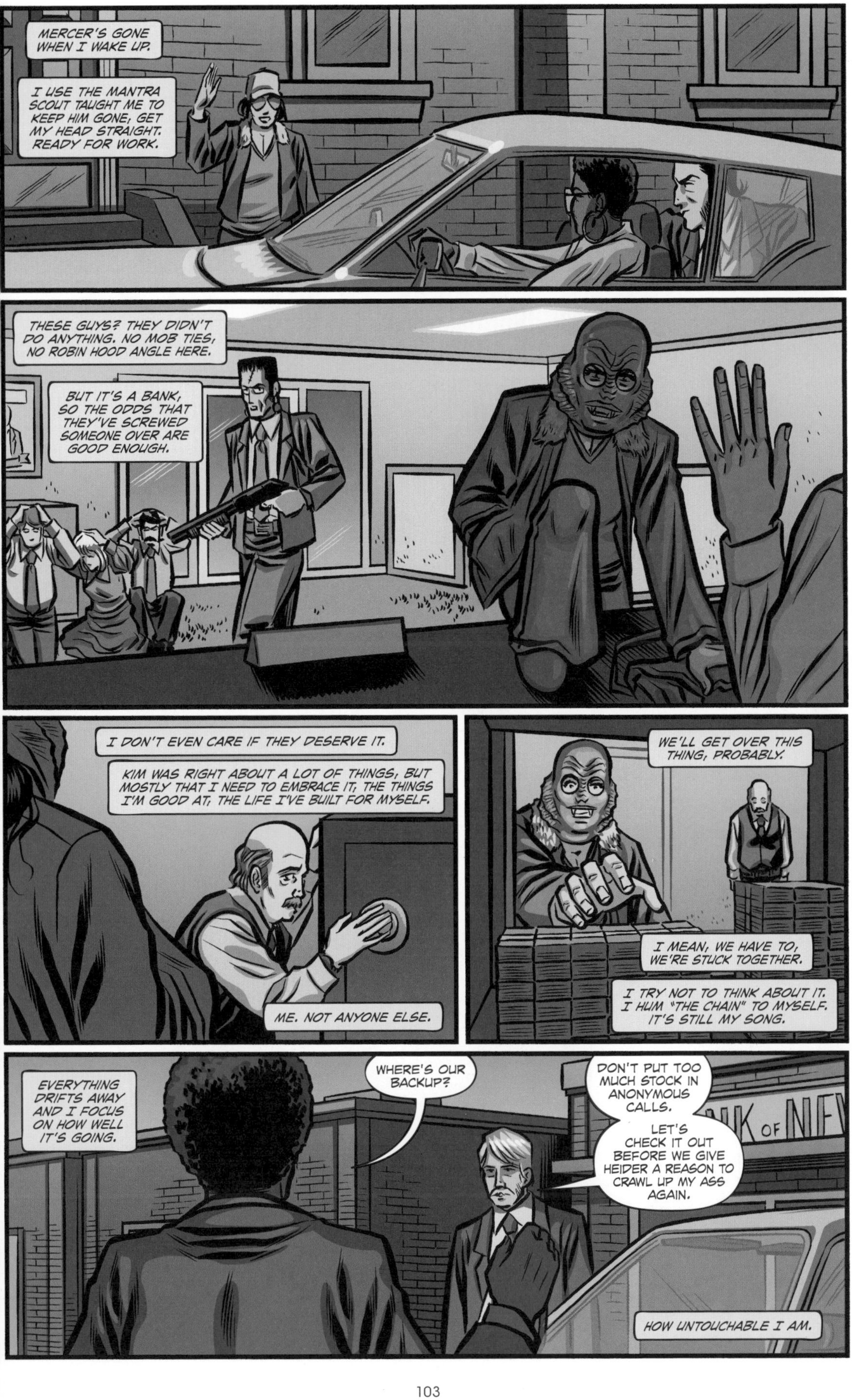
MERCER'S GONE WHEN I WAKE UP.
I USE THE MANTRA SCOUT TAUGHT ME TO KEEP HIM GONE; GET MY HEAD STRAIGHT. READY FOR WORK.
THESE GUYS? THEY DIDN'T DO ANYTHING. NO MOB TIES, NO ROBIN HOOD ANGLE HERE.
BUT IT'S A BANK, SO THE ODDS THAT THEY'VE SCREWED SOMEONE OVER ARE GOOD ENOUGH.
I DON'T EVEN CARE IF THEY DESERVE IT.
KIM WAS RIGHT ABOUT A LOT OF THINGS, BUT MOSTLY THAT I NEED TO EMBRACE IT, THE THINGS I'M GOOD AT, THE LIFE I'VE BUILT FOR MYSELF.
ME. NOT ANYONE ELSE.
WE'LL GET OVER THIS THING, PROBABLY.
I MEAN, WE HAVE TO, WE'RE STUCK TOGETHER.
I TRY NOT TO THINK ABOUT IT. I HUM "THE CHAIN" TO MYSELF. IT'S STILL MY SONG.
EVERYTHING DRIFTS AWAY AND I FOCUS ON HOW WELL IT'S GOING.
WHERE'S OUR BACKUP?
DON'T PUT TOO MUCH STOCK IN ANONYMOUS CALLS.
LET'S CHECK IT OUT BEFORE WE GIVE HEIDER A REASON TO CRAWL UP MY ASS AGAIN.
HOW UNTOUCHABLE I AM.

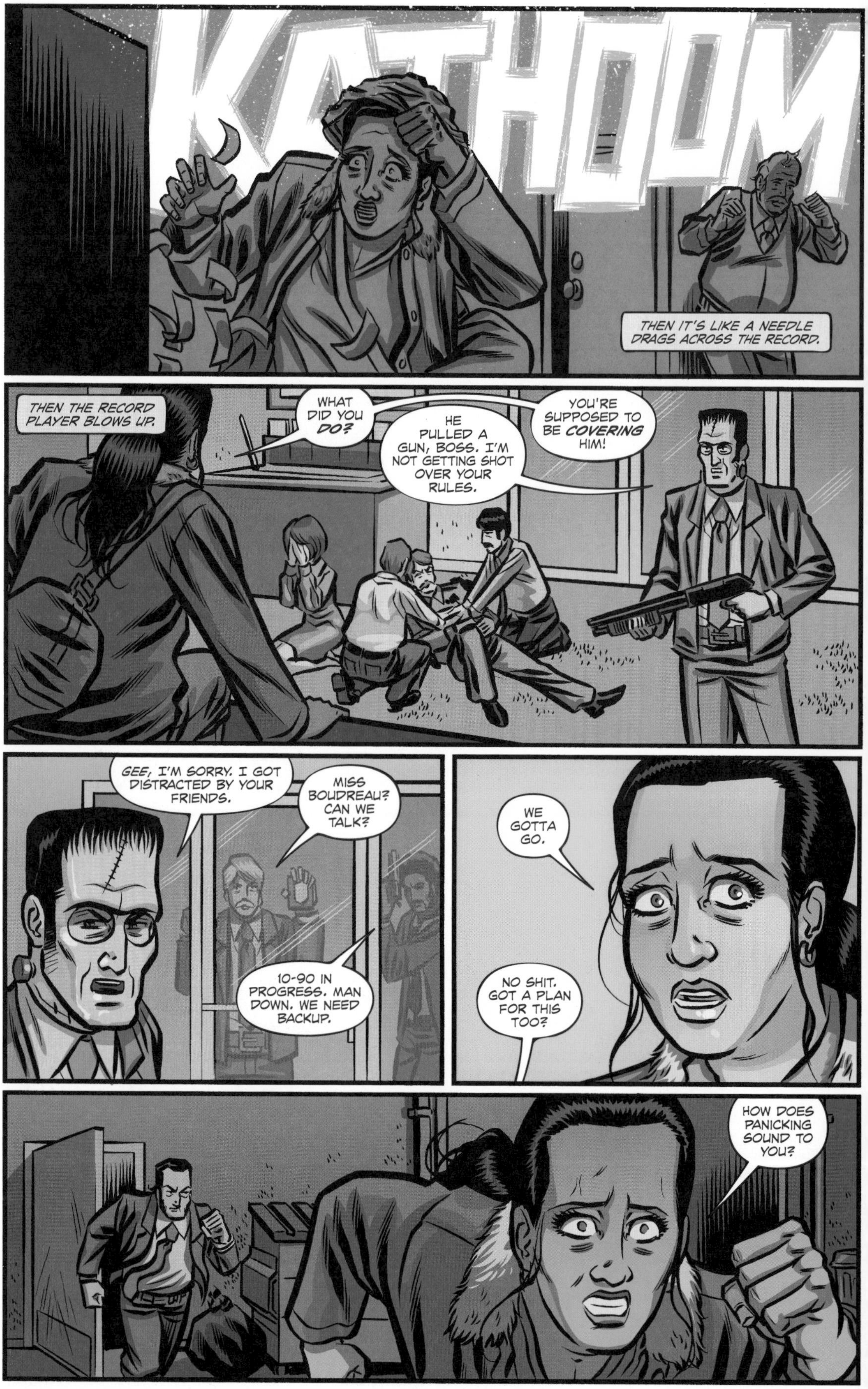
KATHOOM
THEN IT'S LIKE A NEEDLE DRAGS ACROSS THE RECORD.
THEN THE RECORD PLAYER BLOWS UP.
WHAT DID YOU DO?
HE PULLED A GUN, BOSS. I'M NOT GETTING SHOT OVER YOUR RULES.
YOU'RE SUPPOSED TO BE COVERING HIM!
GEE, I'M SORRY. I GOT DISTRACTED BY YOUR FRIENDS.
MISS BOUDREAU? CAN WE TALK?
10-90 IN PROGRESS. MAN DOWN. WE NEED BACKUP.
WE GOTTA GO.
NO SHIT. GOT A PLAN FOR THIS TOO?
HOW DOES PANICKING SOUND TO YOU?

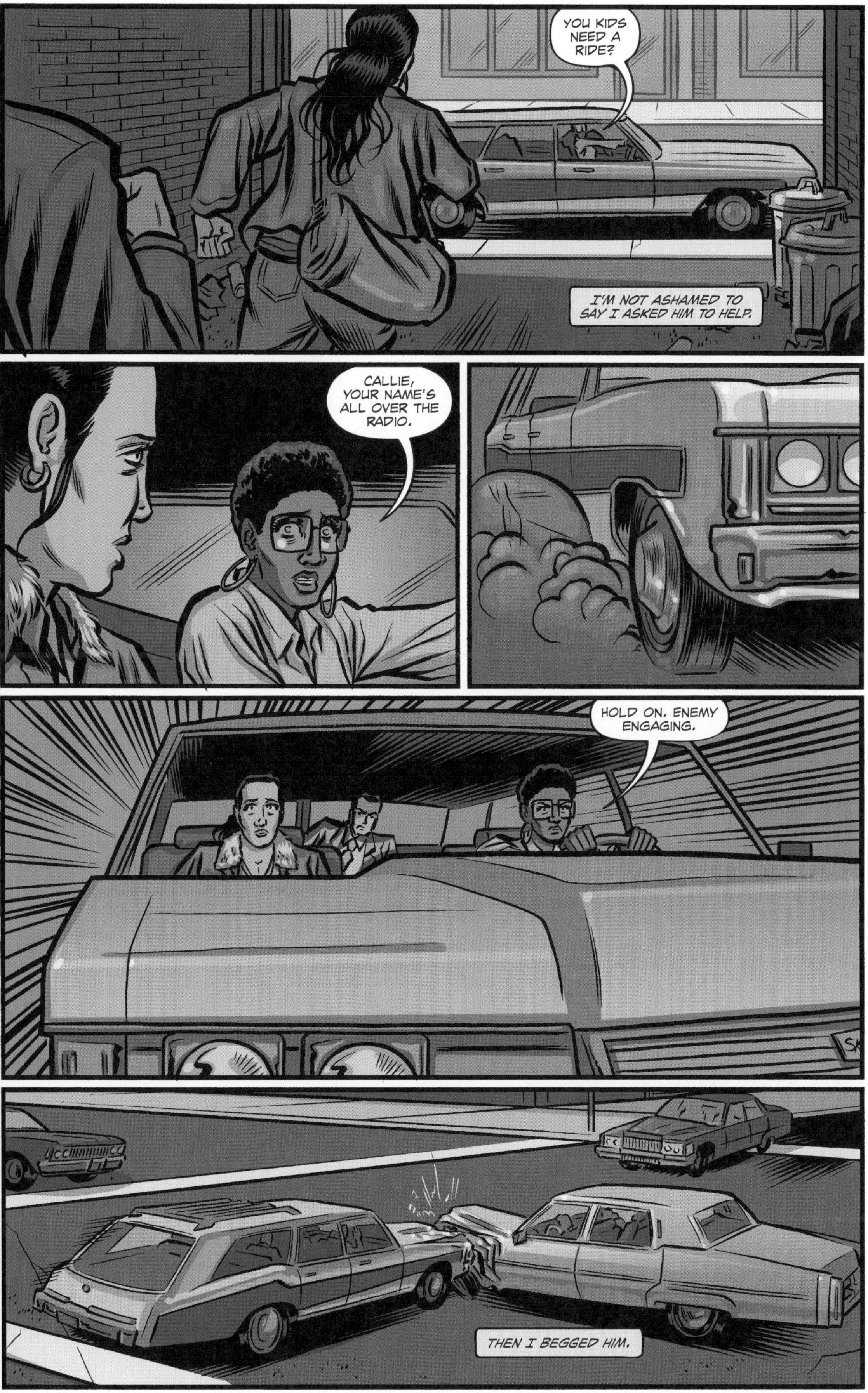
YOU KIDS NEED A RIDE?
I'M NOT ASHAMED TO SAY I ASKED HIM TO HELP.
CALLIE, YOUR NAME'S ALL OVER THE RADIO.
HOLD ON. ENEMY ENGAGING.
THEN I BEGGED HIM.

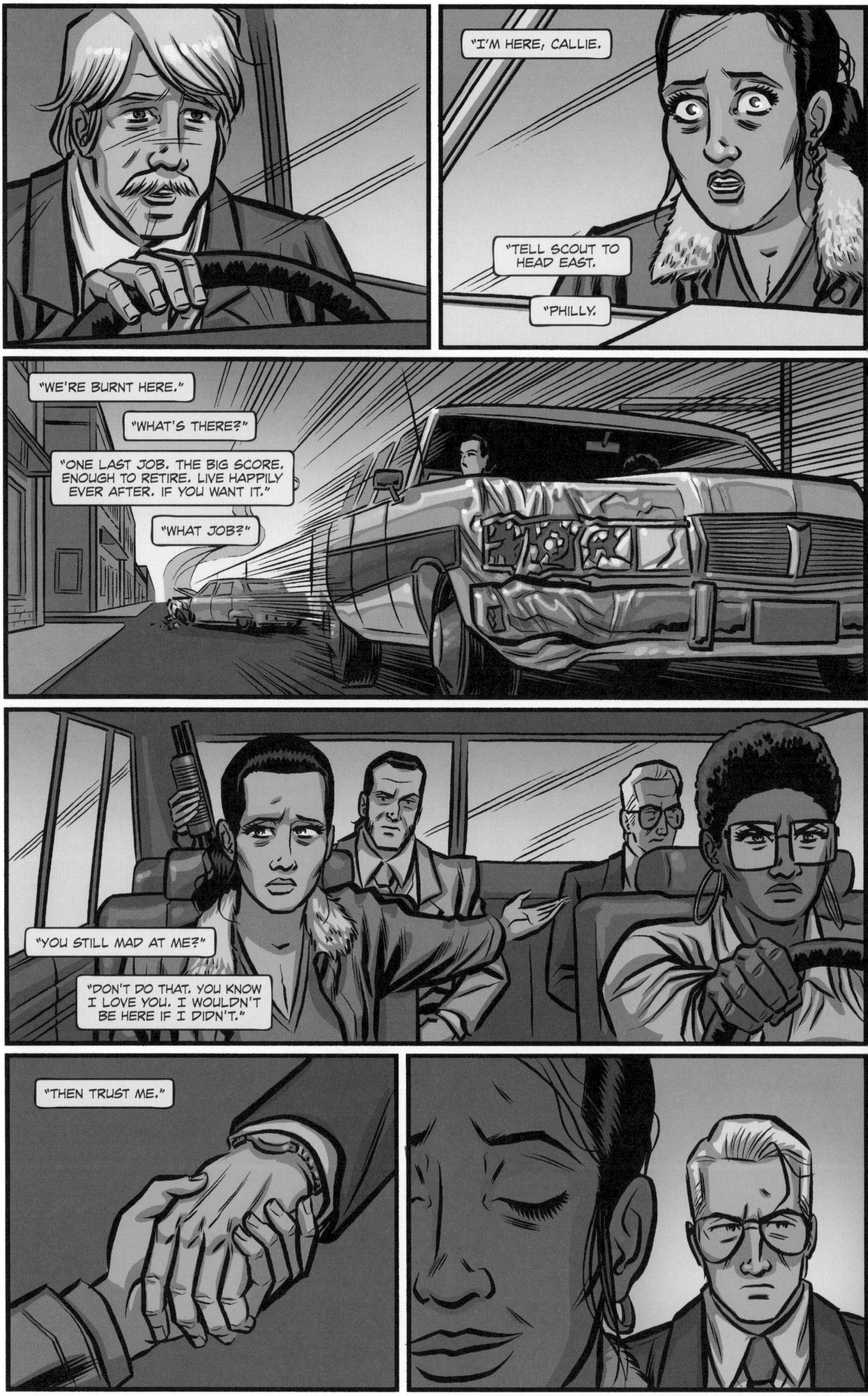
"I'M HERE, CALLIE.
"TELL SCOUT TO HEAD EAST.
"PHILLY.
"WE'RE BURNT HERE."
"WHAT'S THERE?"
"ONE LAST JOB. THE BIG SCORE. ENOUGH TO RETIRE. LIVE HAPPILY EVER AFTER. IF YOU WANT IT."
"WHAT JOB?"
"YOU STILL MAD AT ME?"
"DON'T DO THAT. YOU KNOW I LOVE YOU. I WOULDN'T BE HERE IF I DIDN'T."
"THEN TRUST ME."

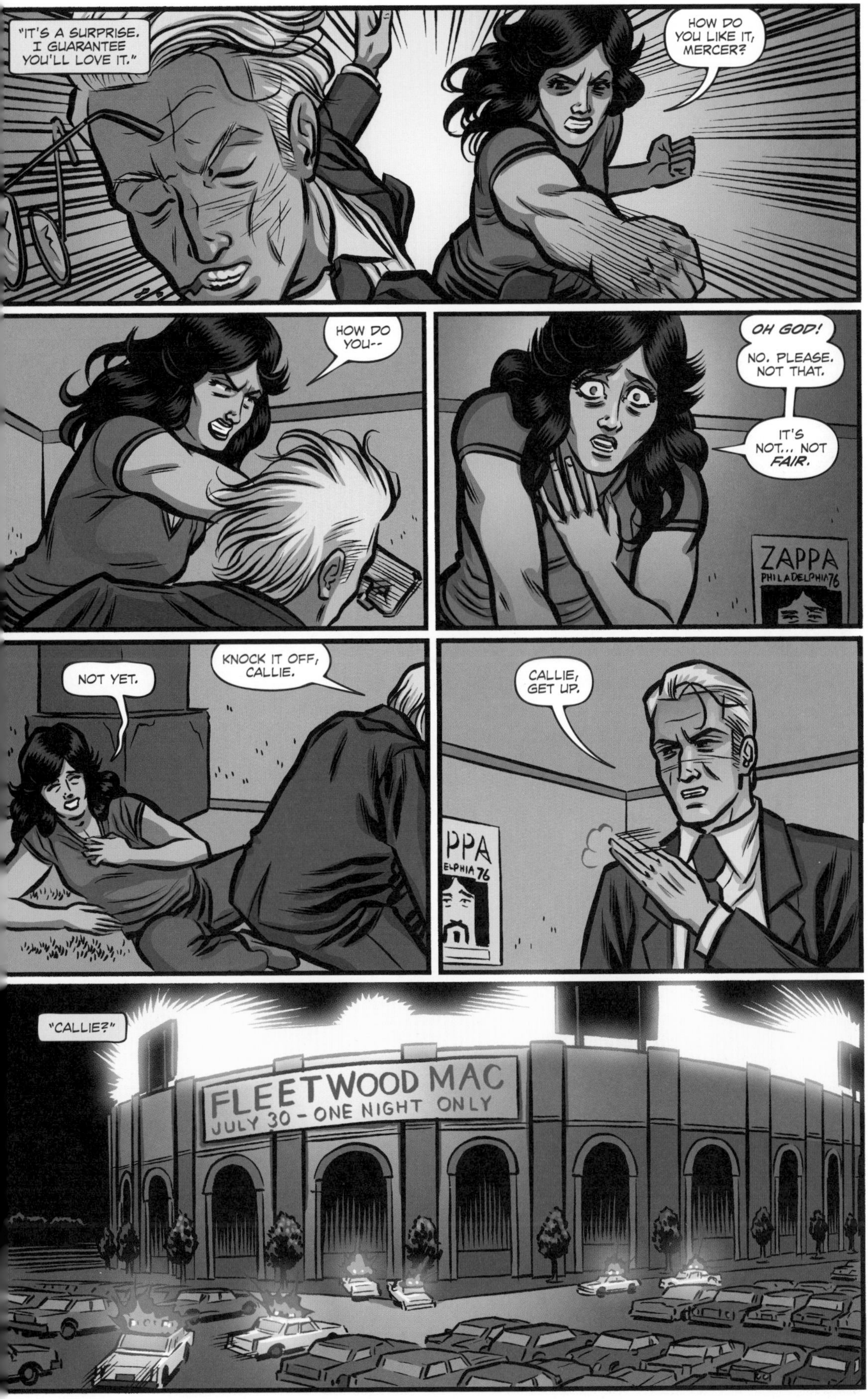
"IT'S A SURPRISE. I GUARANTEE YOU'LL LOVE IT."
HOW DO YOU LIKE IT, MERCER?
HOW DO YOU--
OH GOD!
NO. PLEASE. NOT THAT.
IT'S NOT... NOT FAIR.
ZAPPA PHILADELPHIA 76
NOT YET.
KNOCK IT OFF, CALLIE.
CALLIE, GET UP.
"CALLIE?"
FLEETWOOD MAC
JULY 30 - ONE NIGHT ONLY

# CHAPTER 5

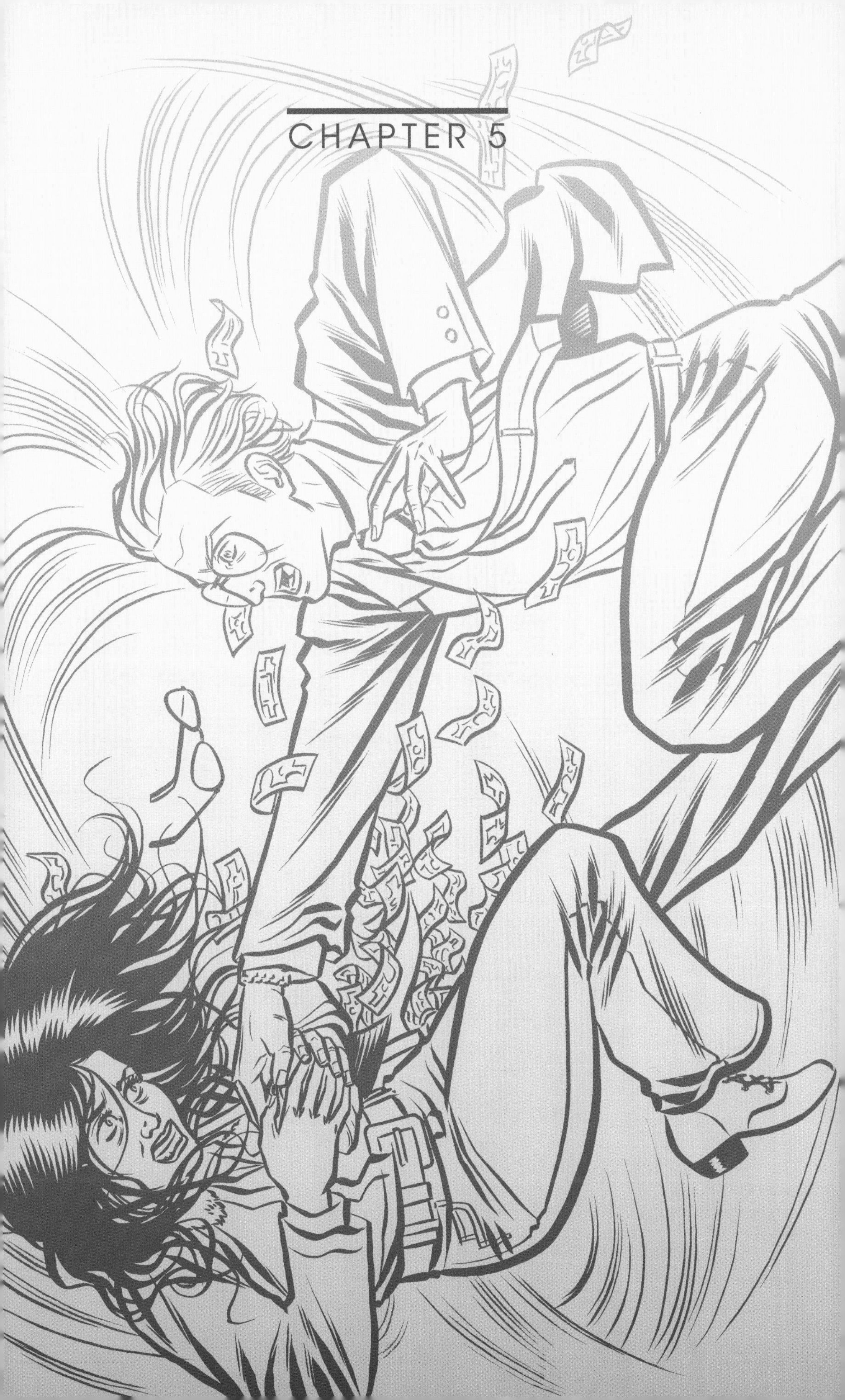

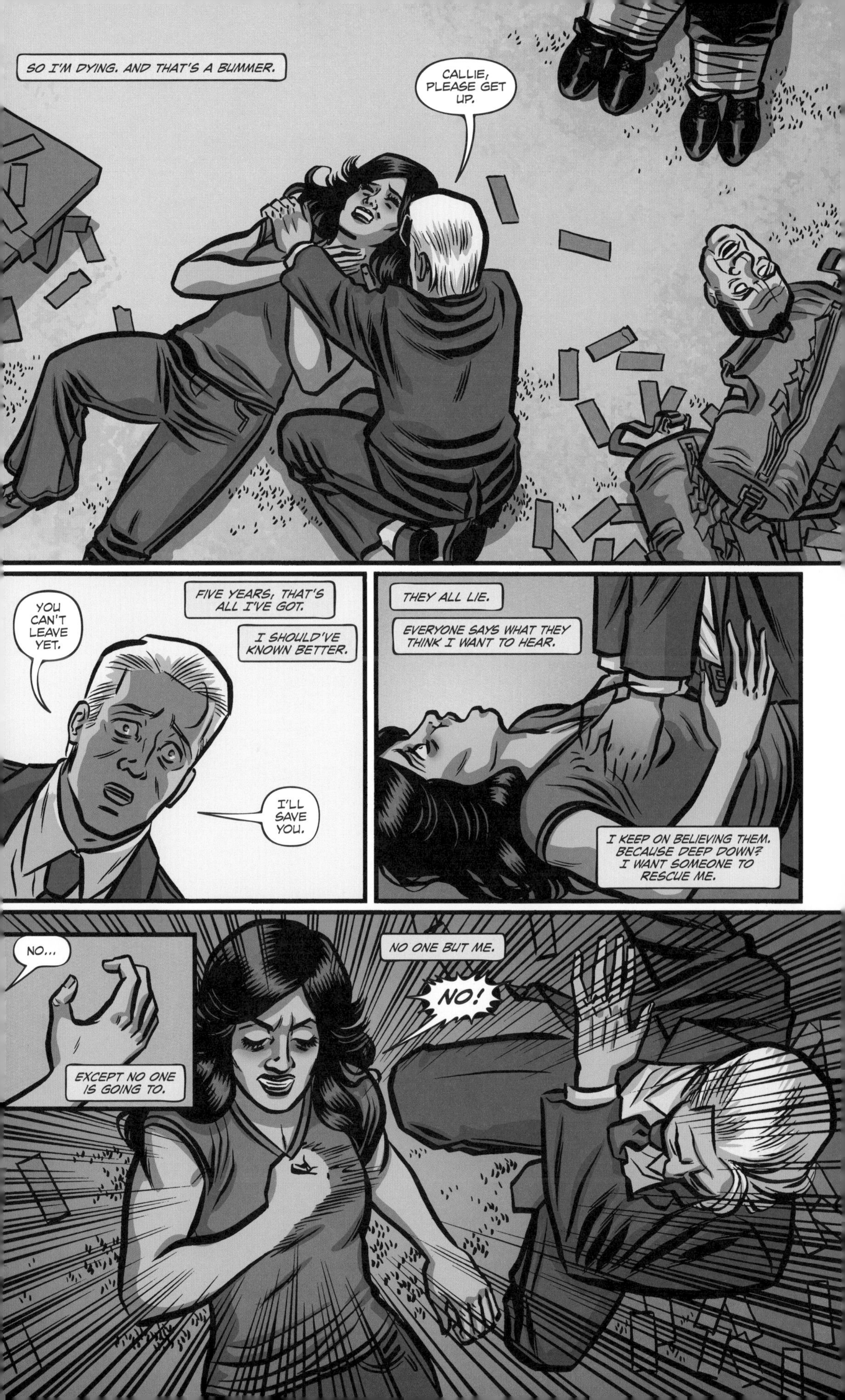
SO I'M DYING. AND THAT'S A BUMMER.
CALLIE, PLEASE GET UP.
FIVE YEARS; THAT'S ALL I'VE GOT.
I SHOULD'VE KNOWN BETTER.
YOU CAN'T LEAVE YET.
I'LL SAVE YOU.
THEY ALL LIE.
EVERYONE SAYS WHAT THEY THINK I WANT TO HEAR.
I KEEP ON BELIEVING THEM. BECAUSE DEEP DOWN? I WANT SOMEONE TO RESCUE ME.
NO...
EXCEPT NO ONE IS GOING TO.
NO ONE BUT ME.
NO!

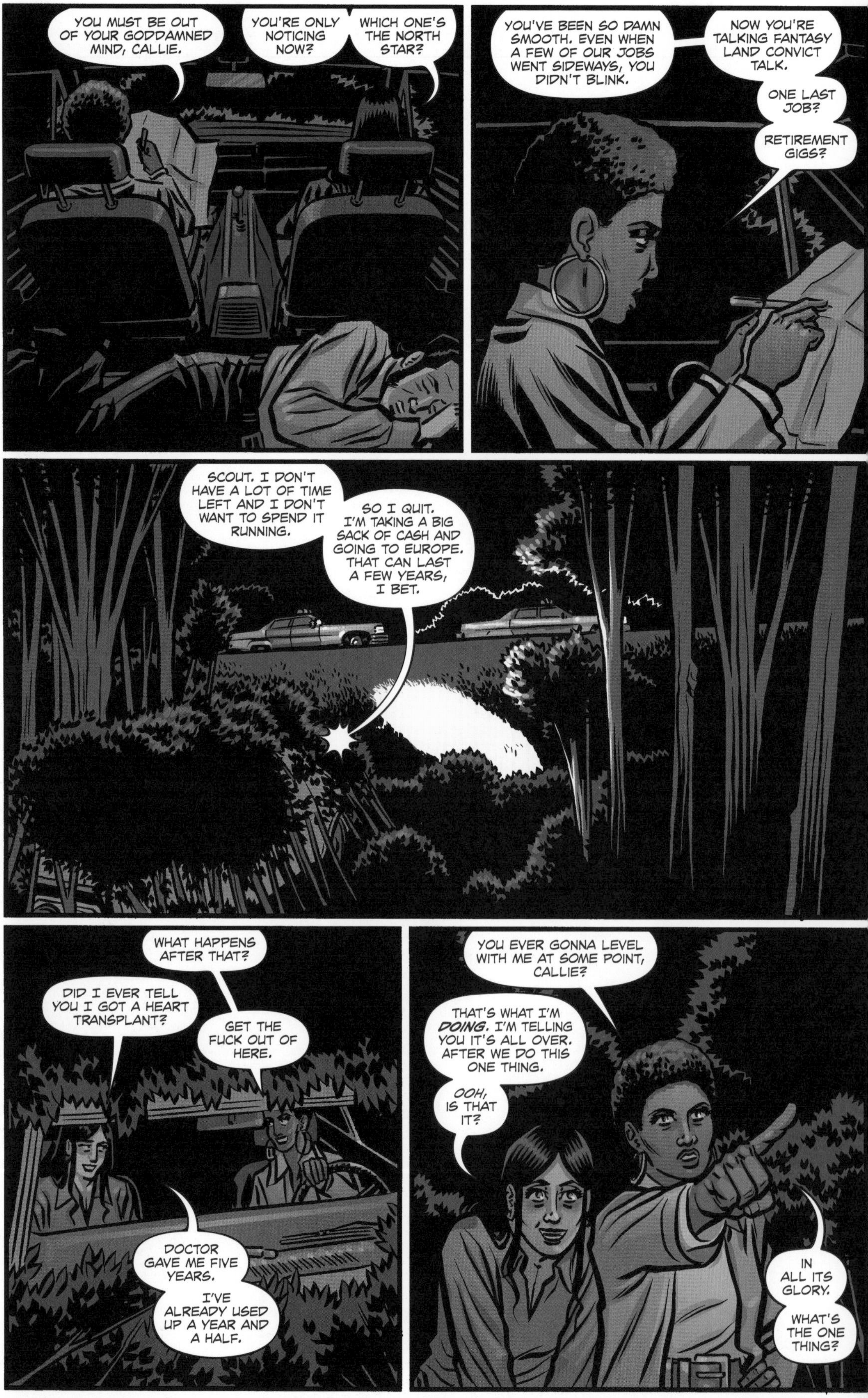
YOU MUST BE OUT OF YOUR GODDAMNED MIND, CALLIE.
YOU'RE ONLY NOTICING NOW?
WHICH ONE'S THE NORTH STAR?
YOU'VE BEEN SO DAMN SMOOTH. EVEN WHEN A FEW OF OUR JOBS WENT SIDEWAYS, YOU DIDN'T BLINK.
NOW YOU'RE TALKING FANTASY LAND CONVICT TALK.
ONE LAST JOB?
RETIREMENT GIGS?
SCOUT. I DON'T HAVE A LOT OF TIME LEFT AND I DON'T WANT TO SPEND IT RUNNING.
SO I QUIT. I'M TAKING A BIG SACK OF CASH AND GOING TO EUROPE. THAT CAN LAST A FEW YEARS, I BET.
WHAT HAPPENS AFTER THAT?
DID I EVER TELL YOU I GOT A HEART TRANSPLANT?
GET THE FUCK OUT OF HERE.
DOCTOR GAVE ME FIVE YEARS.
I'VE ALREADY USED UP A YEAR AND A HALF.
YOU EVER GONNA LEVEL WITH ME AT SOME POINT, CALLIE?
THAT'S WHAT I'M DOING. I'M TELLING YOU IT'S ALL OVER. AFTER WE DO THIS ONE THING.
OOH, IS THAT IT?
IN ALL ITS GLORY.
WHAT'S THE ONE THING?

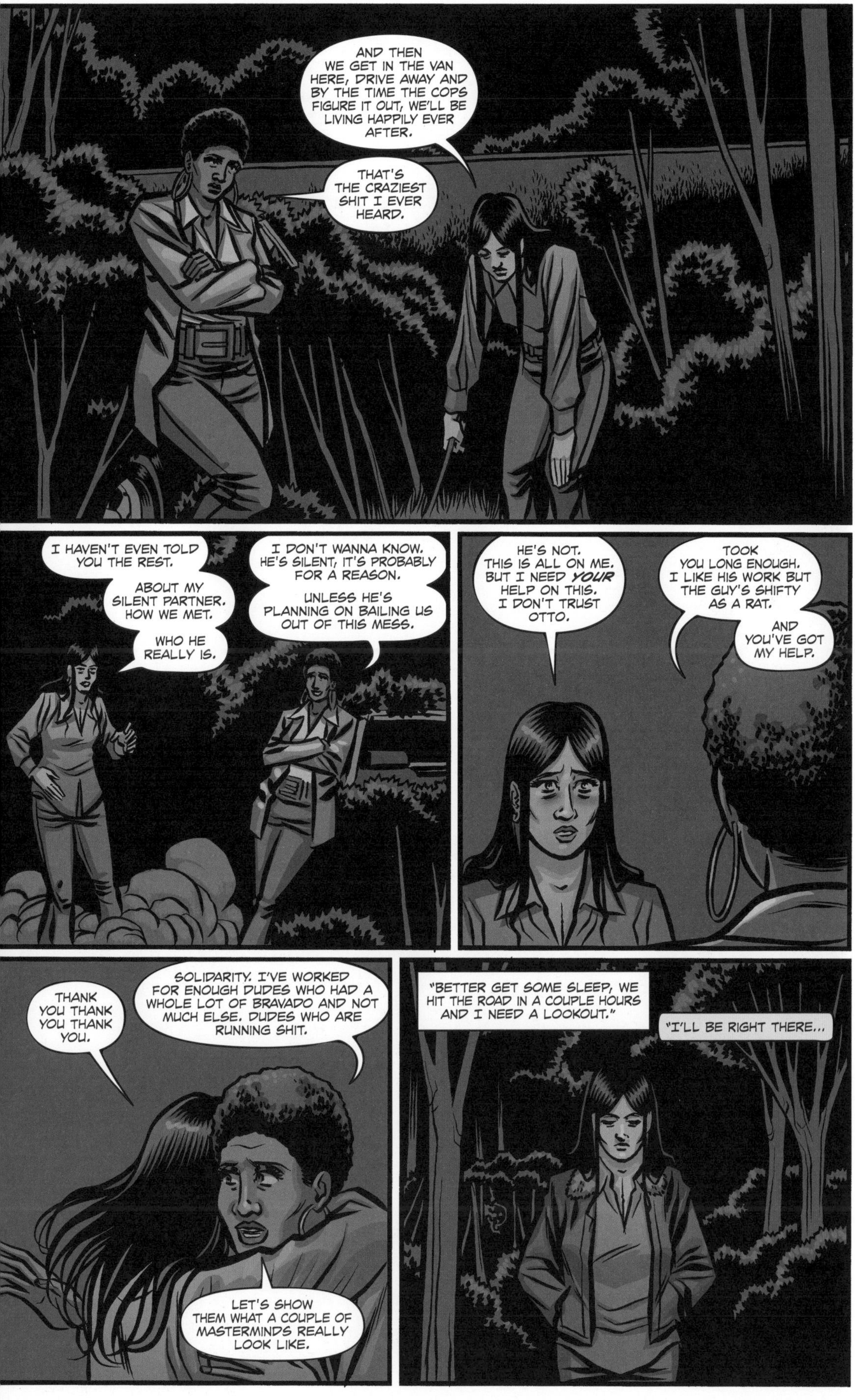
AND THEN WE GET IN THE VAN HERE, DRIVE AWAY AND BY THE TIME THE COPS FIGURE IT OUT, WE'LL BE LIVING HAPPILY EVER AFTER.
THAT'S THE CRAZIEST SHIT I EVER HEARD.
I HAVEN'T EVEN TOLD YOU THE REST.
ABOUT MY SILENT PARTNER. HOW WE MET.
WHO HE REALLY IS.
I DON'T WANNA KNOW. HE'S SILENT, IT'S PROBABLY FOR A REASON.
UNLESS HE'S PLANNING ON BAILING US OUT OF THIS MESS.
HE'S NOT. THIS IS ALL ON ME. BUT I NEED *YOUR* HELP ON THIS. I DON'T TRUST OTTO.
TOOK YOU LONG ENOUGH. I LIKE HIS WORK BUT THE GUY'S SHIFTY AS A RAT.
AND YOU'VE GOT MY HELP.
THANK YOU THANK YOU THANK YOU.
SOLIDARITY. I'VE WORKED FOR ENOUGH DUDES WHO HAD A WHOLE LOT OF BRAVADO AND NOT MUCH ELSE. DUDES WHO ARE RUNNING SHIT.
LET'S SHOW THEM WHAT A COUPLE OF MASTERMINDS REALLY LOOK LIKE.
"BETTER GET SOME SLEEP, WE HIT THE ROAD IN A COUPLE HOURS AND I NEED A LOOKOUT."
"I'LL BE RIGHT THERE...

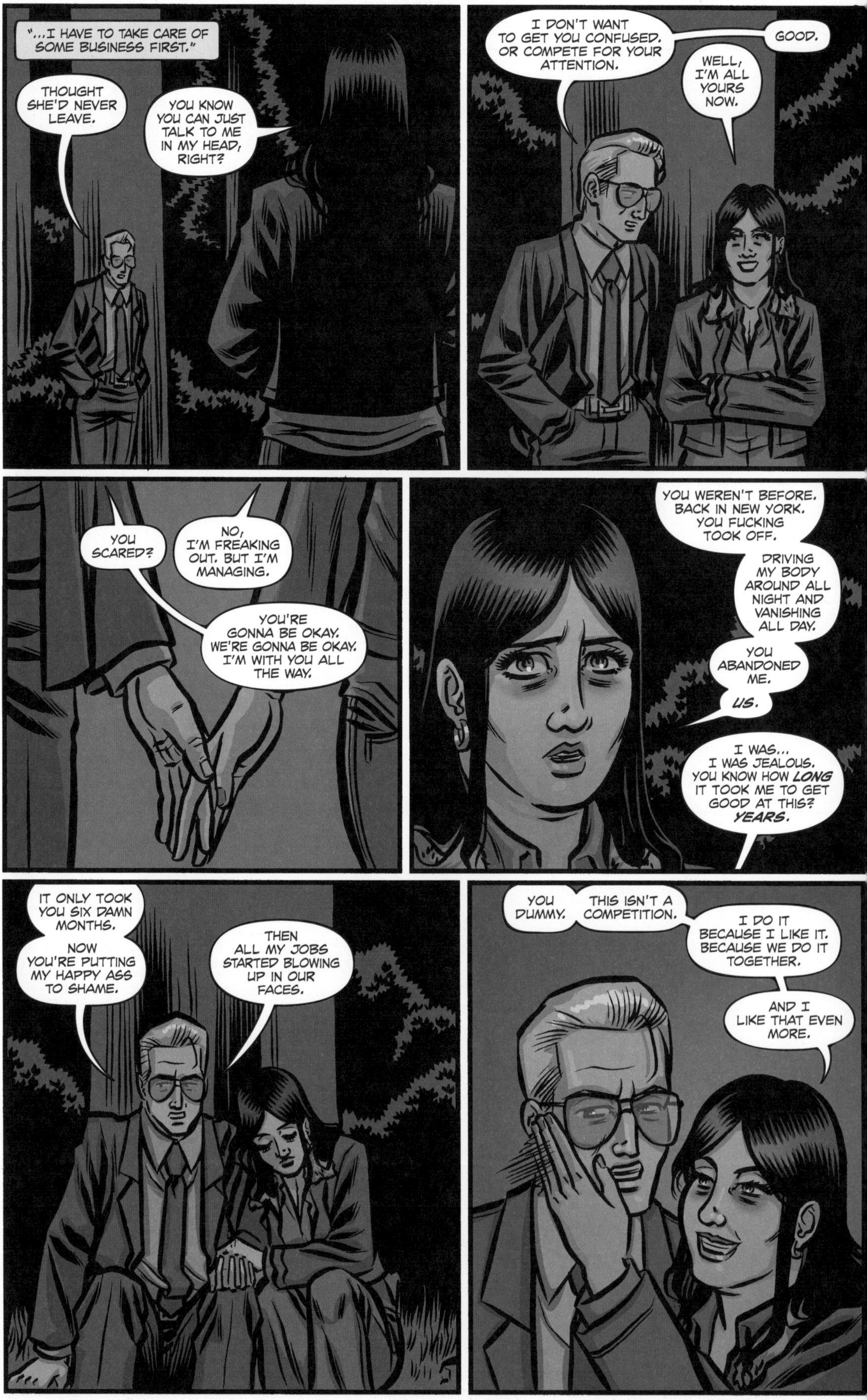
"...I HAVE TO TAKE CARE OF SOME BUSINESS FIRST."
THOUGHT SHE'D NEVER LEAVE.
YOU KNOW YOU CAN JUST TALK TO ME IN MY HEAD, RIGHT?
I DON'T WANT TO GET YOU CONFUSED. OR COMPETE FOR YOUR ATTENTION.
GOOD.
WELL, I'M ALL YOURS NOW.
YOU SCARED?
NO, I'M FREAKING OUT. BUT I'M MANAGING.
YOU'RE GONNA BE OKAY. WE'RE GONNA BE OKAY. I'M WITH YOU ALL THE WAY.
YOU WEREN'T BEFORE. BACK IN NEW YORK. YOU FUCKING TOOK OFF.
DRIVING MY BODY AROUND ALL NIGHT AND VANISHING ALL DAY.
YOU ABANDONED ME.
US.
I WAS... I WAS JEALOUS. YOU KNOW HOW LONG IT TOOK ME TO GET GOOD AT THIS? YEARS.
IT ONLY TOOK YOU SIX DAMN MONTHS.
NOW YOU'RE PUTTING MY HAPPY ASS TO SHAME.
THEN ALL MY JOBS STARTED BLOWING UP IN OUR FACES.
YOU DUMMY.
THIS ISN'T A COMPETITION.
I DO IT BECAUSE I LIKE IT. BECAUSE WE DO IT TOGETHER.
AND I LIKE THAT EVEN MORE.

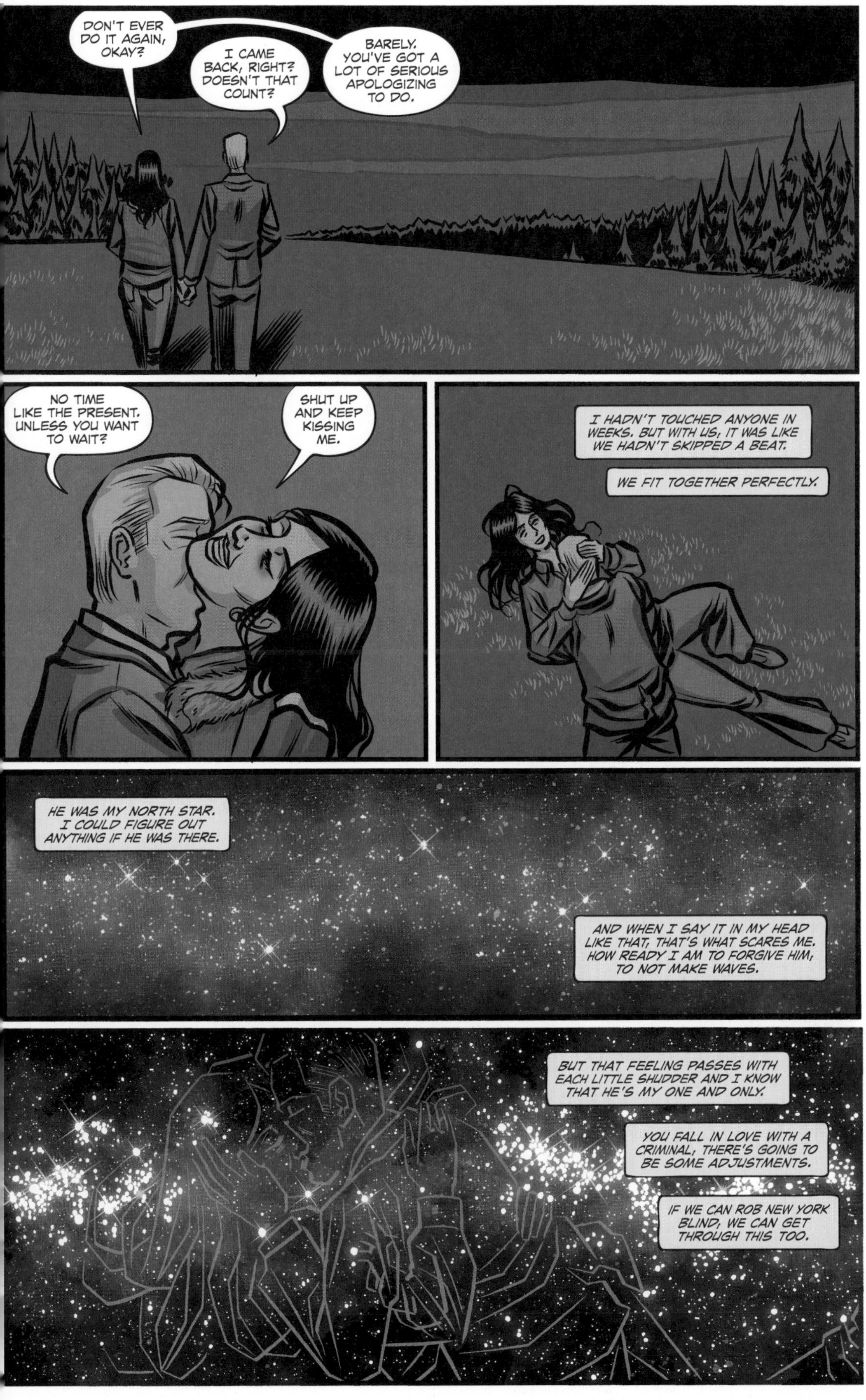
DON'T EVER DO IT AGAIN, OKAY?
I CAME BACK, RIGHT? DOESN'T THAT COUNT?
BARELY. YOU'VE GOT A LOT OF SERIOUS APOLOGIZING TO DO.
NO TIME LIKE THE PRESENT. UNLESS YOU WANT TO WAIT?
SHUT UP AND KEEP KISSING ME.
I HADN'T TOUCHED ANYONE IN WEEKS. BUT WITH US, IT WAS LIKE WE HADN'T SKIPPED A BEAT.
WE FIT TOGETHER PERFECTLY.
HE WAS MY NORTH STAR. I COULD FIGURE OUT ANYTHING IF HE WAS THERE.
AND WHEN I SAY IT IN MY HEAD LIKE THAT, THAT'S WHAT SCARES ME. HOW READY I AM TO FORGIVE HIM, TO NOT MAKE WAVES.
BUT THAT FEELING PASSES WITH EACH LITTLE SHUDDER AND I KNOW THAT HE'S MY ONE AND ONLY.
YOU FALL IN LOVE WITH A CRIMINAL, THERE'S GOING TO BE SOME ADJUSTMENTS.
IF WE CAN ROB NEW YORK BLIND, WE CAN GET THROUGH THIS TOO.

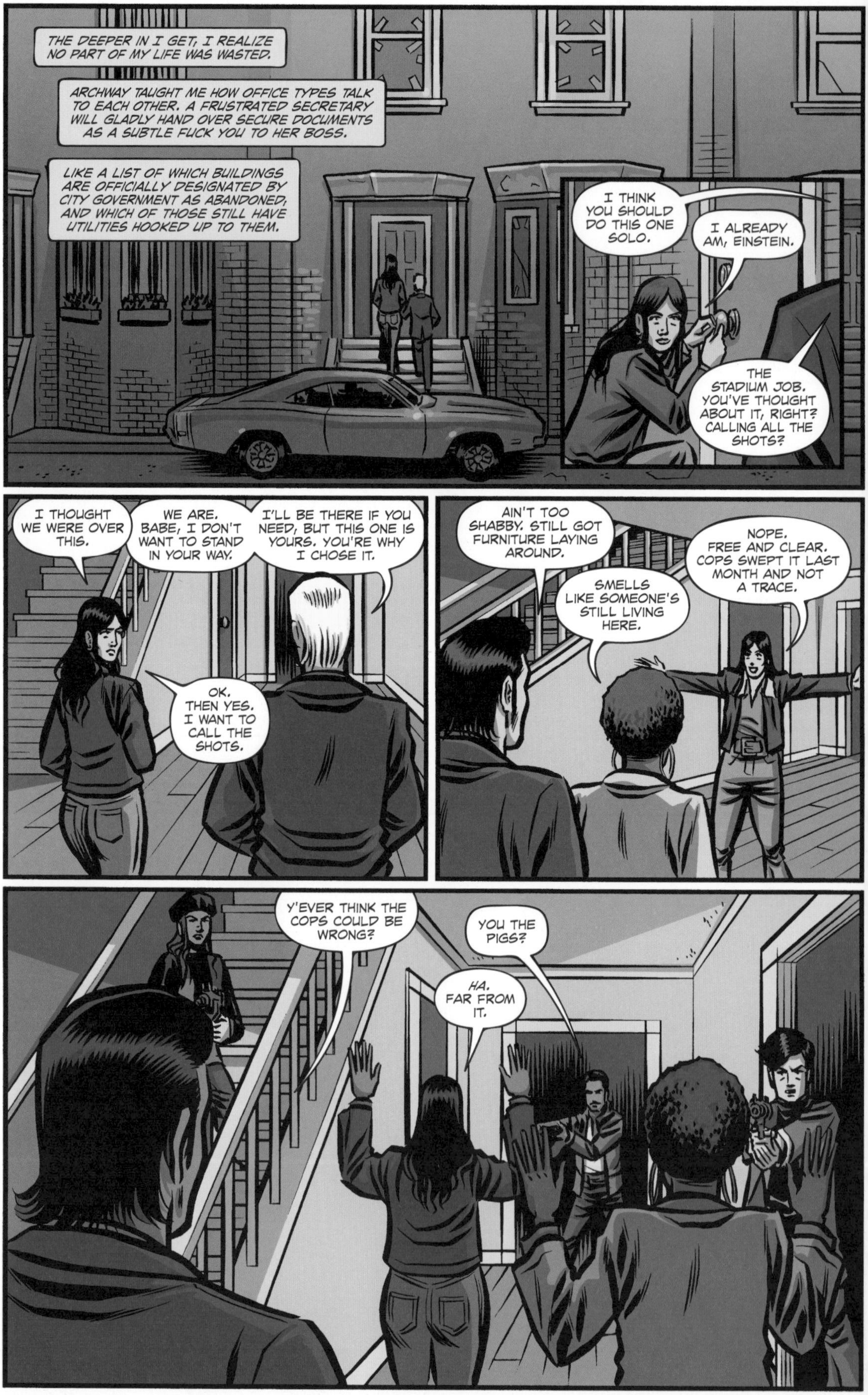
THE DEEPER IN I GET, I REALIZE NO PART OF MY LIFE WAS WASTED.
ARCHWAY TAUGHT ME HOW OFFICE TYPES TALK TO EACH OTHER. A FRUSTRATED SECRETARY WILL GLADLY HAND OVER SECURE DOCUMENTS AS A SUBTLE FUCK YOU TO HER BOSS.
LIKE A LIST OF WHICH BUILDINGS ARE OFFICIALLY DESIGNATED BY CITY GOVERNMENT AS ABANDONED, AND WHICH OF THOSE STILL HAVE UTILITIES HOOKED UP TO THEM.
I THINK YOU SHOULD DO THIS ONE SOLO.
I ALREADY AM, EINSTEIN.
THE STADIUM JOB. YOU'VE THOUGHT ABOUT IT, RIGHT? CALLING ALL THE SHOTS?
I THOUGHT WE WERE OVER THIS.
WE ARE. BABE, I DON'T WANT TO STAND IN YOUR WAY.
I'LL BE THERE IF YOU NEED, BUT THIS ONE IS YOURS. YOU'RE WHY I CHOSE IT.
OK. THEN YES. I WANT TO CALL THE SHOTS.
AIN'T TOO SHABBY. STILL GOT FURNITURE LAYING AROUND.
SMELLS LIKE SOMEONE'S STILL LIVING HERE.
NOPE. FREE AND CLEAR. COPS SWEPT IT LAST MONTH AND NOT A TRACE.
Y'EVER THINK THE COPS COULD BE WRONG?
YOU THE PIGS?
HA. FAR FROM IT.

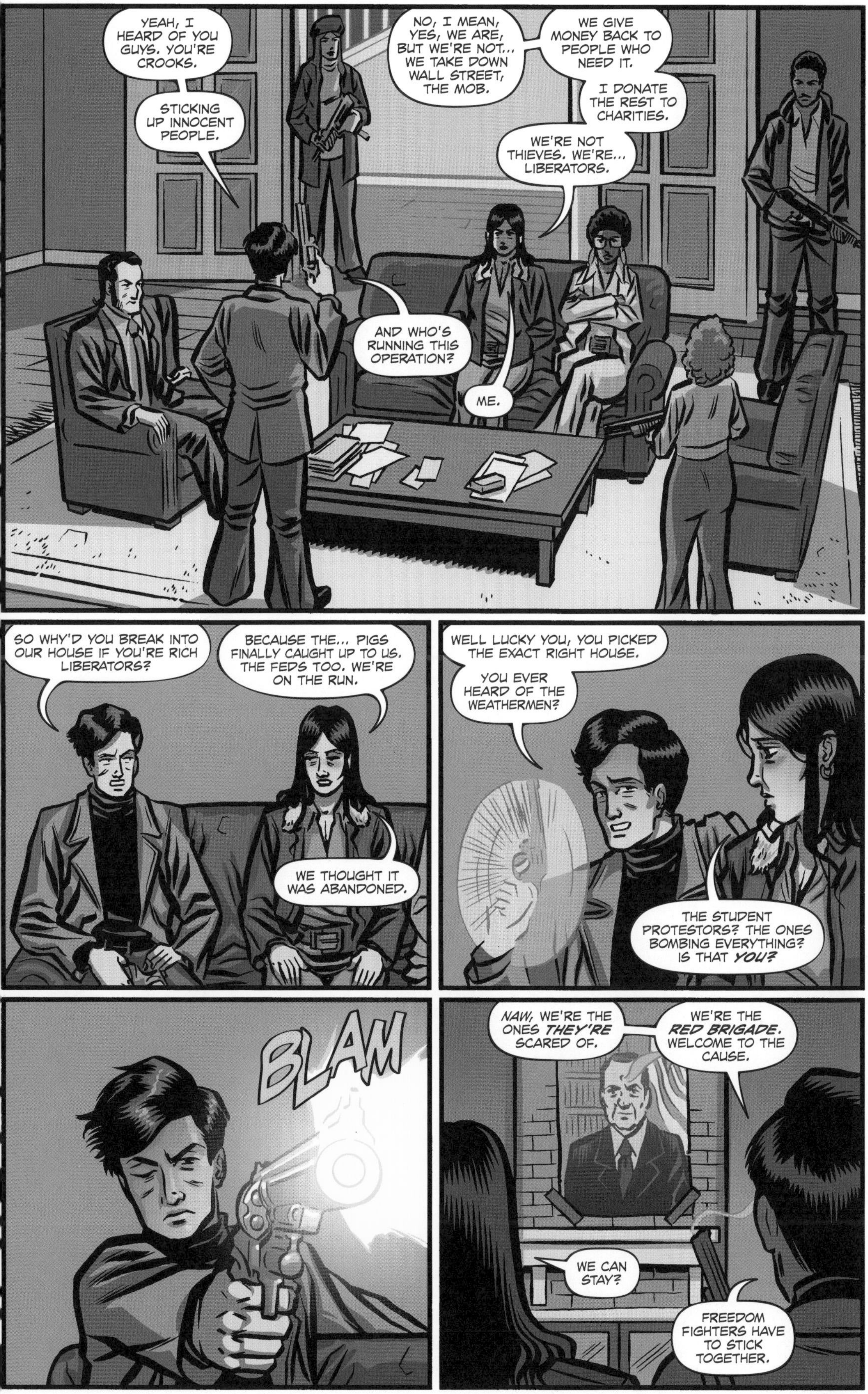
YEAH, I HEARD OF YOU GUYS. YOU'RE CROOKS.
STICKING UP INNOCENT PEOPLE.
NO, I MEAN, YES, WE ARE, BUT WE'RE NOT... WE TAKE DOWN WALL STREET, THE MOB.
WE GIVE MONEY BACK TO PEOPLE WHO NEED IT.
I DONATE THE REST TO CHARITIES.
WE'RE NOT THIEVES. WE'RE... LIBERATORS.
AND WHO'S RUNNING THIS OPERATION?
ME.
SO WHY'D YOU BREAK INTO OUR HOUSE IF YOU'RE RICH LIBERATORS?
BECAUSE THE... PIGS FINALLY CAUGHT UP TO US. THE FEDS TOO. WE'RE ON THE RUN.
WE THOUGHT IT WAS ABANDONED.
WELL LUCKY YOU, YOU PICKED THE EXACT RIGHT HOUSE.
YOU EVER HEARD OF THE WEATHERMEN?
THE STUDENT PROTESTORS? THE ONES BOMBING EVERYTHING? IS THAT *YOU?*
BLAM
*NAW*, WE'RE THE ONES *THEY'RE* SCARED OF.
WE'RE THE ***RED BRIGADE***. WELCOME TO THE CAUSE.
WE CAN STAY?
FREEDOM FIGHTERS HAVE TO STICK TOGETHER.

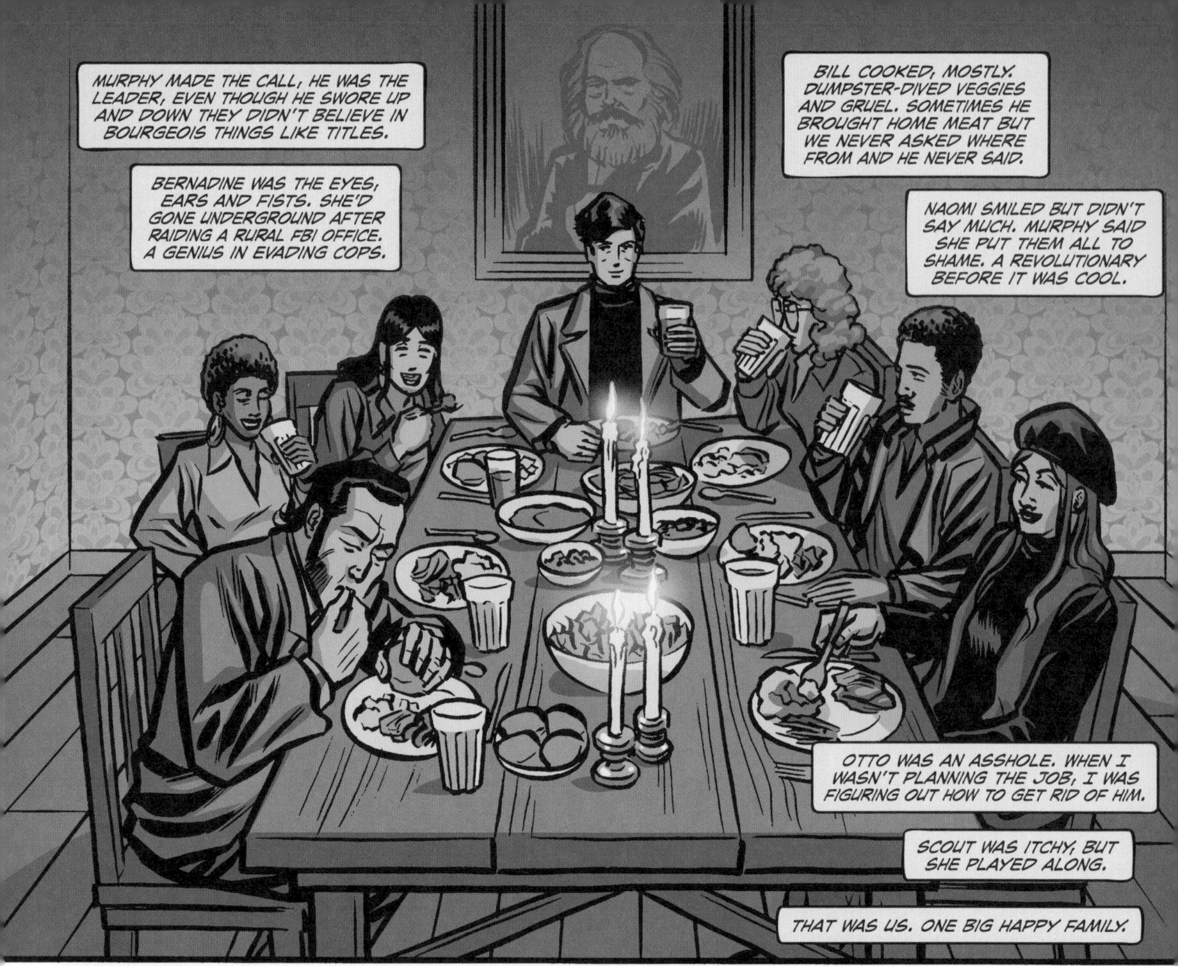
MURPHY MADE THE CALL, HE WAS THE LEADER, EVEN THOUGH HE SWORE UP AND DOWN THEY DIDN'T BELIEVE IN BOURGEOIS THINGS LIKE TITLES.
BERNADINE WAS THE EYES, EARS AND FISTS. SHE'D GONE UNDERGROUND AFTER RAIDING A RURAL FBI OFFICE. A GENIUS IN EVADING COPS.
BILL COOKED, MOSTLY. DUMPSTER-DIVED VEGGIES AND GRUEL. SOMETIMES HE BROUGHT HOME MEAT BUT WE NEVER ASKED WHERE FROM AND HE NEVER SAID.
NAOMI SMILED BUT DIDN'T SAY MUCH. MURPHY SAID SHE PUT THEM ALL TO SHAME. A REVOLUTIONARY BEFORE IT WAS COOL.
OTTO WAS AN ASSHOLE. WHEN I WASN'T PLANNING THE JOB, I WAS FIGURING OUT HOW TO GET RID OF HIM.
SCOUT WAS ITCHY, BUT SHE PLAYED ALONG.
THAT WAS US. ONE BIG HAPPY FAMILY.

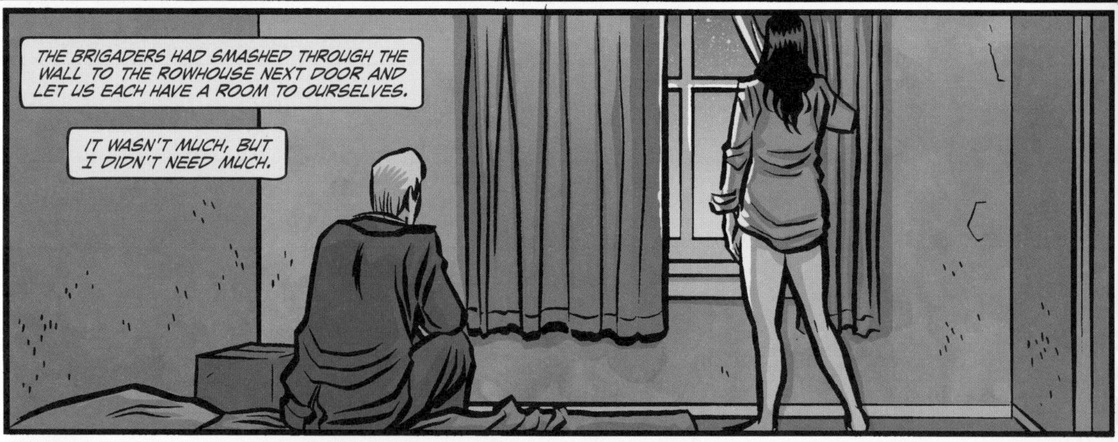
THE BRIGADERS HAD SMASHED THROUGH THE WALL TO THE ROWHOUSE NEXT DOOR AND LET US EACH HAVE A ROOM TO OURSELVES.
IT WASN'T MUCH, BUT I DIDN'T NEED MUCH.

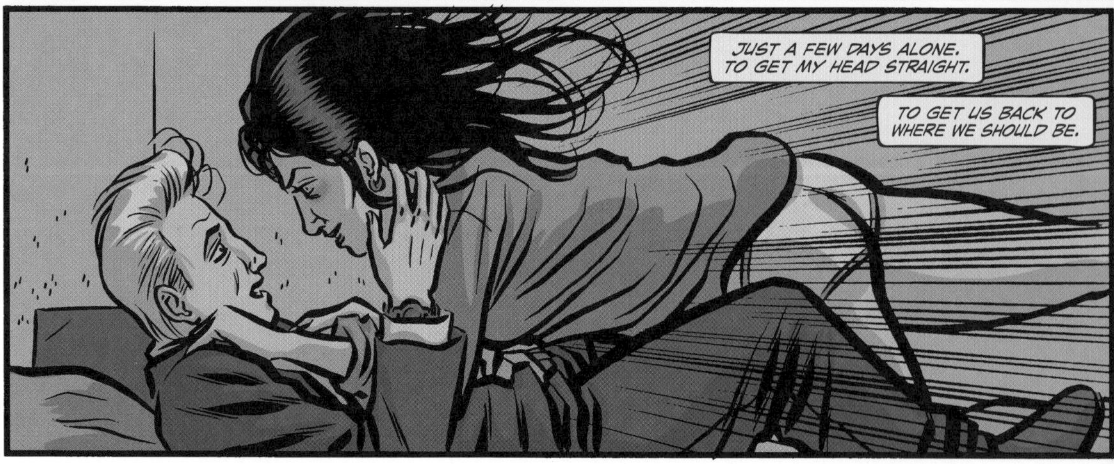
JUST A FEW DAYS ALONE. TO GET MY HEAD STRAIGHT.
TO GET US BACK TO WHERE WE SHOULD BE.

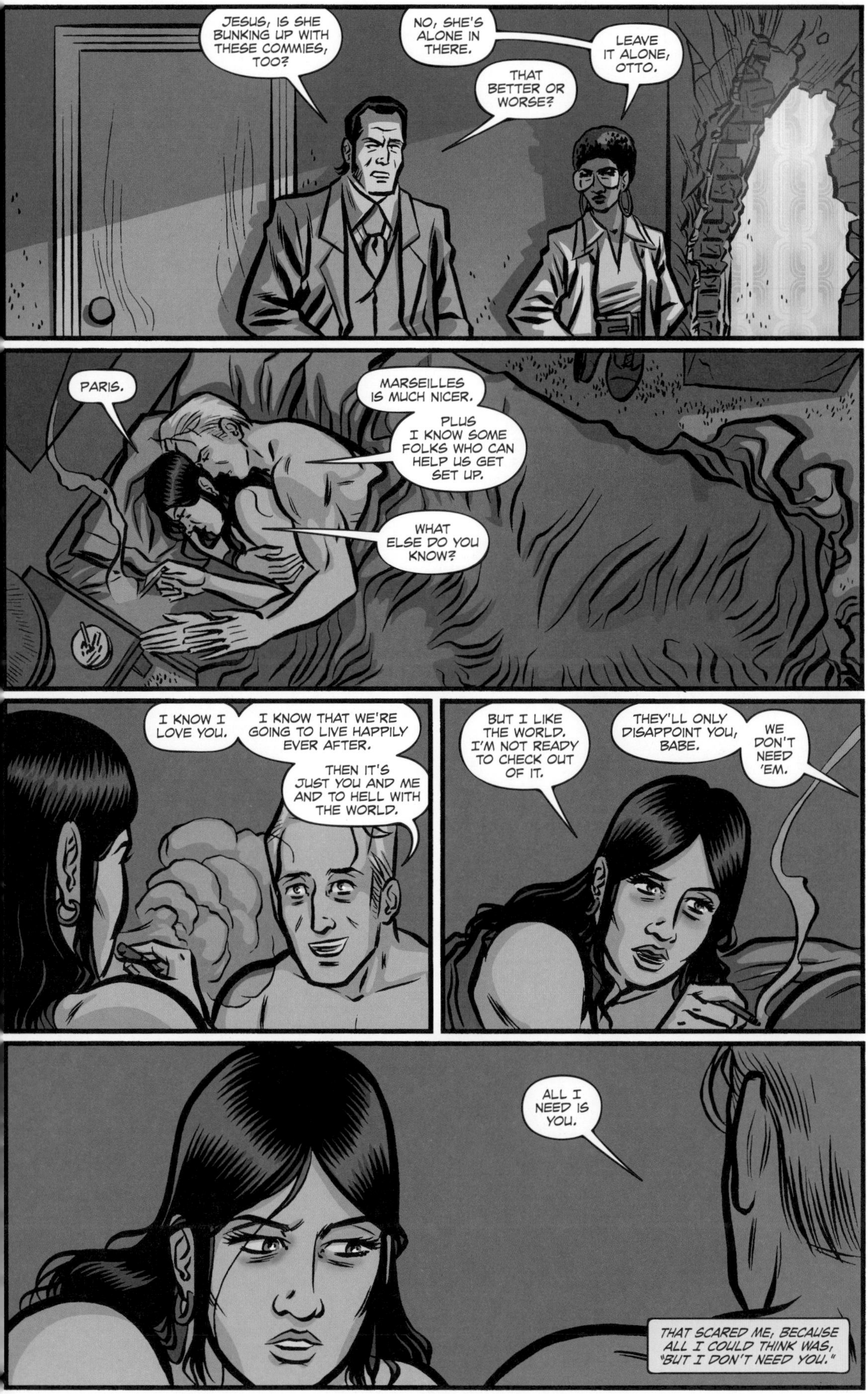
JESUS, IS SHE BUNKING UP WITH THESE COMMIES, TOO?
NO, SHE'S ALONE IN THERE.
LEAVE IT ALONE, OTTO.
THAT BETTER OR WORSE?
PARIS.
MARSEILLES IS MUCH NICER.
PLUS I KNOW SOME FOLKS WHO CAN HELP US GET SET UP.
WHAT ELSE DO YOU KNOW?
I KNOW I LOVE YOU.
I KNOW THAT WE'RE GOING TO LIVE HAPPILY EVER AFTER.
THEN IT'S JUST YOU AND ME AND TO HELL WITH THE WORLD.
BUT I LIKE THE WORLD. I'M NOT READY TO CHECK OUT OF IT.
THEY'LL ONLY DISAPPOINT YOU, BABE.
WE DON'T NEED 'EM.
ALL I NEED IS YOU.
THAT SCARED ME, BECAUSE ALL I COULD THINK WAS, "BUT I DON'T NEED YOU."

IT'S NOT BAD, CALLIE.

FAR AS CRAZY, STUPID PLANS GO. NO OFFENSE.

THANKS, BUDDY.

FLEETWOOD MAC
JULY 30 - ONE NIGHT ONLY

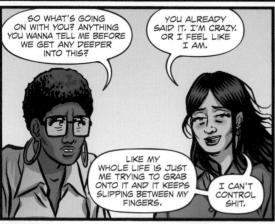

SO WHAT'S GOING ON WITH YOU? ANYTHING YOU WANNA TELL ME BEFORE WE GET ANY DEEPER INTO THIS?

YOU ALREADY SAID IT. I'M CRAZY. OR I FEEL LIKE I AM.

LIKE MY WHOLE LIFE IS JUST ME TRYING TO GRAB ONTO IT AND IT KEEPS SLIPPING BETWEEN MY FINGERS.

I CAN'T CONTROL SHIT.

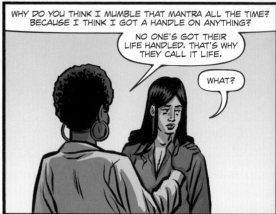

WHY DO YOU THINK I MUMBLE THAT MANTRA ALL THE TIME? BECAUSE I THINK I GOT A HANDLE ON ANYTHING?

NO ONE'S GOT THEIR LIFE HANDLED. THAT'S WHY THEY CALL IT LIFE.

WHAT?

FEEL THAT? THAT'S FORCE, GRINDING AWAY AT US. IF WE WEREN'T BELTED IN, WE'D BE THROWN ALL OVER. YOU CAN'T FIGHT IT.

THE BRAIN IS FUNNY. IT CAN DO ALL SORTS OF THINGS ALL AT ONCE WITHOUT SKIPPING A BEAT.

BUT SHOW IT SOMETHING SHINY, SOMETHING FOUL, YOU GIVE IT A HICCUP, KNOCK IT OUT OF THE LOOP.

WILL YOU TEACH ME YOUR MANTRA?

I'LL DO YOU ONE BETTER...

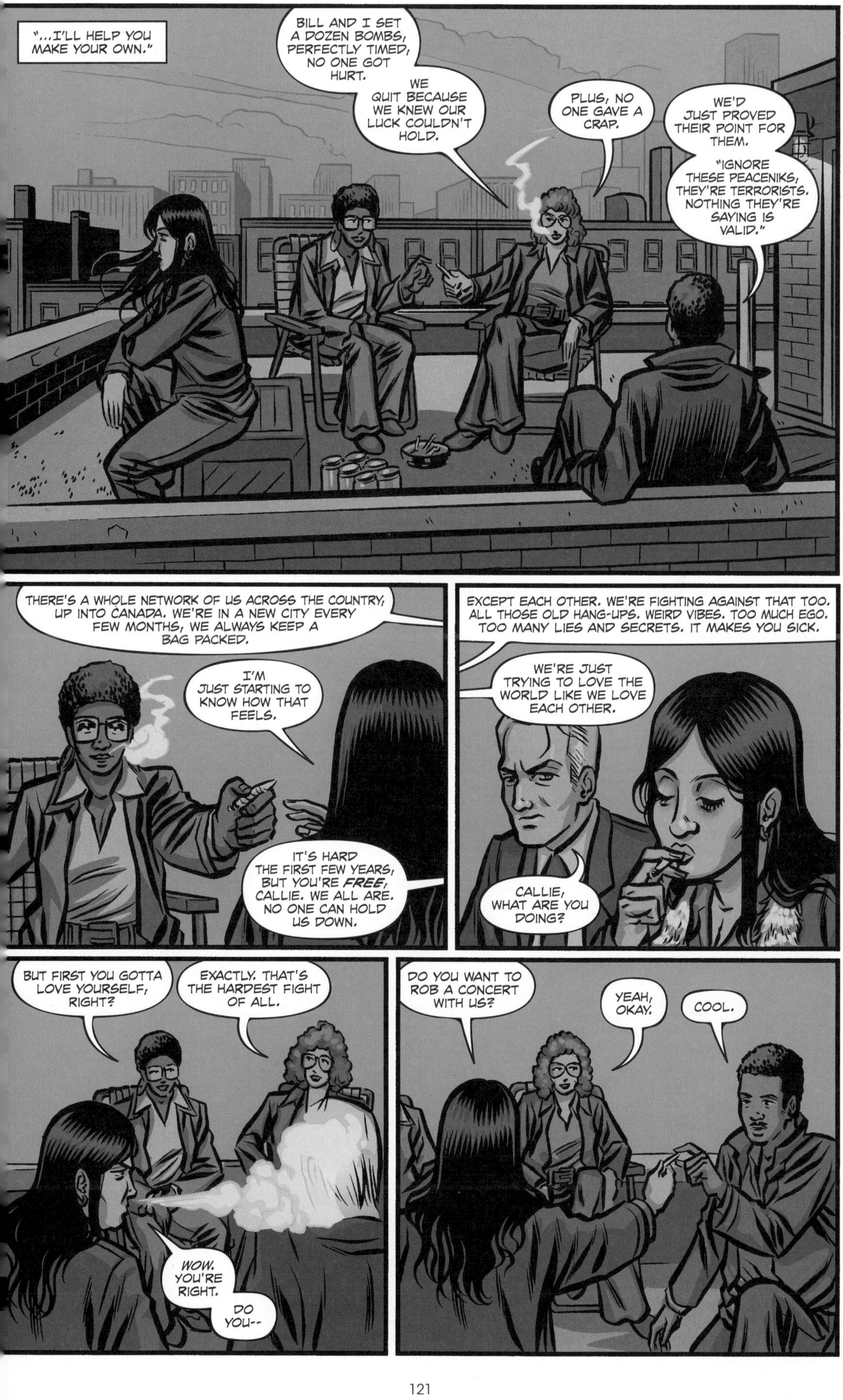
"...I'LL HELP YOU MAKE YOUR OWN."
BILL AND I SET A DOZEN BOMBS, PERFECTLY TIMED, NO ONE GOT HURT.
WE QUIT BECAUSE WE KNEW OUR LUCK COULDN'T HOLD.
PLUS, NO ONE GAVE A CRAP.
WE'D JUST PROVED THEIR POINT FOR THEM.
"IGNORE THESE PEACENIKS, THEY'RE TERRORISTS. NOTHING THEY'RE SAYING IS VALID."
THERE'S A WHOLE NETWORK OF US ACROSS THE COUNTRY, UP INTO CANADA. WE'RE IN A NEW CITY EVERY FEW MONTHS, WE ALWAYS KEEP A BAG PACKED.
I'M JUST STARTING TO KNOW HOW THAT FEELS.
IT'S HARD THE FIRST FEW YEARS, BUT YOU'RE *FREE*, CALLIE. WE ALL ARE. NO ONE CAN HOLD US DOWN.
EXCEPT EACH OTHER. WE'RE FIGHTING AGAINST THAT TOO. ALL THOSE OLD HANG-UPS. WEIRD VIBES. TOO MUCH EGO. TOO MANY LIES AND SECRETS. IT MAKES YOU SICK.
WE'RE JUST TRYING TO LOVE THE WORLD LIKE WE LOVE EACH OTHER.
CALLIE, WHAT ARE YOU DOING?
BUT FIRST YOU GOTTA LOVE YOURSELF, RIGHT?
EXACTLY. THAT'S THE HARDEST FIGHT OF ALL.
*WOW.* YOU'RE RIGHT.
DO YOU--
DO YOU WANT TO ROB A CONCERT WITH US?
YEAH, OKAY.
COOL.

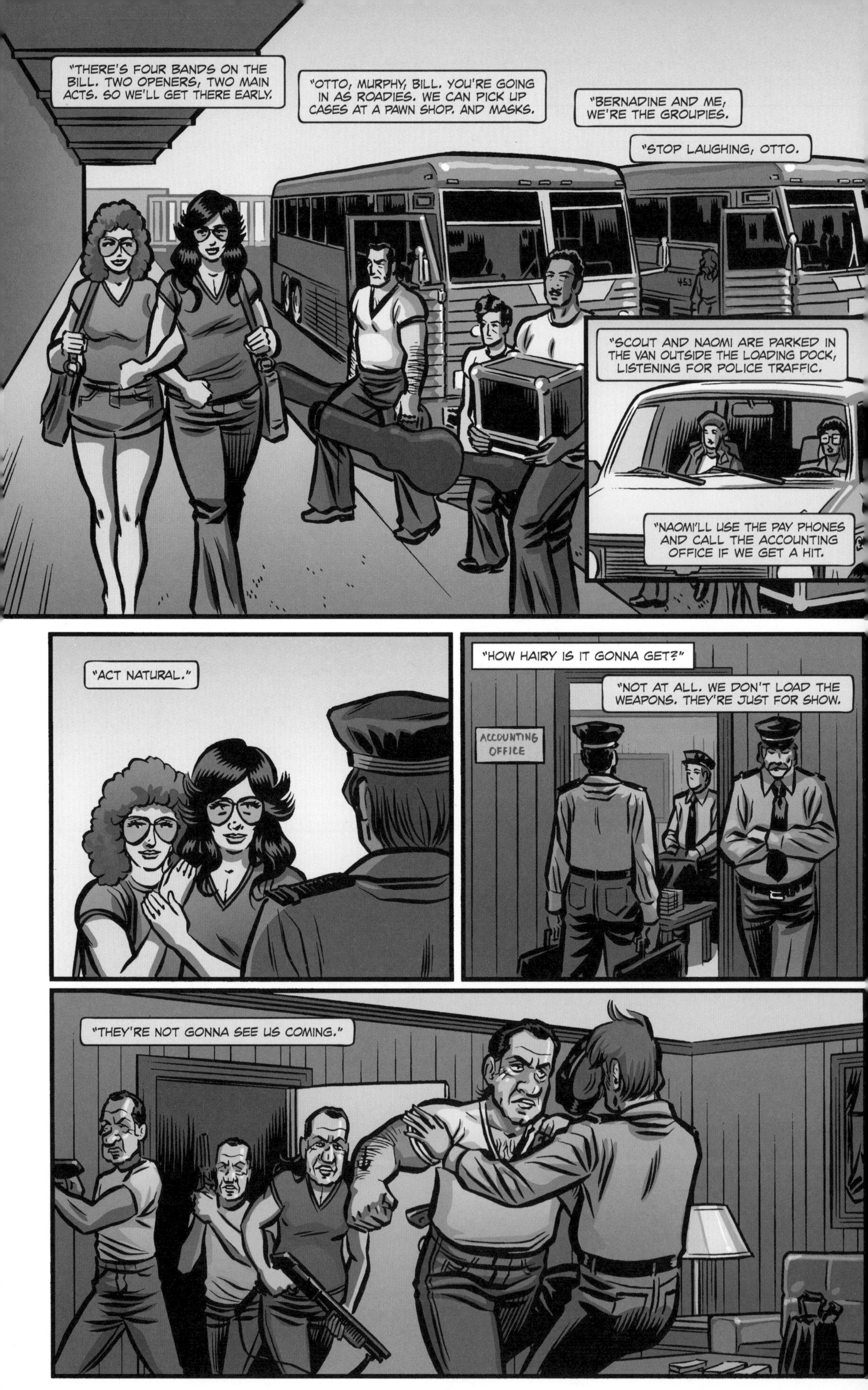
"THERE'S FOUR BANDS ON THE BILL. TWO OPENERS, TWO MAIN ACTS. SO WE'LL GET THERE EARLY.
"OTTO, MURPHY, BILL. YOU'RE GOING IN AS ROADIES. WE CAN PICK UP CASES AT A PAWN SHOP. AND MASKS.
"BERNADINE AND ME, WE'RE THE GROUPIES.
"STOP LAUGHING, OTTO.
453
"SCOUT AND NAOMI ARE PARKED IN THE VAN OUTSIDE THE LOADING DOCK, LISTENING FOR POLICE TRAFFIC.
"NAOMI'LL USE THE PAY PHONES AND CALL THE ACCOUNTING OFFICE IF WE GET A HIT.
"ACT NATURAL."
"HOW HAIRY IS IT GONNA GET?"
"NOT AT ALL. WE DON'T LOAD THE WEAPONS. THEY'RE JUST FOR SHOW.
ACCOUNTING OFFICE
"THEY'RE NOT GONNA SEE US COMING."

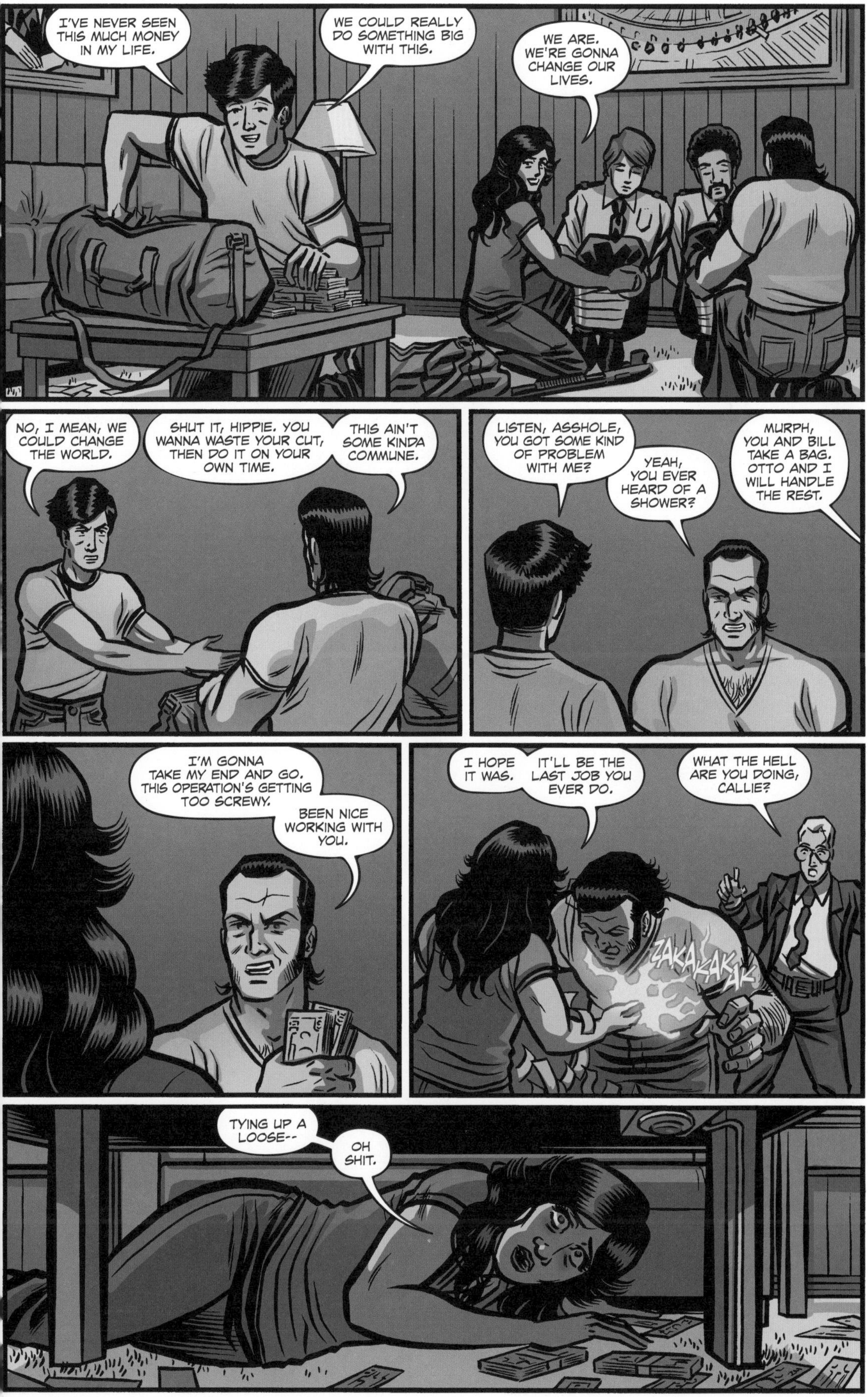

I'VE NEVER SEEN THIS MUCH MONEY IN MY LIFE.
WE COULD REALLY DO SOMETHING BIG WITH THIS.
WE ARE. WE'RE GONNA CHANGE OUR LIVES.
NO, I MEAN, WE COULD CHANGE THE WORLD.
SHUT IT, HIPPIE. YOU WANNA WASTE YOUR CUT, THEN DO IT ON YOUR OWN TIME.
THIS AIN'T SOME KINDA COMMUNE.
LISTEN, ASSHOLE, YOU GOT SOME KIND OF PROBLEM WITH ME?
YEAH, YOU EVER HEARD OF A SHOWER?
MURPH, YOU AND BILL TAKE A BAG. OTTO AND I WILL HANDLE THE REST.
I'M GONNA TAKE MY END AND GO. THIS OPERATION'S GETTING TOO SCREWY.
BEEN NICE WORKING WITH YOU.
I HOPE IT WAS.
IT'LL BE THE LAST JOB YOU EVER DO.
WHAT THE HELL ARE YOU DOING, CALLIE?
ZAKAKAKAKAK
TYING UP A LOOSE--
OH SHIT.

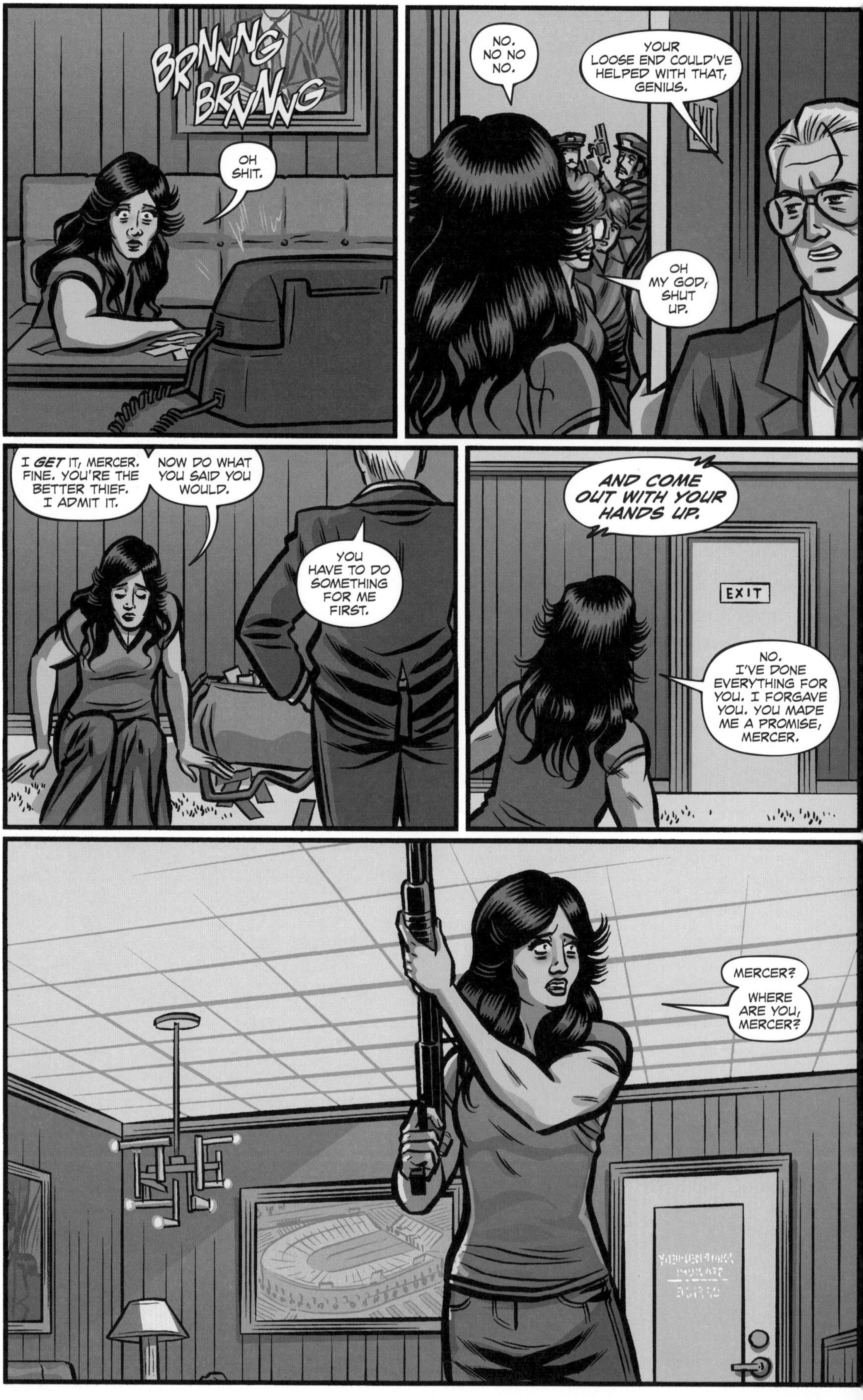
BRNNNG BRNNNG
OH SHIT.
NO. NO NO NO.
YOUR LOOSE END COULD'VE HELPED WITH THAT, GENIUS.
OH MY GOD, SHUT UP.
I GET IT, MERCER. FINE. YOU'RE THE BETTER THIEF. I ADMIT IT.
NOW DO WHAT YOU SAID YOU WOULD.
YOU HAVE TO DO SOMETHING FOR ME FIRST.
AND COME OUT WITH YOUR HANDS UP.
EXIT
NO. I'VE DONE EVERYTHING FOR YOU. I FORGAVE YOU. YOU MADE ME A PROMISE, MERCER.
MERCER?
WHERE ARE YOU, MERCER?

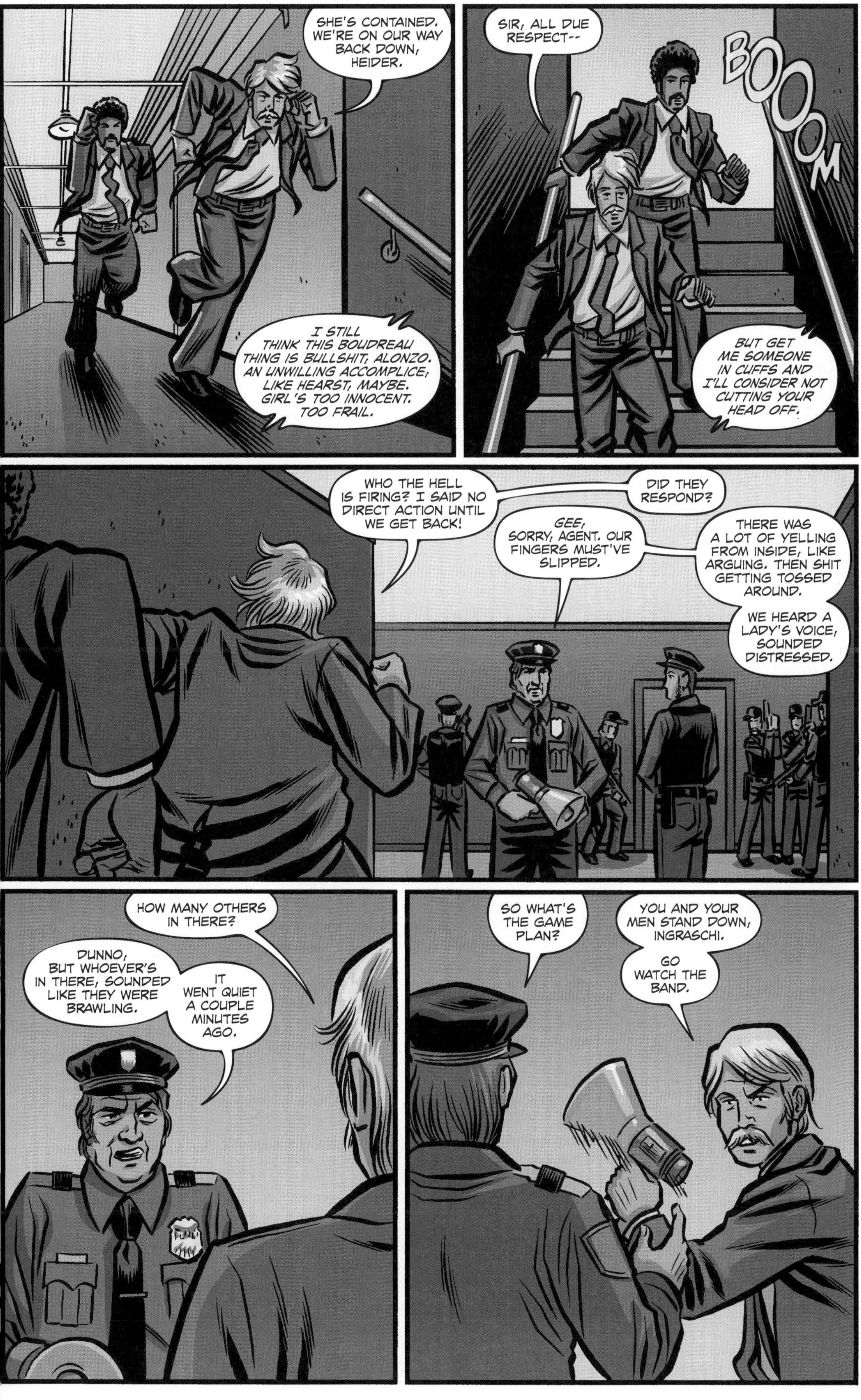
SHE'S CONTAINED. WE'RE ON OUR WAY BACK DOWN, HEIDER.
I STILL THINK THIS BOUDREAU THING IS BULLSHIT, ALONZO. AN UNWILLING ACCOMPLICE; LIKE HEARST, MAYBE. GIRL'S TOO INNOCENT. TOO FRAIL.
SIR, ALL DUE RESPECT--
BOOOOM
BUT GET ME SOMEONE IN CUFFS AND I'LL CONSIDER NOT CUTTING YOUR HEAD OFF.
WHO THE HELL IS FIRING? I SAID NO DIRECT ACTION UNTIL WE GET BACK!
GEE, SORRY, AGENT. OUR FINGERS MUST'VE SLIPPED.
DID THEY RESPOND?
THERE WAS A LOT OF YELLING FROM INSIDE, LIKE ARGUING. THEN SHIT GETTING TOSSED AROUND.
WE HEARD A LADY'S VOICE, SOUNDED DISTRESSED.
HOW MANY OTHERS IN THERE?
DUNNO, BUT WHOEVER'S IN THERE, SOUNDED LIKE THEY WERE BRAWLING.
IT WENT QUIET A COUPLE MINUTES AGO.
SO WHAT'S THE GAME PLAN?
YOU AND YOUR MEN STAND DOWN, INGRASCHI.
GO WATCH THE BAND.

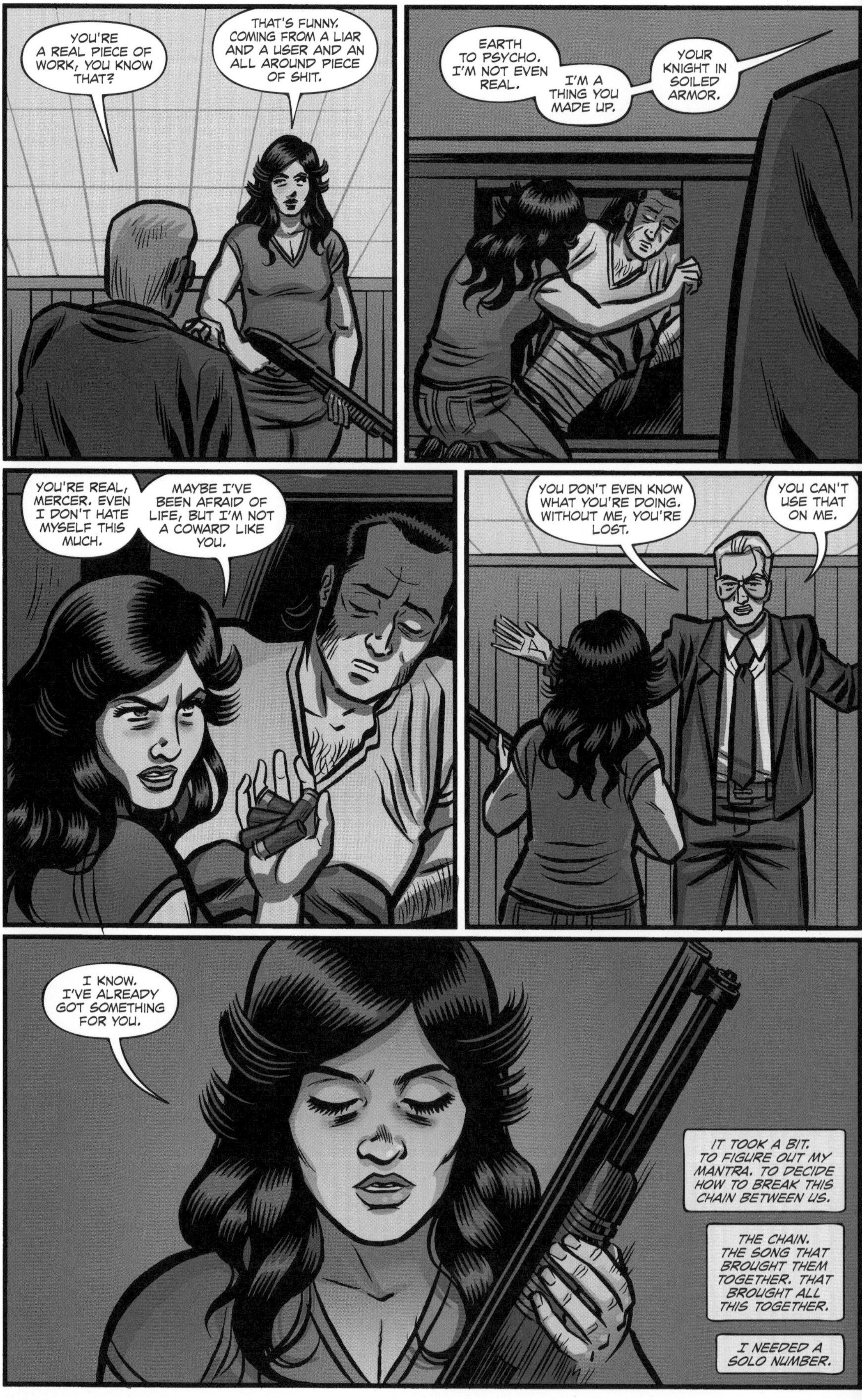
YOU'RE A REAL PIECE OF WORK, YOU KNOW THAT?
THAT'S FUNNY. COMING FROM A LIAR AND A USER AND AN ALL AROUND PIECE OF SHIT.
EARTH TO PSYCHO. I'M NOT EVEN REAL.
I'M A THING YOU MADE UP.
YOUR KNIGHT IN SOILED ARMOR.
YOU'RE REAL, MERCER. EVEN I DON'T HATE MYSELF THIS MUCH.
MAYBE I'VE BEEN AFRAID OF LIFE, BUT I'M NOT A COWARD LIKE YOU.
YOU DON'T EVEN KNOW WHAT YOU'RE DOING. WITHOUT ME, YOU'RE LOST.
YOU CAN'T USE THAT ON ME.
I KNOW. I'VE ALREADY GOT SOMETHING FOR YOU.
IT TOOK A BIT. TO FIGURE OUT MY MANTRA. TO DECIDE HOW TO BREAK THIS CHAIN BETWEEN US.
THE CHAIN. THE SONG THAT BROUGHT THEM TOGETHER. THAT BROUGHT ALL THIS TOGETHER.
I NEEDED A SOLO NUMBER.

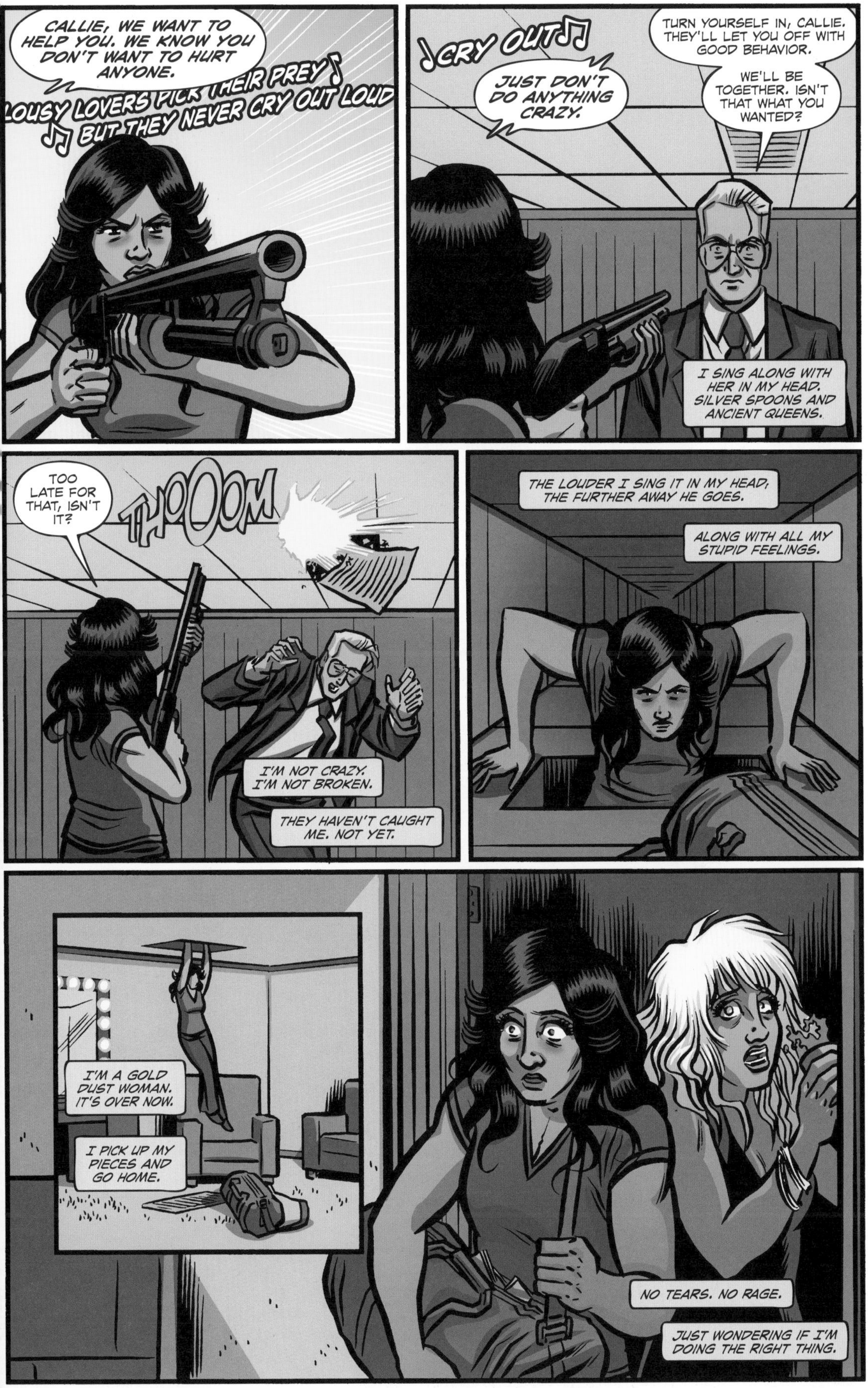
CALLIE, WE WANT TO HELP YOU. WE KNOW YOU DON'T WANT TO HURT ANYONE.
LOUSY LOVERS PICK THEIR PREY BUT THEY NEVER CRY OUT LOUD
CRY OUT
JUST DON'T DO ANYTHING CRAZY.
TURN YOURSELF IN, CALLIE. THEY'LL LET YOU OFF WITH GOOD BEHAVIOR.
WE'LL BE TOGETHER. ISN'T THAT WHAT YOU WANTED?
I SING ALONG WITH HER IN MY HEAD. SILVER SPOONS AND ANCIENT QUEENS.
TOO LATE FOR THAT, ISN'T IT?
THOOOM
I'M NOT CRAZY. I'M NOT BROKEN.
THEY HAVEN'T CAUGHT ME. NOT YET.
THE LOUDER I SING IT IN MY HEAD, THE FURTHER AWAY HE GOES.
ALONG WITH ALL MY STUPID FEELINGS.
I'M A GOLD DUST WOMAN. IT'S OVER NOW.
I PICK UP MY PIECES AND GO HOME.
NO TEARS. NO RAGE.
JUST WONDERING IF I'M DOING THE RIGHT THING.

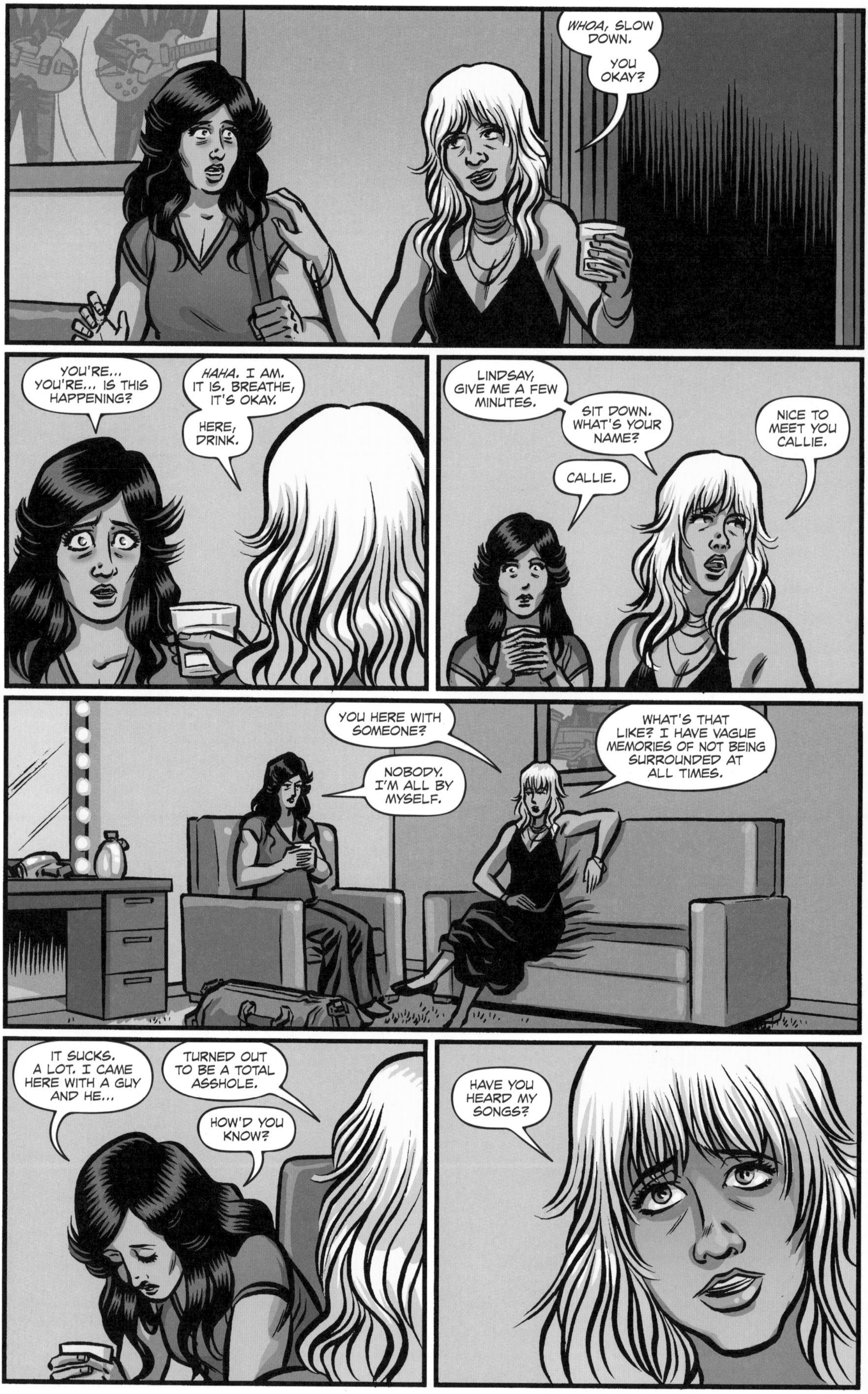
WHOA, SLOW DOWN.
YOU OKAY?
YOU'RE... YOU'RE... IS THIS HAPPENING?
HAHA. I AM. IT IS. BREATHE, IT'S OKAY.
HERE, DRINK.
LINDSAY, GIVE ME A FEW MINUTES.
SIT DOWN. WHAT'S YOUR NAME?
CALLIE.
NICE TO MEET YOU CALLIE.
YOU HERE WITH SOMEONE?
NOBODY. I'M ALL BY MYSELF.
WHAT'S THAT LIKE? I HAVE VAGUE MEMORIES OF NOT BEING SURROUNDED AT ALL TIMES.
IT SUCKS. A LOT. I CAME HERE WITH A GUY AND HE...
TURNED OUT TO BE A TOTAL ASSHOLE.
HOW'D YOU KNOW?
HAVE YOU HEARD MY SONGS?

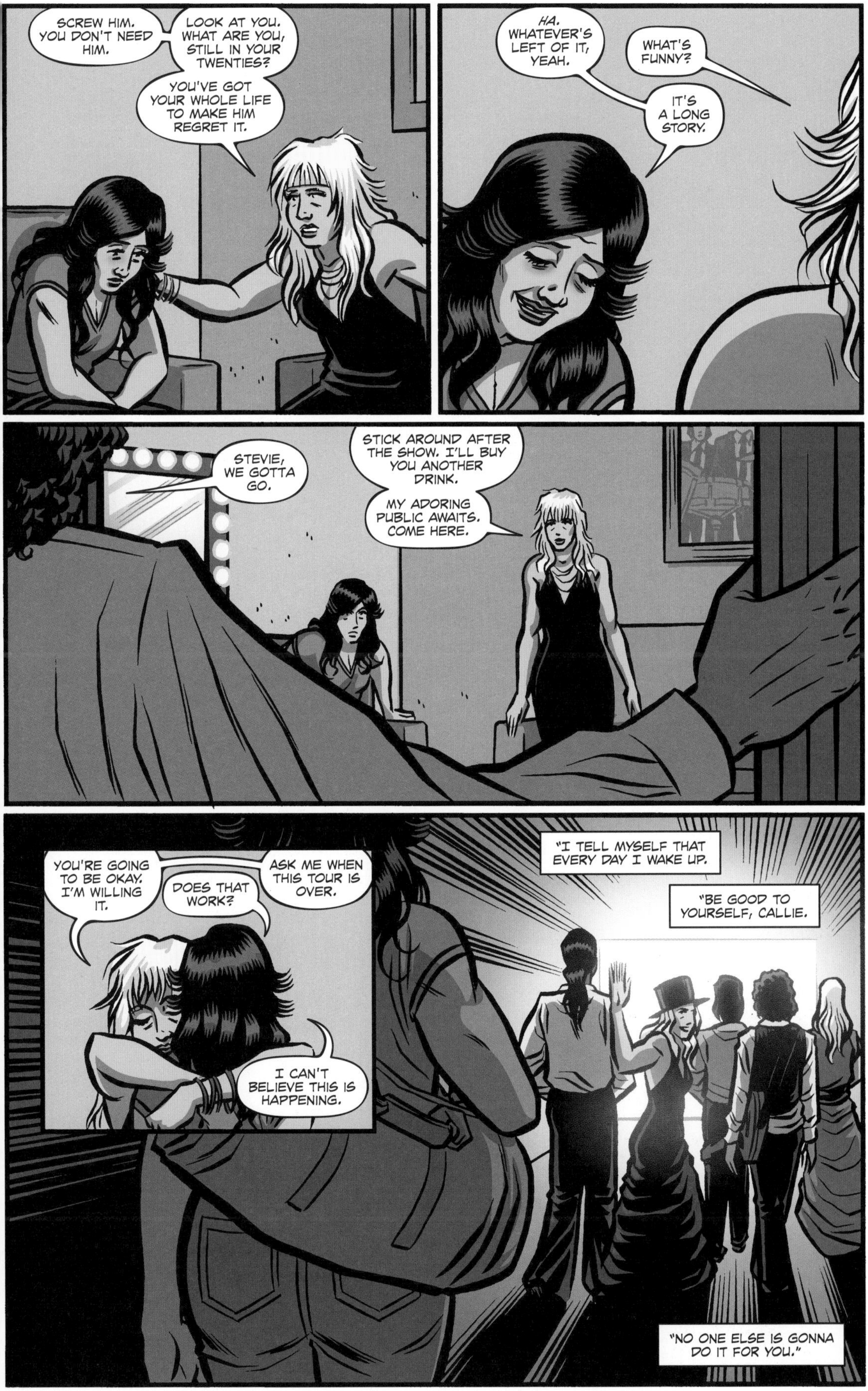
SCREW HIM. YOU DON'T NEED HIM.
LOOK AT YOU. WHAT ARE YOU, STILL IN YOUR TWENTIES?
YOU'VE GOT YOUR WHOLE LIFE TO MAKE HIM REGRET IT.
HA. WHATEVER'S LEFT OF IT, YEAH.
WHAT'S FUNNY?
IT'S A LONG STORY.
STEVIE, WE GOTTA GO.
STICK AROUND AFTER THE SHOW. I'LL BUY YOU ANOTHER DRINK.
MY ADORING PUBLIC AWAITS. COME HERE.
YOU'RE GOING TO BE OKAY. I'M WILLING IT.
DOES THAT WORK?
ASK ME WHEN THIS TOUR IS OVER.
I CAN'T BELIEVE THIS IS HAPPENING.
"I TELL MYSELF THAT EVERY DAY I WAKE UP.
"BE GOOD TO YOURSELF, CALLIE.
"NO ONE ELSE IS GONNA DO IT FOR YOU."

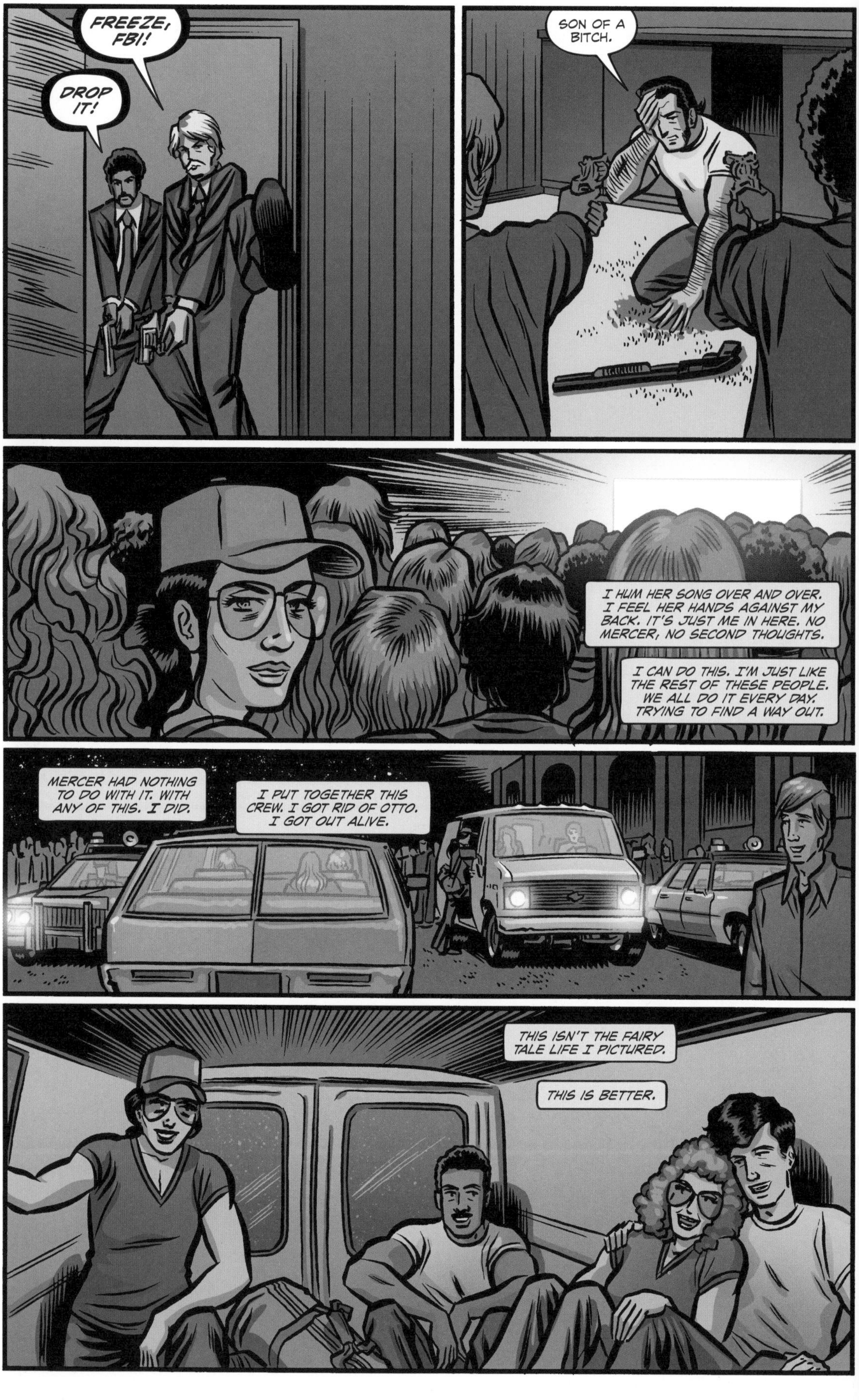
FREEZE, FBI!
DROP IT!
SON OF A BITCH.
I HUM HER SONG OVER AND OVER. I FEEL HER HANDS AGAINST MY BACK. IT'S JUST ME IN HERE. NO MERCER, NO SECOND THOUGHTS.
I CAN DO THIS. I'M JUST LIKE THE REST OF THESE PEOPLE. WE ALL DO IT EVERY DAY. TRYING TO FIND A WAY OUT.
MERCER HAD NOTHING TO DO WITH IT. WITH ANY OF THIS. I DID.
I PUT TOGETHER THIS CREW. I GOT RID OF OTTO. I GOT OUT ALIVE.
THIS ISN'T THE FAIRY TALE LIFE I PICTURED.
THIS IS BETTER.

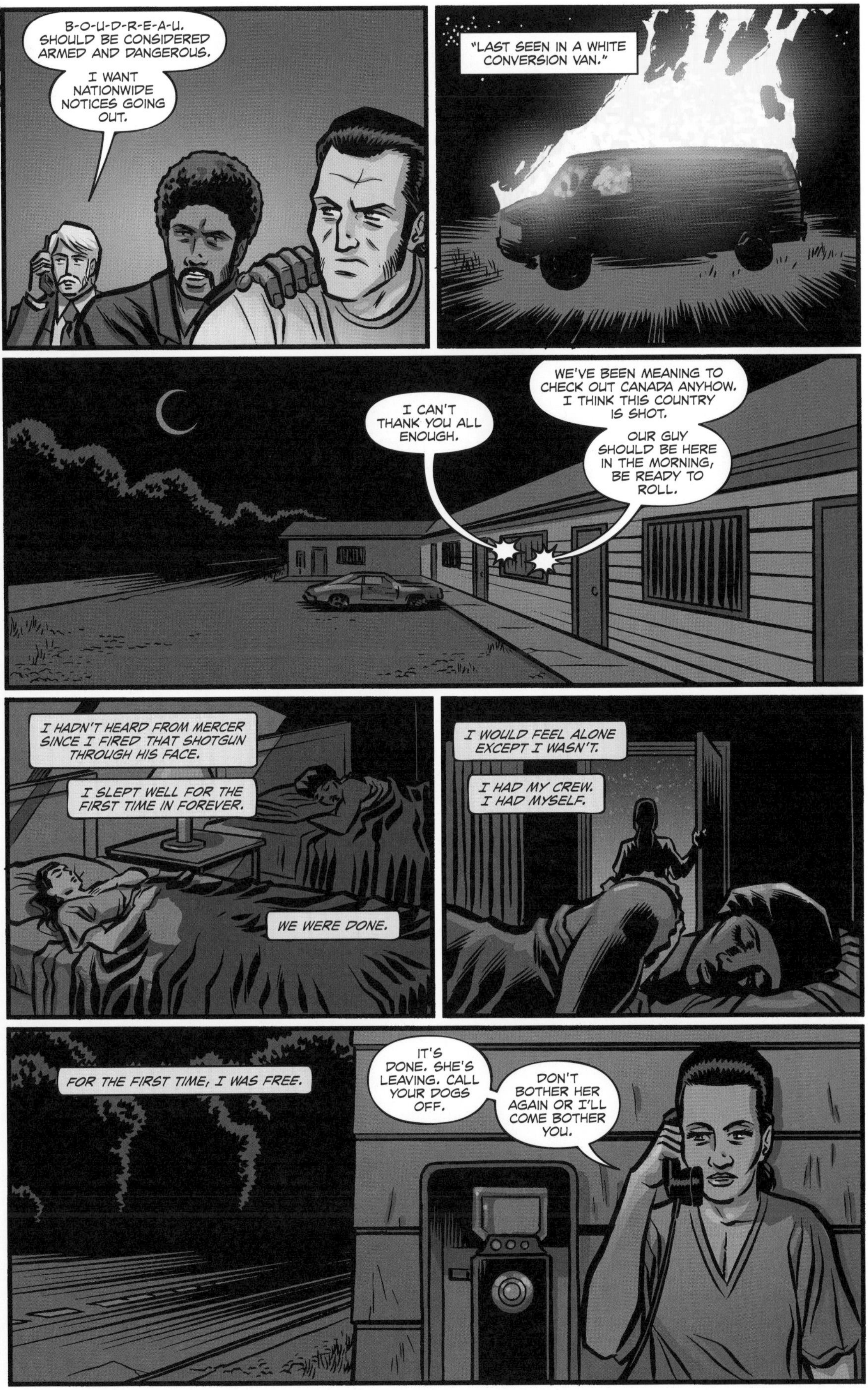
B-O-U-D-R-E-A-U. SHOULD BE CONSIDERED ARMED AND DANGEROUS.
I WANT NATIONWIDE NOTICES GOING OUT.
"LAST SEEN IN A WHITE CONVERSION VAN."
I CAN'T THANK YOU ALL ENOUGH.
WE'VE BEEN MEANING TO CHECK OUT CANADA ANYHOW. I THINK THIS COUNTRY IS SHOT.
OUR GUY SHOULD BE HERE IN THE MORNING, BE READY TO ROLL.
I HADN'T HEARD FROM MERCER SINCE I FIRED THAT SHOTGUN THROUGH HIS FACE.
I SLEPT WELL FOR THE FIRST TIME IN FOREVER.
WE WERE DONE.
I WOULD FEEL ALONE EXCEPT I WASN'T.
I HAD MY CREW. I HAD MYSELF.
FOR THE FIRST TIME, I WAS FREE.
IT'S DONE. SHE'S LEAVING. CALL YOUR DOGS OFF.
DON'T BOTHER HER AGAIN OR I'LL COME BOTHER YOU.

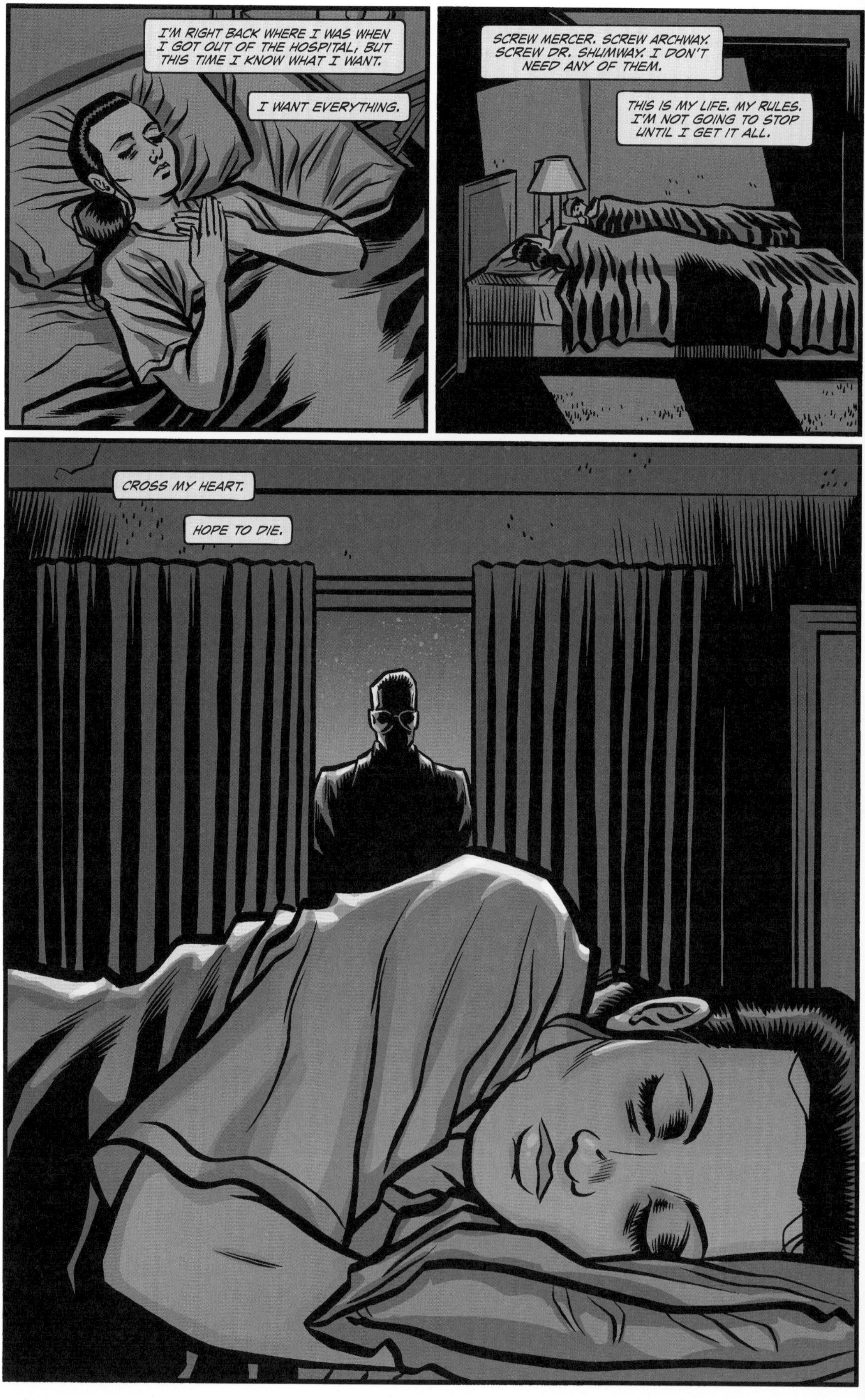
I'M RIGHT BACK WHERE I WAS WHEN I GOT OUT OF THE HOSPITAL, BUT THIS TIME I KNOW WHAT I WANT.
I WANT EVERYTHING.
SCREW MERCER. SCREW ARCHWAY. SCREW DR. SHUMWAY. I DON'T NEED ANY OF THEM.
THIS IS MY LIFE. MY RULES. I'M NOT GOING TO STOP UNTIL I GET IT ALL.
CROSS MY HEART.
HOPE TO DIE.

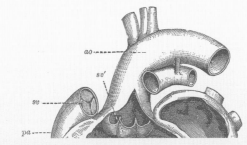

DAMN YOUR LOVE / DAMN YOUR LIES

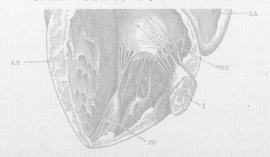

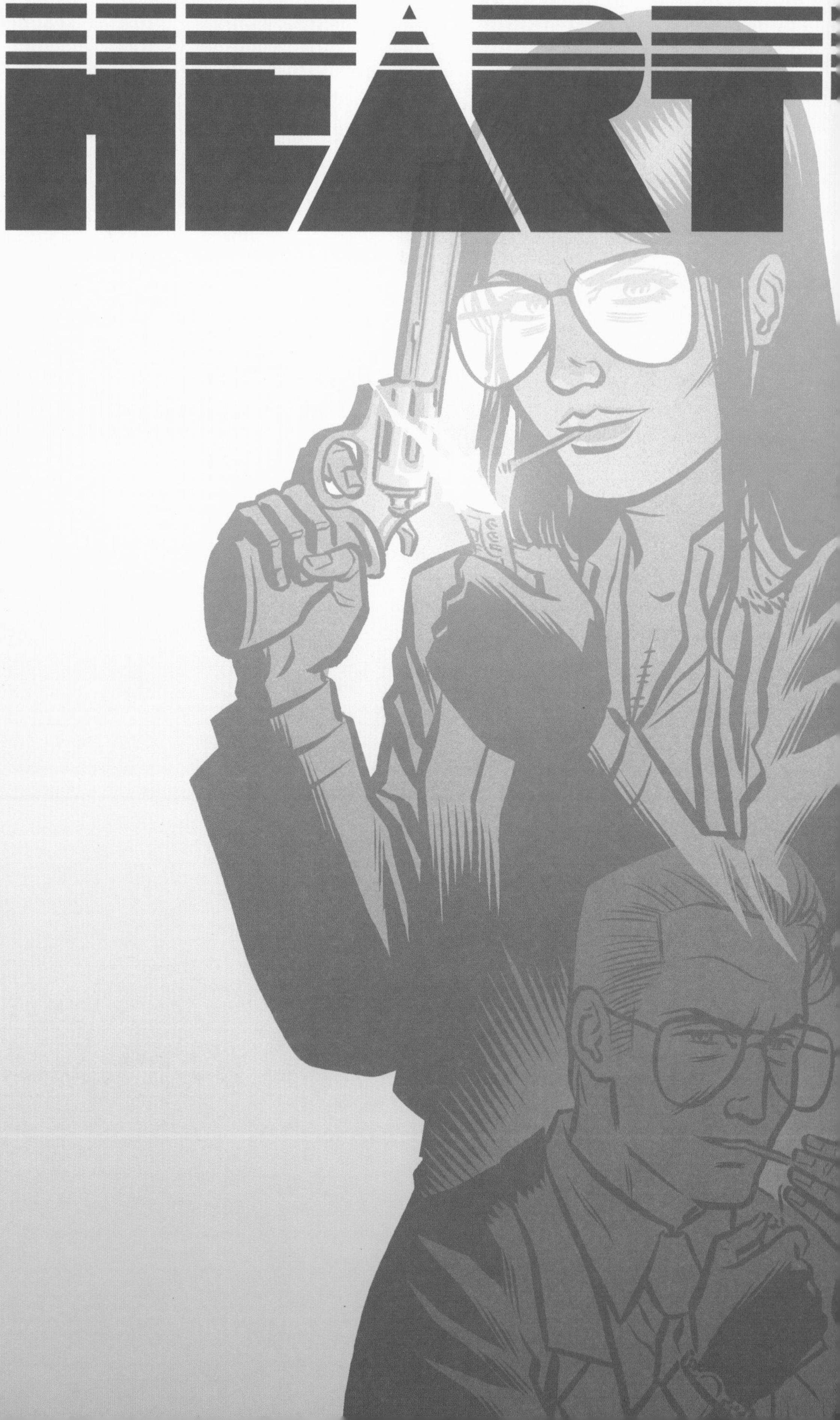
HEART